MARGARET LLEWELYN DAVIES

MARGARET LLEWELYN DAVIES

With Women for a New World

RUTH COHEN

MERLIN PRESS

The Merlin Press Ltd
Central Books Building
Freshwater Road
Dagenham
RM8 1RX

www.merlinpress.co.uk

First published 2020

© Ruth Cohen, 2020

Cover: Photo of Margaret Llewelyn Davies from Llewelyn Davies family papers, courtesy of Jane Wynne Willson; bottom photo, courtesy of Co-operative Women's Guild Collection, University of Hull.

All rights reserved. No part of this publication may be reproduced, stored in a retrieval system, or transmitted in any form or by any means, electronic, mechanical, photocopying, recording or otherwise, without the prior permission of the publisher.

The author's moral rights have been asserted.

ISBN. 978-0-85036-759-1

A CIP record of this book is available from the British Library

Printed in the UK by Imprint Digital, Exeter

Contents

Introduction: Discovering Margaret Llewelyn Davies 1

Section One: Beginning

Crompton/Llewelyn Davies Family Tree 6
Chapter 1: Radical Relations 7
Chapter 2: Early Days, 1861-1883 16
    Part One: Growing up in Marylebone 16
    Part Two: Girton Girl 23
Chapter 3: Finding the Guild, 1883-1889 28

Section Two: Growing

Chapter 4: Changes, 1889-1892 43
Chapter 5: Public Success, Private Grief, 1892-1895 56
Chapter 6: Making a Mark, 1895-1904 67
Chapter 7: Reaching the Poorest, 1899-1905 81
Chapter 8: Entr'acte: Untimely Deaths, 1905-1910 94

Section Three: Flying

Chapter 9: In Their Prime: Margaret and the Guild, 1906-1914 107
Chapter 10: Votes for Which Women? 1904-1914 121
    Part One: 1904-1909 122
    Part Two: 1909-1914 131
Chapter 11: Better Wages and More, 1906-1913 140
Chapter 12: Gender Politics in the Home, 1909-1914 153
Chapter 13: Mothers First! 1911 onward 168
    Part One: Money for Mothers 168
    Part Two: Money is Not Enough 175
    Part Three: Mothers and Babies in Wartime 182

Chapter 14: In Time of War, 1914-1918 187
    Part One: Margaret's Home Front 187
    Part Two: Margaret and the Guild 189
    Part Three: War and Peace 194
Chapter 15: Entr'acte 2: Lilian 202

Section Four: Winding Down

Chapter 16: Leaving, 1918-1922 209
Chapter 17: After the Guild, 1922-1933 222
Chapter 18: The Final Years, 1933-1944 232
Conclusion: Margaret's Afterlife 239

Appendix: The Co-operative Movement of Margaret's Time . . 242
Acknowledgements 243
Bibliography 245
Abbreviations Used in the Notes 253
Notes 254
Index 271

INTRODUCTION

Discovering Margaret Llewelyn Davies

One sunny morning in June 1922, Virginia Woolf and her husband Leonard left their peaceful Sussex home for Brighton's imposing Dome. She was singularly unimpressed both by the building – 'a gaudy kind of tea caddy, all arabesques and horseshoes and chandeliers'[1] – and by the overwhelmingly male gathering: 'innumerable hard-headed drab'. Nevertheless, the 1,700 delegates represented a powerful social organisation with over four and a half million members, running local shops and manufacturing enterprises across the country, and with its own weekly newspaper and political party.[2] The Woolfs had come to the annual Co-operative Congress.

This Bloomsbury incursion into a bastion of working-class self-organisation might be surprising, not to say incongruous. True, the Woolfs both had links with co-operation, but they came today for a special reason. Their good friend Margaret Llewelyn Davies was due to preside over the Congress and had been widely hailed as the first woman ever to do so.

Margaret had recently retired as General Secretary of the Women's Co-operative Guild and, over the years, had battled time and again with the male dominated co-operative leadership. Now, it seemed, times had changed. She saw the invitation to chair the Congress as a long overdue recognition of women's part in the co-operative movement, and made a point of accepting the honour not for herself but on behalf of 'that host of women without whom she would have been nothing'.[3]

Margaret came onto the stage that morning, as Virginia Woolf noted, 'very cool and distinguished looking ... all in grey, but with a dash of kingfisher blue about the bonnet'. She was greeted by a standing ovation. This was indeed a novel occasion, and delegates were urged to remember that the Chair was a lady. There was some confusion about how to address her: Madame President? Lady President? Missus President? Mr Chairman? But overall, it went off smoothly, and a commentary in the weekly *Co-*

operative News described Margaret as 'the best man of the conference ... sweet, sympathetic and smart'. She was later presented with an illuminated address, accompanied by flowers and chocolates – then, as now, considered suitable gifts for a lady.[4]

Her opening address, however, may not have been quite what Virginia Woolf, or indeed, many of the delegates, expected. At this time of economic and political crisis, Margaret argued, capitalism was 'on ... trial as never before', and the peaceful extension of co-operation would provide a revolutionary solution: 'Co-operation is far more than a reformist movement. We are working for no patchwork modifications, for no "reconciliation of capital and labour" ...We are laying the foundations of a new industrial civilisation.' When she went on to speak of the importance of international Co-operative trade, she highlighted trade with Bolshevik Russia.

Moving closer to home, Margaret pulled no punches. She criticised the barriers which women still faced when trying to progress within co-operative organisations, took a swipe at bureaucracy, argued for greater grass-roots democracy, and demanded better treatment of employees.[5] All in all, she 'stood up to the [Central] Board and the movement and flicked them very energetically ... her vitality, her vigour ... conquered all'.[6]

Who was this formidable woman?

Born in 1861, Margaret Llewelyn Davies came from a remarkable upper middle-class family which was embedded in radical and reforming intellectual circles of the time. Outraged by the social injustice which she saw around her, as a young adult she became committed to the co-operative movement, believing that this could, potentially, provide a peaceful path to socialism. As we have seen in her Congress speech, this conviction was if anything strengthened with the passing of time. And Margaret was also a passionate supporter of women's rights; her feminism, as we would call it today, was inextricably intertwined with her co-operative and socialist beliefs.

In his authoritative history, G.D.H. Cole affirmed that Margaret was 'by far the greatest woman ... actively involved in the British Co-operative movement'.[7] Leonard Woolf admired her too, and saw her as one of the most eminent women he had ever known.[8] Her greatest achievement was her visionary work in the Women's Co-operative Guild.

Guild members were primarily home-based married women from better off sections of the working class. They had to manage household finances, keep up a respectable home, and look after their husband and children –

the last, at this period, an unending, backbreaking struggle. Initially, many had to struggle even for the right to venture out to Guild meetings: as one male co-operator put it, his wife should instead 'stay at home and wash my moleskin trousers'.[9]

But Margaret, herself unmarried, educated and comfortably off, insisted that things could be different. She greatly admired the wives and mothers of the Guild, whom she saw as 'heroines of the home', and believed they could and should play a part in the co-operative movement and in the wider public world. Once elected General Secretary, she introduced a system of education, discussion and campaigning which soon struck a chord. The Guild not only provided women with an outlet but began to change lives. As one member put it, 'from a shy, nervous woman, the Guild made me a fighter'.[10] By 1914 there were over 32,000 members across England and Wales, and the *Manchester Guardian* called the Guild 'perhaps the most remarkable women's organisation in the world'.[11]

By the time she retired, in 1921, Margaret had been the Guild's General Secretary for over thirty years. During this time, thanks greatly to her visionary leadership, the Guild became a unique public voice for working-class women, campaigning on a whole range of issues: everything from fair trade policies in co-operative shops to votes for women. When the Russian revolutionary Alexandra Kollontai visited a Guild meeting in 1913, she concluded that these women gave the lie to the accepted wisdom that housewives could not be politicised.[12]

Influenced by what she learned from Guildswomen about their hard lives, Margaret's campaigns began to highlight married women's unpaid domestic labour, and alongside this the impact of poverty and even hidden domestic abuse within the home. In the campaigns for divorce law reform and maternity provision she did something unique, and indeed shocking, at the time, by gathering and publishing Guildswomen's intimate stories about their lives. This provided a unique public space in which their voices could be heard directly.

As a middle-class woman of this period, Margaret was not alone in her lifelong commitment to a working-class women's organisation, but she is a particularly interesting example. Re-elected as the Guild's General Secretary annually for over thirty years, her success was underpinned by a remarkable rapport with women from a different class, and with very different life experience from her own. This partly reflected her legendary persuasive ability; Virginia Woolf commented that Margaret could 'compel a steamroller to waltz'[13]. But there was much more to it, on both sides of her relationship with Guildswomen. Especially important were the commonly held beliefs and ideals which underlay this cross-class partnership.

Margaret was not just a single-minded campaigner. Good-looking, and by all accounts extremely charming, she made a powerful impression. A loving and conscientious daughter, sister and aunt, she never married but stayed at home until her father died, helping to care for him during his final years. Then, in her fifties, she went on to live happily with her friend and co-worker Lilian Harris for the rest of her life.

Margaret was sociable, intensely interested in people, and had a wide circle of friends. She loved discussing ideas, and especially politics; but she also liked music, poetry – and nice clothes, preferably in some shade of blue. Like many campaigners, she sometimes irritated her friends with her intensity and single-mindedness. Nevertheless, they often found her idealism and unflagging commitment inspiring, and admired her warmth, gaiety and vitality. Finally, perhaps surprisingly, she seems to have had a lifelong weakness for terrible jokes.

This is the first full-scale biography of Margaret Llewelyn Davies, and soon after I started work I began to understand why. The fact that she left few private papers seemed, initially, an insurmountable obstacle. The public and private Margaret were obviously intertwined and I worried that a lack of personal information would make for a very one-dimensional picture.

Fortunately, a family memoir by Margaret's great niece Jane Wynne Willson proved to be a lifeline, as did a cache of letters to Margaret from her mother. More family letters and reminiscences appear in a memoir collated by her nephew Peter, one of the orphaned 'lost boys' informally adopted by J. M. Barrie. And I was delighted to discover her own voice coming through in letters which survive in the archives of several eminent friends.

While each of these sources spotlighted Margaret and her life in a particular period and from a particular angle, this threw into sharper relief the lack of material directly from her closest women friends, or from the pioneering working-class women of the Guild with whom she worked so closely. However, the lively women's pages of the weekly *Co-operative News* turned out to be a goldmine. In thirty years of articles, reports of debates and letters to the editor, Guildswomen sprang into life. They have quietly moved to centre stage in this biography. Margaret would absolutely have approved.

Section One

BEGINNING

Crompton/Llewelyn Davies Family Tree

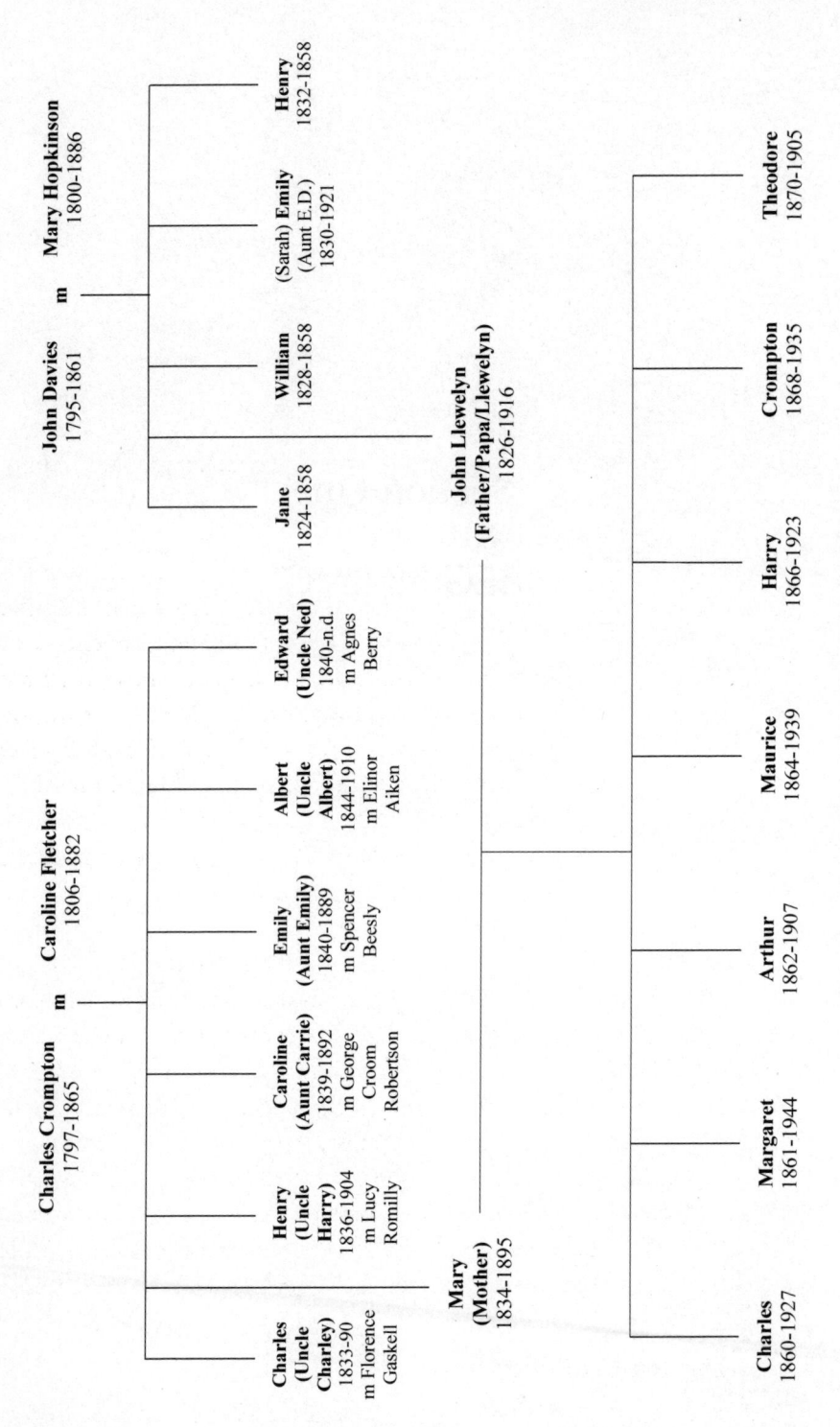

John Davies 1795-1861 m **Mary Hopkinson** 1800-1886

Children:
- **Jane** 1824-1858
- **William** 1828-1858
- **(Sarah) Emily (Aunt E.D.)** 1830-1921
- **Henry** 1832-1858

Charles Crompton 1797-1865 m **Caroline Fletcher** 1806-1882

Children:
- **Charles (Uncle Charley)** 1833-90, m Florence Gaskell
- **Henry (Uncle Harry)** 1836-1904, m Lucy Romilly
- **Caroline (Aunt Carrie)** 1839-1892, m George Croom Robertson
- **Emily (Aunt Emily)** 1840-1889, m Spencer Beesly
- **Albert (Uncle Albert)** 1844-1910, m Elinor Aiken
- **Edward (Uncle Ned)** 1840-n.d., m Agnes Berry

John Llewelyn (Father/Papa/Llewelyn) 1826-1916 m **Mary (Mother)** 1834-1895

Children:
- **Charles** 1860-1927
- **Margaret** 1861-1944
- **Arthur** 1862-1907
- **Maurice** 1864-1939
- **Harry** 1866-1923
- **Crompton** 1868-1935
- **Theodore** 1870-1905

Adapted from *The Chain of Love*, Jane Wynne Willson

CHAPTER 1

Radical Relations

Looking back at the age of seventy, Margaret explained her family background like this:

> My father, a Greek scholar and translator of Plato's Republic, was the rector of a very large and poor parish in London. He was one of the 'Broad Church' leaders, and among his friends and correspondents were Professor F.D. Maurice, the well-known theologian whose teaching undermined the belief in Hell, Charles Kingsley, T.H. Huxley, Browning and Carlyle. My aunt, Emily Davies, was a pioneer of middle-class women's education, and the originator of Girton College. My mother, daughter of a Judge, was a Unitarian, while some of my uncles were English Positivists, and great supporters of the legalisation of Trade Unions, then a most unpopular cause.[14]

Although hers was a superficially conventional middle-class Victorian family with connections to the Church, law and business, it was far from typical. Margaret's parents, aunts and uncles were part of a liberal, even radical, intelligentsia. They had, between them, a wide-ranging network of eminent friends and acquaintances – J.S. Mill, George Eliot, Ruskin, Carlyle, Marx, Elizabeth Garrett Anderson, and more.

In their world, social reform – especially the advancement of women – was not just debated. It was taken for granted that both men and women could and should intervene in public affairs in the interest of others; that they had the right to be listened to; that they had the power to make things happen.

Introducing the Cromptons

In the summer of 1864 Margaret was nearly three, her older brother

Charley, was four and little Arthur, eighteen months. With her mother about to give birth to a fourth child, the family decamped from London's summer heat and bustle to the peace of Eardiston in Worcestershire, her grandparents' country house. During the visit, the doting grandmother created a sketchbook for the children, which Margaret carefully preserved all her life.

This introduces us to grandparents Sir Charles and Lady Crompton along with two of their servants, and several of Margaret's aunts and uncles.[15] Although Uncle Charley, the oldest of these, wasn't around for this visit, there is a sketch of his wife, Aunt Florence – daughter of the novelist Mrs Gaskell – playing with the children. Uncle Charley became a QC and was also a Liberal MP for a time.

Uncle Harry is shown in one picture 'jump[ing] for joy' as the children and parents arrive and, in another, helping four-year-old Charley climb up a ladder which looks dangerously high. A barrister, he was to promote various radical, controversial causes; for example, in 1865 he supported the call to prosecute Governor Eyre for his brutal repression of a rebellion in Morant Bay, Jamaica. During the 1860s and '70s, he worked with trade unions to improve their legal position and became a personal friend of some union leaders. Uncle Harry was to marry Lucy Romilly, another supporter of trade unions.

Harry was also an ardent Positivist. Based on the ideas of French philosopher Auguste Comte, and with its associated 'religion of humanity', Positivism was extremely influential in Britain at this time. Prominent believers or sympathisers included J.S. Mill, G.H. Lewes, George Eliot, Harriet Martineau, Thomas Hardy, Leslie Stephen and Annie Besant. Beatrice Webb, very attracted by Positivism in her youth, wrote in her autobiography that she like many others had been convinced by Comte that 'altruism alone can enable us to live in the highest and truest sense'.[16] Comte also taught that the working classes played the central role in social development, and that political action should always aim to advance their interests.

Aunt Carrie appears in the sketchbook looking surprised, as four-year-old Charley, supported on the ladder by Uncle Harry, greets her at a first floor window. She provides a link with a rather different kind of radicalism. Aunt Carrie married the distinguished philosopher Professor George Croom Robertson, who, like her, supported campaigns for women's suffrage and university education. Carrie was secretary to the Girton College Council for several years and, later, the salaried bursar, taking on a degree of financial and business responsibility highly unusual for women at this time. Margaret and Carrie were to become particularly close.

Emily, Margaret's youngest Crompton aunt, was to marry Uncle Harry's friend, Professor Spencer Beesly, bringing a famous – or infamous – Positivist into the family. Beesly worked with Harry supporting trade unions and was a prominent, outspoken speaker and writer. In 1864 he chaired an historic meeting which led to the formation of the International Working Men's Association (otherwise known as the First International), and Karl Marx described him as a 'very capable and courageous man'.[17] Beesly and Harry both attracted particular hostility in 1867 by protesting at the draconian treatment of Fenian (Irish nationalist) prisoners. Later that year, when he compared recent violence by Sheffield trade unionists to the brutal killings by the British army in Jamaica, *The Globe* newspaper suggested that Beesly wanted to be 'the Marat of the English Revolution', and there were attempts to get him sacked from his university post.

As his marriage approached, Beesly assured Marx that Aunt Emily was 'heartily sympathetic with my political and social views and there is no fear that I shall have to become respectable'. Emily, who never became a Positivist herself, was active in the Women's Liberal Association for some time, and showed her sympathy for Irish Home Rule by writing new lyrics for *The Wearing of the Green*.[18]

The sketchbook also shows Uncle Albert careering downhill in a bath chair, aided by the children and the dog. Albert trained as a barrister and helped Harry to advise the TUC but, later, joined a Liverpool shipping firm run by relatives. He became a very pious Positivist and, from 1890, was the leader of the Positivist Church of Humanity in Liverpool. Uncle Ned, the youngest, followed a different path from his brothers, becoming a successful engineer.

While the Crompton grandparents' Unitarianism connected the family with current reforming ideas about education and the rights of women, Grandfather Charles, an eminent judge, also provided a link with earlier radical, even revolutionary, traditions. Joking with some pride that the last judge in the family had tried a 'very illustrious prisoner', he traced his Puritan ancestry back to Lord Bradshaw, who signed King Charles I's death warrant. He stood for Parliament in the first election after the 1832 Reform Act on a platform which included demands such the removal of property qualifications for the vote, later put forward by the Chartists. Margaret must have been proud of this, as she carefully kept a copy of his election address; a link with the turbulent politics of the early 1830s.

Grandfather Charles had a highly successful career at the Bar, was knighted and became 'the archetype of the liberal-minded, supremely competent mid-Victorian judge'.[19] He married Caroline Fletcher, from a circle of prominent Unitarian business families in Liverpool. Caroline's sister married into the Booth family, and her nephew, Charles Booth, would become became a pioneer of social investigation. Grandmother Caroline, a woman of parts, actively supported women's education. After she was widowed in 1864, she spent a great deal of time with Margaret's family and they had regular holidays at her country house. Towards the end of her life, she moved in with them, staying until she died in 1882 after a long drawn out illness. She was very fond of her granddaughter: the year before her death, when Margaret had just returned to university after the holidays, she wrote, '... how I miss you. My darling, it is so sad not to have you coming in + out of my room'.[20]

Margaret's parents also put in an appearance in the sketchbook. Papa, waving a croquet mallet, enthusiastically applauds her as she gesticulates with excitement while sitting on a horse under the supervision of Dawson, the coachman; Mama rests decorously under a tree, as befits her heavily pregnant state. After the new baby, Maurice, has arrived, Margaret is depicted pleading with a nameless nurse to be allowed to hold him.

This was a secure, loving and privileged world.

Introducing the Davies family

Margaret's father's side of the family provided quite a contrast.

She never knew her paternal grandfather, Canon John Llewelyn Davies, who died, suddenly, a few days after she was born. Three of his five children had already died young, all in 1858: Jane and Henry of tuberculosis, and William, a naval chaplain, of wounds sustained in the Crimea. Only Margaret's father, John, always known in the family as Llewelyn, and his sister, Sarah Emily, known as Emily, survived beyond their thirties.

Born in 1795, Margaret's grandfather was the son of a humble Cardiganshire farmer who, after working as a tutor and school teacher from the age of thirteen, managed to get to Oxford and then to Cambridge and became an Anglican clergyman. He married Mary Hopkinson, the daughter of a local manufacturer, and the family eventually settled in Gateshead. Grandfather John later became a canon at Durham, rapidly establishing himself as a theologian and publishing a number of books and pamphlets on religious topics. Conservative in politics and Evangelical in theology, he confided to his diary in true, self-critical, Evangelical fashion that his disposition was one of 'natural vehemence, pride and impetuosity'.[21]

After Grandfather John died, his widow moved with Emily to London, where Llewelyn found them a house near him and his family, and lived on for more than twenty years. Margaret will have seen a lot of her while she was growing up.

Grandmother Mary's story is interesting. Initially, she was an able, unobtrusive, provincial wife and mother, deeply religious, whose life was bounded by family, a few close friends and relations, and church concerns. But after she moved to London with her daughter her world began to expand. Surprisingly, she became more radical as she grew older, enthusiastically supporting Emily's work in the growing women's movement of the time. She took an interest in Emily's plans, helped out with practical work, was on good terms with friends and campaigning colleagues, gave her opinion on difficult decisions, and made no objection when her daughter had to stay away from home on business.[22]

Unusually for the times, then, Margaret had an example in the family of an independent single woman who was active and effective in public life. Aunt Emily Davies was, arguably, Margaret's most distinguished relative – and certainly the one who left the most lasting legacy.

Born in 1830, Emily had been bitterly frustrated by her lack of opportunities as a girl and young woman. While their brothers were sent to public school and on to Cambridge or legal training, Emily and her sister received only a scrappy education. After she grew up, she found herself still largely trapped in domesticity, and cared for her sister and brother during their final illnesses.

In her mid-twenties, however, Emily Davies made contact with the emergent women's movement in London. Once she moved there, in 1862, her campaigning work took off and women's education soon became her over-riding preoccupation. With friend and fellow feminist Barbara Bodichon she was a moving spirit in establishing Girton College, the first to provide women with university level studies, which was based initially in Hitchin and then just outside Cambridge. This alone was an immense achievement, but Emily Davies also fought successfully for its women students to study and be assessed on exactly the same terms as their male Cambridge peers – though the university did not officially grant degrees to women until after the Second World War. An eminent Girton graduate, writing of her extraordinary gift for organisation, concluded: 'she could be utterly intransigent and disastrously mistaken. Yet the driving force which she alone commanded was that which brought the New Jerusalem down to Hitchin Hill.'[23]

Emily Davies believed in reforms for women on the basis of common humanity with men, rather than, as some feminists did, on their essentially different and superior moral qualities. She had no patience with the rosy Victorian ideal of the joys of home and family, and argued, for example, that for single women – and even some married ones – work outside the home was essential to happiness. These were radical ideas for the time, but Emily was otherwise conservative with a small as well as a capital C. She sometimes made herself unpopular at Girton by her insistence on perceived propriety and decorum; though this may have been necessary because many saw Girton and other pioneering women's colleges as scandalous.

Towards the end of the nineteenth century, Emily Davies became closely involved in the movement for votes for women. She lived long enough to cast her vote, for the very first time, in the 1918 General Election, dying in 1921.

Emily combined her active public life with close family attachments. She cared deeply for her mother and brother, proving a doting, even proprietary, aunt to his children. Llewelyn supported her campaigning and, thanks to his diverse contacts in the Church, Cambridge and elsewhere, could usefully open doors. On the other hand, his sister expanded Llewelyn's horizons, putting him in touch with new feminist ideas and campaigns, some of which he actively supported. While she often asked for his advice, and usually seems to have acted on it, there is no suggestion that either had any sense of inequality. When writing about her brother, Emily Davies maintained a cool and ironical stance, for example reporting that he 'was so excited all last week about Miss Garrett's candidature [for the London School Board] that he could not write his sermon & was obliged to preach an old one.'[24] Elizabeth Garrett, later Elizabeth Garrett Anderson and a trailblazing woman doctor, was part of Emily's close feminist network, and as a result became friendly with the Llewelyn Davies family.

Introducing Papa

Mary Crompton and John Llewelyn Davies met and married in 1859. They went on to produce six sons and one daughter – Margaret.

Born in 1826, John Llewelyn Davies was a prominent Anglican clergyman and theological scholar who distinguished himself first at Trinity College, Cambridge and, later, with a widely praised translation of Plato's *Republic*. A few years after he was ordained, he became the rector at Christ Church, Marylebone, a large, mostly very poor, London parish. The living was in the gift of the Crown, and Llewelyn later became honorary Chaplain to the Queen. Although he was said to possess 'all the necessary background, connections, and learning for a fine Victorian bishop,'[25] he remained at Christ Church, apparently contentedly, for over thirty years without receiving promotion.

Llewelyn was part of the liberal 'broad church' wing of Anglicanism, and a leading adherent of Christian Socialism. The latter had emerged during the bitter class conflicts of the 1840s, when a small but influential group of intellectuals came together hoping to promote cross-class harmony. Putting into practice their belief in the importance of working-class education and moral improvement, they established the Working Men's College in London's Red Lion Square, which aimed to foster Christian brotherhood between lecturers and students. Llewelyn was actively involved there for many years. The Christian Socialists were also supporters of the co-operative movement, and some tried to help workers to organise small-scale co-operatives. Several, including Llewelyn's close friend Thomas Hughes, author of *Tom Brown's School Days*, were actively involved in the movement at national level.

Through Christian Socialism, Llewelyn became a long-term disciple and friend of the theologian F D Maurice. 'The Prophet', as Maurice was known to his adherents, was said to be revered in the Llewelyn Davies household; he was godfather to Margaret, and her younger brother was named after him. Maurice rejected the evangelical belief in hell and salvation, emphasising instead a God of 'righteousness and love'. He proclaimed that 'social behaviour which recognises Christ in a brother creature [is] a form of reverence to God himself'.[26] His vision of human brotherhood across class boundaries, and of the crucial moral importance of personal, loving relationships has a distinctly modern, humanist tinge.[27] We shall see later how, in her own way, Margaret put this into practice in the Guild.

Llewelyn's social ideas were generally liberal. He believed in compulsory state education, was a member of the London School Board for a time, and took an active part in debates about religious education in schools. As well as backing his sister Emily's campaigns for women's education, he helped Elizabeth Garrett Anderson in her efforts to found the New Hospital for Women, of which he was Chair for a period, and backed votes for women. He occasionally spoke out in support of trade unions, most controversially when he backed the agricultural labourers' union in the early 1870s. And he attacked the gulf between rich and poor, as in this 1854 letter to *The Spectator* criticising a speech by the Bishop of London (presumably not a wise career move, as he was a mere London curate at the time): 'Artisans and labourers, and poor people generally, do not want condolence; they want common hopes and a common purpose with their richer fellow-countrymen.'[28]

However, like his mentor Maurice and, indeed, other Christian Socialists,

Llewelyn did not look for changes to the basic structure of society. He believed that God had ordained an unequal order of society, and that all should have 'the *best* and not the *most equal* opportunities possible'.[29] And perhaps surprisingly, given his other ideas, he actively supported the Charity Organisation Society's punitive approach to charitable help and poor law relief.

John Llewelyn Davies was always busy and active; when he was a young curate in London's East End, his housekeeper summed him up as 'always in and out, like a dog at a fair'.[30] As well as running his large parish, he took on committee and campaigning work, published theological treatises and numerous articles, and regularly debated in the letters columns of *The Times* and other papers. He was a prolific correspondent with friends and acquaintances, including many of the liberal minded great and good of his time.

In photographs, Llewelyn – always shown with a beard – has a piercing, even intimidating, gaze. He could apparently be reserved, or even stern.[31] But he was not the stereotype of the Victorian paterfamilias; nor indeed was Mary Davies the humble, adoring wife. Her letters to Margaret, usually referring to him as 'Pa' or 'Papa', give the distinct impression that she was more than ready to puncture any tendency to self-importance: 'Papa is very coy over his L.T. shoes. Can't you fancy. They [sons] enjoy hearing him chaffed a bit, + he smiles serenely.'[32]

Introducing Mama

Margaret's father's busy public and professional life contrasts with her mother's more restricted world. But her delightfully idiosyncratic voice and perceptive observations shine through in her surviving letters.

Born Mary Crompton in 1834, Mary was well educated, thanks to her Unitarian parents. She was knowledgeable about politics and literature, could speak and read French and possibly other languages, and was a talented amateur musician. She was pretty and charming; and soon after they met, John Llewelyn Davies romantically compared her to a white pink.[33] For ten years after they married, her life was dominated by childbearing and rearing; she produced seven children between 1860 and 1870.

Mary Davies had a special gift for getting on with people and was particularly good with children. Fourteen-year-old Dolly Parry was taken ill while visiting the family, and fifty years on still recalled her kindness, her 'remarkable brain, and great knowledge and love of literature and poetry.'[34]

For Mary Davies, family definitely came first. She was very close to her own parents, sisters and brothers; her mother, as we know, came to live with her towards the end of her life, and she also nursed both her sisters in their last illnesses. She was devoted to her children too, missing them dreadfully when they went off to boarding school and university.

Her letters are often full of self-deprecation but also of a teasing refusal to take others too seriously. On a summer's day: 'I am not having tea outside – as that sort of thing does not I know fit in with the Davies soul.'[35] She was certainly more than capable of sending up her more serious-minded relatives. Emily Davies reported that on one occasion, when sending out letters canvassing support for women to be admitted to London university degrees, 'It was thought best not to give my Christian names in full, M. Ll D [Mary Davies] remarking that "they'd think it was some horrid woman in spectacles"' (Emily added wryly that, as a result, she received many replies addressed to 'S.E. Davies Esq.').[36]

Unlike her sister Carrie and sister-in-law Emily, Margaret's mother was not herself actively involved with feminist campaigns. She was much taken up with seven children and a busy household, often having to entertain visiting churchmen or other contacts of Llewelyn's. When she did put her toe in the water on occasion, she lacked confidence; writing to Margaret 'Don't you think I'm bold to attempt it, + Papa wet blankets!' about helping a relative with a meeting about women's trade unions.[37]

So Margaret grew up with strong connections to earlier reforming traditions, and particularly to three major intellectual currents of the mid to late nineteenth century: her father's Christian Socialism, her uncle's Positivism, and the activist feminism of Emily Davies and other relatives. It was to be a potent mix.

CHAPTER 2

Early Days, 1861-1883

Part One: Growing up in Marylebone

The Llewelyn Davies children loved nicknames and, for some reason, 'Little Toast' was Margaret's for a while. She was not at all happy with it. The family story goes that when she was particularly cross about this one breakfast time, one of her brothers 'picked a small slice of toast and disappeared into the garden. He reappeared a few minutes later, and, with great solemnity, announced, "I have buried Little Toast".'[38] That put an end to it.

Until Margaret was in her late twenties, the family lived in a small enclave of pleasant, leafy squares north of London's Marylebone Road. In its heyday the area was literary, artistic and cosmopolitan. Writer Mary Lamb, the actress Sarah Bernhardt and Kossuth, the Hungarian revolutionary had all lived there at different times, as did Barbara Bodichon, Emily Davies' friend and a leading feminist campaigner. The Llewelyn Davies's most notable neighbour, however, was George Eliot who lived with her common law husband G.H. Lewes just a couple of doors away. As the wife of a clergyman, Margaret's mother could not call on Eliot because she was 'living in sin'. But she greatly admired Eliot's work, and it is said that she made a point of touching the front gate in homage whenever she went by.

For most of Margaret's childhood, the family lived in Blandford Square with its attractive central lawn and trees, built in the 1830s on the site of a botanical garden. When she was seventeen, the family moved to a slightly larger house in nearby Dorset Square, probably needing the extra space to house Grandmother Caroline and her servants. This was only temporary, though, and, after she died the family moved back to Blandford Square, buying the lease to number 5 from Barbara Bodichon.[39] This was to be their home until they left London in 1889. The house disappeared soon afterwards when part of Blandford Square was pulled down to make way for Marylebone station.

Comfortable though it was, Blandford Square was on the fringes of the notorious slums of Lisson Grove, which dominated Llewelyn's Christ Church parish. Respectable, even fashionable, in the early nineteenth century, Lisson Grove had deteriorated as its population increased. Overcrowding was rife, with dilapidated houses split into single-room tenements. By the time Margaret's family moved into Blandford Square, Lisson Grove was described as the worst part of St Marylebone: a byword for crime and grinding poverty. Margaret's father's duties necessarily took him there frequently, but although Margaret did some charitable work in Lisson Grove later on, there is no suggestion that she and her brothers knew the area while they were growing up. Like better-off Londoners before and since, they probably grew up unaware of the realities of day to day life just one or two streets away.

Whilst comfortably within the professional upper middle class, the Llewelyn Davies family did not consider itself well off. The houses in Blandford Square were large and attractive, but not huge by middle-class standards for a family of nine plus the three or four living-in servants considered normal at their social level. The boys all went to public schools, but ones which offered reduced fees for the children of clergymen. Extra money gained from scholarships at school and university was definitely appreciated. When 12-year- old Theodore won a Junior Scholarship at Marlborough public school, brother Charles wrote to him, 'How pleased they will all be at home. You have the proud satisfaction of earning £60 for the family.'[40] In 1876, explaining Uncle Charley's plan to give Margaret a present of a 'best' winter dress, her mother wrote, 'I congratulate you on having a new dress! No cast-offs this time!'[41]

However, there is no indication that money was ever really short. Grandmother Caroline may well have helped out, and, over time, the family's finances were boosted by bequests from her and from the Davies grandparents. There was certainly enough money to rule out any question of Margaret earning her own living.

Family life

Margaret's childhood experience as the big sister of a brood of boys may well have stood her in good stead later on. The arrival of baby brothers, to join older brother Charles, punctuated her childhood. Arthur was born when she was eighteen months old, followed by Maurice, Henry (Harry), Crompton and, finally, Theodore in 1870, when Margaret was nine.

Although Mary Davies had the help of at least one nursery maid, she was still involved with looking after the children day to day. She was terribly upset when the doctor insisted that she was not strong enough to nurse nine-year-old Crompton during a bout of scarlet fever. 'It cost me a great deal to give up my dear little boy into the hands of a stranger.'[42] She found it equally difficult to part with the boys when they went off to boarding school. They clearly felt the same, following her round from room to room as she did their packing.[43]

The large family and frequent visitors generated a great deal of work and, on occasion, Mary Davies had to roll up her sleeves alongside the servants. She complained to fifteen-year-old Margaret, away on holiday at the time, 'Annie and I had *such* a grand turn out of your room one day! Such stores and hoards of rubbish as you had there Madam!'[44] (original emphasis and spelling).

Margaret's mother was clearly highly competent at running the household but it is significant that the servants do not seem to have stayed with the family long-term.[45] This may have been her choice; but they may also have voted with their feet, as servants often did in this period, looking for higher pay or a less demanding employer. We do know, however, that Mary Davies could be sympathetic to their precarious position, especially that of young women; for whom a single event like losing a job without a reference, falling ill, or becoming pregnant could easily trigger a descent into destitution:

> That poor Marianne … has been in hospital ever since I went to see her …. + I wrote to tell her that when she came out I would take her in here till she got a place. I was so afraid of her getting into harm + I thought I *might* help to get her into a quiet safe situation.[46] [original emphasis]

The Victorian maxim that children should be seen and not heard definitely did not apply in the Llewelyn Davies home. Thomas Hughes reported calling while Llewelyn was out, only to discover the boys 'at high jinks besieging and defending the big armchair in the dining room.'[47] And although less involved with the children than his wife, John Llewelyn Davies was a fond and, for his time, liberal father. When teenage Margaret wrote home from a trip to Europe with Aunt Carrie, her mother reported how

> Papa rushed up to me with the letter …. first I read it all aloud + then Papa read it to me! …… Papa reads the letters with such interest, his specs perched on his nose! + he looks out all the places + excursions in his Murray, + the flowers in his Botany book.[48]

There were many visitors to this busy household, including Llewelyn's Christian Socialist friends, along with others of his and his wife's extended acquaintance and of course, uncles and aunts. Judging from the assistance Llewelyn gave Emily Davies and her friend Elizabeth Garrett, various feminist campaigns were also planned from the Llewelyn Davies drawing room. He loved all this, but it seems that it was sometimes too much for his wife, especially from the late 1870s onward when she had worrying bouts of ill-health. However, she was devoted to her Crompton relations and outings, visits and holiday breaks with them were a regular feature of Margaret's routine as a child. On the Davies side, too, Grandmother Mary and Aunt Emily Davies (referred to in letters as 'Aunt E.D.', presumably to distinguish her from Emily Beesly on the other side of the family) were regular visitors.

Perhaps aware that Margaret might be isolated as the only daughter, her parents encouraged her to visit her Crompton aunts, and one highlight of her teenage years was the extended trip to Europe with Aunt Carrie, with whom she had a particular bond. Interestingly, though, there is no evidence that Emily Davies and Margaret, her only niece, were particularly close.

Looking back, Margaret praised the way her parents encouraged the children to express their own ideas freely. With their mother retaining a discreet loyalty to Unitarianism, the parents practised a non-sectarian religious approach, and apart from Charley the other children all appear to have rejected organised religion as adults.[49] They will have benefited from listening to debates among the many visitors and, as they grew older, there were lively political disputes, for example on home rule for Ireland and republicanism. When the family moved from Dorset Square back to Blandford, Mary Davies teased 21-year-old Margaret: 'You'll be glad to hear that the [picture of the] dear Queen was successfully hung this evening. Tell it not among the Radicals!'[50]

Margaret and her brothers

The Llewelyn Davies children all grew up to be good-looking, and the adult Margaret was often described as beautiful. A studio photograph, probably taken in her early teens, already shows something of this, although the serious and thoughtful girl portrayed here could also be extremely lively, not to say boisterous. When fifteen-year-old Margaret visited one of her aunts, her mother wrote, 'I only hope you will have mercy upon her when you give her your goodnight hugs'.[51] Not long before, Mary Davies reported that the servants would be delighted to see 'the lively one' back.[52] At this time Margaret was nearly fifteen, and the three youngest boys – surely lively as well? – were still living at home.

There was another side to Margaret, too. Throughout her life, her capacity for great enjoyment would be combined with a heightened, even guilty, sensitivity to others' misfortunes. Her grandmother Davies suffered for years from acute neuralgia, and fourteen-year-old Margaret wrote from a happy summer holiday at her other grandmother s country house:

> The roses this year are splendid. We have got glass ornaments in the rooms filled with ... beautiful dark red ones, with the 'Gloire de Dijon' and pinky-white ones all mixed together with maidenhair. How I wish you had them on your table instead of ours! I don't see why we should have everything delightful while we are enjoying ourselves so much, and you only your horrid pain! [53]

Margaret was clearly well able to hold her own with her brothers. Throughout their lives, the siblings retained a strong bond, although when they were children, jokes and teasing were evidently part of day to day family life. Margaret might have been upset at her nickname of 'Little Toast', but what did stocky Maurice think of being called 'Hippo'?

Harry, deemed less academic than the others, went on to technical college and a highly successful career in engineering. His brothers all went from public school to Oxford or Cambridge, walking off with scholarships capped by first class degrees.

Margaret's strength of will and staying power as an adult may have been forged by her childhood experience as the only girl in this large family; but she also probably benefited from extra attention, especially from her mother.

Queen's College

The women Margaret was later to meet in the Women's Co-operative Guild's earlier years had mostly grown up before the advent of state-funded and organised education. Often starting work aged eleven, or even younger, they had received what formal education they could at small local 'dame schools', and/or from local charitable schools, often associated with the Church. They had to supplement this by educating themselves, as many did.

While things were very different for Margaret, most girls of her generation and social class still suffered from the lack of opportunities which had frustrated the young Emily Davies decades earlier. Although academic education for girls was beginning to expand, it still reached only a tiny minority. Middle-class girls were taught at home by their mothers, by private tutors or governesses, and/or in small day or boarding schools.

For most, whatever teaching they received was primarily designed to equip them with the ladylike behaviour and accomplishments they needed in order to attract a husband, along with the virtues required to provide moral and religious guidance within the family.[54]

Thanks to her parents, Margaret escaped these restrictions and benefited from an advanced level of education for a girl of her time. While she was probably taught at home by her mother until she was ten, she then went to Queen's College School, moving up to the main College when she was thirteen and staying there for another five years.

By the time Margaret arrived, Queen's College had been going for nearly twenty-five years. Something of a hybrid between a school and an adult college, it was the first to give girls and young women the opportunity to study at the same academic level as boys. Despite its pioneering, wide-ranging academic curriculum, the College operated within a carefully conventional framework. Initiated by Llewelyn's mentor, F.D. Maurice, it had strong Anglican and Christian Socialist connections and, for several years while Margaret was there, her father acted as Principal, leading an all-male governing body. The founders justified women's need for education in fairly traditional terms – 'every lady is and must be a teacher – of some person or other, children, sisters, the poor'.[55] Lecturers were almost invariably male, many connected with King's College, and volunteer Lady Visitors – mostly society women – chaperoned the students at lectures. A Lady Resident acted as the equivalent of head teacher.

Queen's College had a distinctive ethos, which reflected its Christian Socialist roots. At its fiftieth birthday celebrations in 1898, the then Lady Resident announced proudly that it had kept to its principles of non-competition and aimed to inculcate a love of learning 'for its own sake'. Perhaps for this reason, the College's marking system was somewhat vague. As well as traditional female accomplishments like music and drawing, Margaret studied a long list of subjects including arithmetic, geometry, chemistry, languages, English grammar and literature, history, geography, astronomy, church history, Latin and also, for a while, Greek. Her results veered between 'good' and 'very good', with one or two 'excellents' (usually for English, sometimes for Latin), although she struggled at times with arithmetic and algebra.

A number of women who later became prominent in public life and the feminist movement were educated, and/or taught, at Queen's College. They included Frances Buss, Dorothea Beale and other pioneers of girls' schools, Octavia Hill of the Charity Organisation Society, housing reform and the National Trust, and trail-blazing doctor Sophia Jex-Blake. The

College experience evidently encouraged women to venture into new fields. By 1898, its ex-students included journalists, horticulturalists, a surgeon, the head of a boys' preparatory school, and even the managing director of a brewery.[56] We do not know directly how Margaret herself reacted to life there, but judging from this, the College's unusual education for girls helped to develop confidence and initiative as well as academic ability – a good preparation for her future as an activist.

When Margaret was thirteen, her mother wrote from a visit to Emily Davies at Girton College, 'Shall you ever come here I wonder! And inhabit one of these delightful little sets of rooms?'[57]

This was indeed to be Margaret's next step, and would mark the beginning of her adult life.

Growing up in a feminist family – Victorian style

Margaret was spared the mind-numbing domestic restrictions which other girls of her generation and class still found so oppressive, and was given an excellent education for a girl of her time. Yet she was, after all, the daughter of a Church of England clergyman, and the family was embedded in respectable Victorian society. Despite her parents' liberal views, she was definitely treated differently from her brothers.

Being the only girl in the family clearly carried with it with gender-specific responsibilities. Once Margaret reached her early teens, it seems that she, rather than any of the boys, was expected to provide her mother with domestic back-up. This only happened occasionally but when Mary was away from home she would send Margaret messages to be passed on to the servants, or ask her to oversee domestic tasks, for example, to ensure rooms were ready for visitors, or a brother's washing was done; although, needless to say, the actual work was done by the servants.

The Victorian ideal of the sunbeam in the home could rear its head even in this feminist family. When Margaret went on a European trip with Aunt Carrie, the plan had been for the whole family to join her in France. Then, little Crompton fell ill and Mary Davies decided to stay behind. Worried about abandoning the others, she wrote to Margaret, who was then fifteen:

> … it will be quite an opportunity for you to come out in a motherly way, + to try to smooth + soften + make things go very happily. One of my troubles has been that I fear there may be rubs + difficulties + little teasings, wh perhaps if I had been there would not have been, or would have been eased over. Will you try your best to make all things happy. A kind word – a refraining from joining in a laugh against an

unfortunate one, even a standing on his side! ... I shall rejoice if Papa tells me you have been the helper of everyone + the kind friend of all.[58] [original abbreviations]

Part Two: Girton Girl

A year after leaving school, Margaret left home for Girton College, Cambridge. Tall and dark haired, she had her full share of the family good looks; a friend compared her with the female saints in Andrea del Sarto's paintings. She was lively, and above all had a 'great power of enjoyment' which would stay with her throughout her life.[59]

Her mother's regular letters tell us a good deal about Margaret at this time. Frustratingly, we only have her side of the correspondence, but it confirms that Margaret loved college life from the start.

The very first university college for women, Girton had opened its doors in 1869. By 1881, when Margaret arrived, it was well settled on its own site just outside Cambridge, its impressive buildings recently extended to house up to 55 young women. In these early days, Girton students were very aware that they were in the forefront of huge changes. Women were only beginning to claim the right to the same level of education as men, and were still effectively barred from the professions. They faced entrenched opposition in the academic world, and had to challenge the widely accepted opinion that women's brains could not cope with academic work; more, that it would damage their physical and mental health.

It is not surprising, then, that in 1871 there was almost a riot at Girton, when the first three women passed the Cambridge tripos (degree) examinations.

> The students climbed on to the roof and rang the alarm bell, with such effect that the ... police began to get the fire engines ready for action. When the Mistress remonstrated, they fell back on singing *Gaudeamus igitur*, and tying three flags to the chimneys.[60]

By the time Margaret arrived, however, things had calmed down. When several women gained first class results in 1882, celebrations were more sedate, the students contenting themselves with a candlelit procession and singing college songs.

By now, Emily Davies and her colleagues had persuaded the University to agree formal examination arrangements for Girtonians, though they and other women had to wait until 1947 to be officially granted Cambridge degrees. Like the male students, they first had to pass the 'Little-go', a preliminary examination in classics and mathematics which extended to a third part, known as 'Additionals', for anyone aiming for a tripos – that is, a full honours degree. The Little-go's emphasis on classics seriously disadvantaged many women students who, unlike Margaret, had not studied Latin and Greek at school. But although the university had agreed that they could substitute certain other exams, Emily Davies insisted that Girton students should be judged by exactly the same rules as men.

After two terms, Margaret achieved a first in classics, and also passed in mathematics; two terms later, she also got through the Additionals. She went on to the tripos, probably studying history,[61] but occasionally complained about finding the academic work difficult. Each time an examination loomed, it seems, she worried whether she would pass. While Mary Davies tried to encourage her daughter, she also made it clear that she did not have high expectations: '[the Little-go] is not a *vital* matter, though I know how infinitely pleasanter in every way it would be for you to get through + done with it.'[62] [original emphasis].

Margaret performed perfectly well, both at school and at college, so why, when it came to academic work, did she lack confidence? The weight of family tradition may have daunted her. After all, her aunt had been one of Girton's founders and all but one of her brothers regularly walked off with prizes and scholarships. Younger brother Arthur's lordly response to her results says a great deal: 'It is satisfactory that Peg has got through her Little Go, even though she has not got a First Class.'[63]

Girton students were expected to take responsibility for organizing their own studies, and within the college itself had an exceptional amount of freedom compared with young women living at home. However, painfully concerned to preserve the college's reputation, the Girton authorities enforced tight restrictions on any outside contacts. The students were taken to and from university lectures by carriage and had to be chaperoned once there. One later recalled her embarrassment as the only woman student attending a particular course of lectures. She often had to hang around outside the lecture hall because her chaperone was late, thus, ironically, exposing her to the 'mockery of a certain type of undergraduate'.[64]

There were strict rules about all male visitors to the college, who were only allowed into students' rooms if the door remained open, and both parties stayed standing up. Restrictions even applied to contact with close relatives. When Margaret first arrived at Girton, her mother advised that they would have to ask Aunt Emily Davies how she could visit her brother Charley, then at Trinity College. It definitely would not do for Margaret to be seen going up the stairs to his rooms on her own.

Days at Girton followed an established, well-defined routine. Mornings were for studying and attending lectures, which sometimes spilled over into the afternoons. But afternoons were the time for walks, tennis, and seeing friends. After the evening meal there would be meetings of the various college societies, and an hour or two more of study. Then a round of socializing began, which ex-students remembered as a central part of college life. This was always known as 'Tray', because the servants provided each student with a tray, a bun and the makings of cocoa, enabling them to spend the rest of the evening in their rooms, comfortably chatting together in small groups. Like the others, Margaret had her own bedroom and private study/sitting room, and she leapt at this first opportunity to arrange her surroundings as she liked. Her mother responded with vicarious enthusiasm, approving of her purchase of a pot of lobelia and enquiring: 'Is the room (your craze) as beauteous as ever?'[65]

Margaret also took to the social side of Girton with great enthusiasm. Among the thirteen students who started with her, three became life-long friends. Rosalind Shore Smith, Rosie, as she was usually known, loved music, as did Margaret, and they shared similar backgrounds in Marylebone. Rosalind, too, had pioneering women relatives, including Florence Nightingale, of whom she saw a great deal, and Barbara Bodichon. She had been educated at Heath Brow, a progressive school run by the parents of Janet Case, a second kindred spirit at Girton. Janet also grew up with feminist ideas; her Unitarian uncle, the politician Sir James Stansfeld, worked with Josephine Butler on her controversial campaign to repeal the Contagious Diseases Acts, which laid down punitive and degrading treatment for suspected prostitutes. The third of Margaret's closest friends, Ethel Sargant, was daughter of a barrister and she, too, had received an unusually good education for a girl of the time at the pioneering North London Collegiate School. Unlike Margaret and Rosalind, she studied the sciences.

Margaret took part in college activities with her characteristic enthusiasm and energy. She had her first taste of public speaking and organization with stints as Secretary of the Debating Society and head captain in the College's Fire Brigade – and took a leading part in a lighthearted debate which erupted when someone put an anti-Gladstone pamphlet in the students' Reading Room. She was a good tennis player, took part in amateur dramatics and was a talented singer. After her first couple of terms, she persuaded her parents to send up a piano, and became a regular and popular soloist at musical evenings and Choral Society concerts, major features of College social life. Rosalind remembered her singing to friends during Tray get-togethers, with 'youthful grace and feeling'.[66]

It comes as a surprise, then, that Margaret left Girton at the end of the 1883 summer term, missing her third year and the tripos examinations. At this time, however, it was by no means uncommon for Girton students to leave without completing the full degree course; indeed, Rosalind did the same.[67] Achieving the tripos was vital for those women students who would go on to paid work, often as teachers. But it was not the same for others like Margaret, who did not have to earn their living. For all, Girton was not only about gaining qualifications, it was a rare opportunity for young women to escape restrictive family and social expectations, live independently and fulfil their own needs.[68]

On the surface, Margaret's early departure is puzzling, as she did not have any serious academic worries and enormously enjoyed college life. It is interesting that it was her father, rather than Margaret herself, who visited 'Aunt E.D' (Emily Davies) to break the news.[69] As this suggests, her parents supported her decision; indeed it seems that they proposed it because Margaret was needed at home.

Although delighted that her daughter got so much out of Girton, Mary Davies had had mixed feelings all along. She frequently wrote about missing Margaret, and looking forward to her coming home for holidays, with a hint of the emotional dependence which increased over the years. What is more, Margaret's absence at Girton had come at the worst possible time. Not long afterwards, grandmother Crompton had sunk into dementia, and Mary Davies had to cope with her distressing decline. Lady Crompton died in spring 1882, when Margaret had been away for a year.

To make things worse, the youngest boys were now leaving the nest. Harry went in 1881, followed by Crompton and finally Theodore in spring 1883. Their mother found herself much on her own, and, on top of all this, was ill on and off for most of the autumn and winter of 1882 to 1883. Her continuing poor health seems to have been the trigger for the parents to ask Margaret to leave Girton early. Shortly before she did so, Mary Davies wrote:

> 'You are much in my thoughts, in leaving [Girton], + I know your heart will be heavy to say goodbye + to come to the end of a time you have enjoyed so much ... My mind is full of all I should like to do for + with you in the future. If only I were more capable! But no doubt there is some purpose in my incapacity – at any rate I like to think so. It may be to teach me patience + submission – + to bring out something in you ... At any rate, you will be my comfort + right hand, + I am sure a

great pleasure to yr father, who has to suffer from my poor + at times depressing society.[70][original abbreviations]

Not for the last time, Margaret was confronted with a conflict between the demands of her independent life and her family obligations. However, the decision was less straightforward than it might appear. In another letter, Mary acknowledged that her daughter had come home 'partly for me'. And many years later, another side of the story came out. Margaret's niece Theodora Calvert remembered asking her why she had left Girton early.

Margaret explained that really she did not find university study congenial. She enjoyed the sociabilities and made many friends ... But her enormously strong social sense, that she inherited from her father, and [her] desire to ameliorate the conditions of the poor, found no fulfilment in college life.[71]

With hindsight, both of these explanations ring true.

Margaret was not alone in her ardent wish to be make some kind of contribution to society. Many pioneering women students of this era felt the same, and she belonged to a particularly remarkable generation at Girton. Among her fellow students Janet, a notable classicist, and Rosalind, a journalist and writer, both went on to work closely with Margaret in Women's Co-operative Guild campaigns. Helena Sickert (later Swanwick) and Alice Zimmern became activists in the women's suffrage and peace movements, and Adelaide Anderson was later appointed as the first woman factory inspector. Others blazed the trail for women in academia; Ethel Sargant and Ellen McArthur became, respectively, a distinguished botanist and economist, while Katherine Jex-Blake, a classicist, stayed on to become, eventually, Mistress of Girton. Other young women also went on to make significant contributions in education and public service of various kinds.[72]

Girton had given Margaret a great deal, and had shown her a community successfully run for and by women. She left at twenty-one with a solid academic training, the beginnings of her formidable network, and, most importantly, close friends who would nurture and sustain her throughout her life.

CHAPTER 3

Finding the Guild, 1883-1889

Back with home and family

Soon after Margaret came home from Girton, her mother wrote to thirteen-year-old Theodore that 'Papa and Margaret' had just gone out 'to meet and lunch with the Waleses and all the Board schoolchildren of the metropolis'. Later the same day, the two went on to a garden party given by the Archbishop of Canterbury. 'Are they not a gay couple?' enquired Mary Davies, adding ruefully that she herself was too ill to get out of bed.[73]

Although standing in for her mother like this might more often have been a duty rather than a pleasure, it did have its advantages. Presumably Margaret was just a little impressed to meet the Prince of Wales and the Archbishop of Canterbury on the same day. Around the same time, in her own letter to Theodore, Margaret casually mentioned meeting Robert Browning at a party given by Lady Stanley, Bertrand Russell's grandmother, a well-known political hostess as well as a great supporter of Girton. Thanks to the family, she had the entrée to London's intellectual society.

Margaret was also developing her own network, quickly recreating something of what she had found at Girton: a group of female friends, mostly like-minded and from a similar background to her own. Rosalind and Janet both came back to live in London, and the friendships flourished. Another good friend from Girton was Rose Rendel, daughter of a Liberal MP; and Margaret sometimes found herself in even more exalted circles thanks to her friendship with Mary Howard. Mary's father, soon to be Earl of Carlisle, was a Liberal politician and friend of William Morris, while her formidable mother was a feminist and temperance advocate. Margaret stayed with them several times at Castle Howard and Naworth Castle. Mary Howard seems to have been a kindred spirit; she is said to have refused to go to society balls, and she and her husband later shared Margaret's enthusiasm for the co-operative movement.

From what we can tell, Margaret did not provide as much companionship as her mother had earlier hoped. Intensely interested and involved in Margaret's doings, as in those of all the children, Mary Davies gently nagged Margaret about her health and knew all about her friends, following their ups and downs with great interest. She loved to discuss everything that was going on, including clothes: 'So you chose the dark red! I liked that best, + hope it will look well + *be becoming*. Shall you have a 'toque' to match? They're all the rage.'[74] Mary's letters make it clear that Margaret did confide in her, and they kept in touch even when parted for a short time. A few months after leaving, Margaret returned briefly to Girton to take part in what was, for a women's college, a pioneering and high profile project: a production of Sophocles' *Electra* in Greek, in which Janet Case played the lead. Missing her daughter, Mary Davies wrote plaintively: 'Goodnight little girl. Come back soon to yr poor old M.'[75][original abbreviations] Despite their closeness, might her mother's dependency have sometimes felt too much for Margaret?

Getting started

With a pleasant life in a comfortably off household, a close, affectionate family and a wide circle of interesting friends and acquaintances, Margaret might have looked no further. But thanks to the 'enormously strong social sense' which her niece Theodora referred to, this would never have been enough. And Margaret had returned home at a time when new opportunities for young women like her were beckoning.

In the early 1880s, many well-to-do people felt a growing sense of guilt – famously described by Beatrice Webb as a 'new consciousness of sin' – about the ever-increasing unemployment, poverty and misery that surrounded them.[76] As William Morris and HM Hyndman declaimed:

> … vast masses of our countrymen are living on the very verge of starvation … Order exists, morality exists, comfort, happiness, education, as a whole, exist only for the class which has the means of production, at the expense of the class which supplies the labour-force that produces wealth.[77]

Margaret could see for herself, close to her own home, the terrible poverty and distress in London caused by a series of hard winters, combined with the general economic depression. In February 1886, a demonstration of the unemployed turned violent, and there was window-smashing, looting and clashes with the police in the West End, not far from where she lived.

At the same time, socialist ideas and activism were burgeoning, with the birth of organizations like the Fabian Society and the Social Democratic Federation in the early 1880s. New ideas were in the air. There was a 'buzzing utopianism'[78] around the SDF and other smaller socialist groupings; and socialists, feminists and others were discussing the need for personal as well as political change. William Morris, Edward Carpenter and Olive Schreiner were among those beginning to advocate new ways of living, and even new approaches to marriage and sexual relationships.

While Margaret was never part of this world, she was clearly aware of it. A life-long admirer of Morris, she loved not only his designs, but also his ideas about socialism and the importance of art and beauty for human well-being. Later on, she said that she had been 'much addicted' to Carpenter's ideas, too.[79] She may have been drawn towards his advocacy of co-operative production, but possibly more to his emphasis on transforming human relationships, and on socialism as a way of achieving this.

New kinds of philanthropic work were expanding at this time, with a special emphasis on personal service to the very poor. Settlements were opening up in slum areas, where educated middle and upper-class volunteers lived and worked directly with the local people. Idealistic young women like Margaret took up this kind of work in increasing numbers, fulfilling their desire to serve others but also gaining an outlet for their abilities and energies; escaping from family restrictions and, for some, experiencing an exciting frisson from their contact with what they saw as a dangerous and transgressive slum life.

Margaret's parents permitted her a good deal of freedom but, in the last analysis, like other young single women living at home and financially dependent, she was still subject to parental authority; even at the age of twenty-six, she had to seek their permission before she went on holiday abroad. Earlier, a few months after leaving Girton, she wrote to them while away visiting a friend, outlining future plans. Her mother wrote back breaking the news that they both felt they could not support her: 'Papa says he could not do with your going off to Red Lion Square so late in the evening. "I *must* draw the line at that," was his remark.' [80] Whatever this project was, once her parents had vetoed it, that was that.

Shortly after this, however, Margaret found an outlet of which her parents definitely approved. This was a social club for young people in Lisson Grove, a 'unique experiment' in that it welcomed both young men and young women. With Margaret Treasurer and her father, the local vicar, President, the club aimed to provide an alternative to 'the baneful attractions of music-halls ... a more refined but equally cheerful social atmosphere.'[81] Located on the edge of Lisson Grove, it was held in somewhat insalubrious surroundings above a fried fish shop. The district as a whole was seen as dangerous and crime ridden. Elizabeth Haldane, one of Margaret's co-workers, was escorted there and back, at her anxious mother's insistence, by the family butler. Nevertheless, the club aimed to recruit 'hard-working, respectable young lads and lasses,' who had to supply character references and pay a subscription. Unlike many of her peers, Margaret had not chosen to work with the very poor.

Margaret not only acted as Treasurer but also ran sessions with the young people. Their 'high spirits' sometimes needed to be controlled, and Elizabeth Haldane remembered being 'truly alarmed when once or twice Miss Davies could not come to the club and I was left to grapple with it without her very efficient aid'.[82] Not much older than the young people she had to control, Margaret clearly possessed confidence and authority; after all, she had experience with her younger brothers.

At one point she wrote a funding appeal, which provides a rare example of her voice at this time:

> Rich people do not grudge £100 for a single evening party in London. How many evening parties our club could provide for that sum to guests who cannot have them in their own small crowded homes! For, after all, the root of the matter is that much-debated question – the unsatisfactory nature of the working people's homes. These young people want something cheery at the end of their long day's work. They want pleasant social intercourse and amusements, and opportunities for reading and thought, just as much as our young people of the middle-class do. We hope not only to give them present enjoyment, but, by raising their standard of comfort and refinement, to make life permanently brighter and purer for them.[83]

While this last pious hope aimed to appeal to wealthy donors, the piece is notable for its emphasis, partly perhaps reflecting Llewelyn's Christian Socialist ideas, on the contrast between the experience of privilege and the circumscribed lives of the working class.

Another young woman with Margaret's background and contacts might well have gravitated to one of the settlements, or to Octavia Hill's Charity Organisation Society, with which her father was heavily involved locally. Interestingly, there is nothing to suggest that Margaret did so. However, her commitment to the Lisson Grove youth club continued for several years, and she also helped with another club which seems to have been just for girls. Evidently, she was at home in this philanthropic setting, and enjoyed it.

Margaret also said later that she worked as 'a sort of amateur sanitary inspector' at some point.[84] During the late 1880s, volunteer ladies had taken up what they saw as poor people's need for sanitary education with great enthusiasm. As always, Margaret was nothing if not well connected, and through family and friends had contacts with some of the leading organizations in the field. She left no other mention of this work, so she probably did not do it for very long.

From philanthropy to co-operation – and then to the Guild

Margaret joined her local co-operative society in 1886. Her enthusiasm for co-operative sausages became a family joke, but this seemingly small step was to change her life.

The move might seem unexpected, given Margaret's previous work, although she will have grown up knowing something about the co-operative movement through her father's Christian Socialist connections. She later said that she made her decision after reading William Thornton's book, *On Labour*.[85] Thornton, who was an economist, admired the movement, suggesting that in the future it might spread in such a way as to lead, gradually and peacefully, to socialism. This signals a shift in Margaret's ideas. She was beginning to aim not only to help individuals, but to contribute to wider social change.

Co-operation of this time had its roots in working-class movements of the turbulent 1820s, when new ideas and social experiments, most famously associated with the 'utopian' socialism of Robert Owen, had sprung up. Co-operators emphasized the need for workers to educate themselves and for 'propaganda' to spread the word, and their overarching ideal was to change how society was organized: to expand co-operation so that it would eventually replace the poverty and misery of capitalism and create what they termed the Co-operative Commonwealth. Small scale worker co-operatives emerged, particularly among skilled craftsmen, along with a range of other experiments, for example in co-operative housing, and even small co-operatively-run communities.

But in subsequent decades times changed, and so did the movement. Small scale co-operative production did survive, actively supported by influential middle-class Christian Socialists like Llewelyn's friend Thomas Hughes. But it was consumer, or distributive, co-operation which took off from the mid-nineteenth century; expanding with the growth of skilled, relatively well-paid sections of the industrial working class and their 'new model' trade unions, and especially strong in the north. Most famously associated with the Rochdale Pioneers and the shop they set up in 1844, consumer co-operation was based on local societies which ran shops owned and controlled by their members. The magic ingredient was the famous 'divi': each member gained a share of the profits in the form of a regular cash dividend which varied according to the amount they spent.

The co-operative society which Margaret joined was one of well over a thousand around the country run on the Rochdale model, boasting nearly 750,000 members between them. By this time, the co-operative store was a linchpin of working-class communities around the country. Owenite ideas of overall social change were now on the back burner, and co-operation had become associated with respectable Victorian self-help, nonconformist Christianity, and Liberal politics.

However the movement was complex, and differing traditions and currents rubbed shoulders. Significantly, the Rochdale Pioneers themselves, always seen as the emblem of consumer co-operation, were politically radical, and originally had ambitions for co-operative production and house-building, even a self-supporting community, very much in line with the earlier movement. Illustrating how differing values co-existed, banners on display at an 1879 co-operative exhibition in Hebden Bridge could, it seems quite naturally, include both the slogan 'self-help is true help' and 'co-operation is mutual help'.[86]

Many co-operative managers operated much like hard-headed businessmen, and many members may have seen the dividend just as a convenient method of saving. But a commitment to mutual aid had very much survived, and the dream of a Co-operative Commonwealth was still invoked. Education was still, as it always had been, seen as an integral feature of the movement, and a distinctive co-operative culture had grown up, with a rich social and community life that was built around the local co-operative societies.[87]

Co-operators were proud of their movement's democratic structure. However, although in theory men and women had equal rights, everyday practice was often very different. Most societies only allowed one member of a family to join, and this was often the husband. Some formally excluded wives, or required the husband's consent. Women who had become members were often cold shouldered at the crucial quarterly meetings which governed local societies, and it was not until 1884 that the first woman was elected on to any of the committees which ran them and the overall movement. So democracy effectively worked for men only. The women who actually shopped at the stores, and relied on the dividend when times were hard, did not have a voice.

Margaret was about to find out about all this. In December 1886, she went to the first meeting of the Marylebone branch of what was then called the Women's League for the Spread of Co-operation.[88] Immediately attracted by what she found, she agreed to be branch secretary. Little did she know it but she had found a life-long home.

The League had been founded by two women, three years previously. Middle-class Alice Acland, a vicar's daughter, got to know about co-operation whilst travelling in industrial areas with her husband, an Oxford don and progressive Liberal politician. Working-class Mary Lawrenson, the eldest of eleven children, was the daughter of a printer and co-operator and had worked as a teacher when young.

In 1883, Mrs Acland had persuaded the editor of the weekly *Co-operative News* to give space for the first time to a '*Woman's Corner*', in which she cautiously suggested that women might meet together, read, and discuss. Mrs Lawrenson immediately backed this idea, and the League, soon renamed the Women's Co-operative Guild came into being. Its official aims were to persuade more women to use co-operative stores, and to increase the understanding of co-operative principles. An ambitious-sounding additional aim – 'to improve the conditions of women all over the country' – was, as we shall see, effectively about social support rather than public activism. [89]

Within two years, the Guild had 376 members in ten branches attached to local co-operative societies and was steadily growing. It was led by an elected General Secretary and Central Committee, and the weekly *Woman's Corner* in the *Co-operative News* acted informally as a crucial, nationwide channel of communication.[90]

Although middle-class women like Margaret and Mrs Acland were prominent in the Guild leadership, most members were working-class wives and mothers. Except in the north-west, where there was a tradition of married women working in the mills, most had given up regular paid work outside the home once they got married and had children. Coming from 'respectable', better off sections of the working class, they felt themselves – and were felt by others – to be quite distinct from the worst off, those labelled as 'the poor'.

This did not mean that they had easy lives, far from it. While some individual Guildswomen were undoubtedly prosperous, including a number whose fathers were prominent co-operators, for others it was a real struggle to make the money last while keeping up 'respectable' standards –

especially for those with large families. Even a relatively well paid worker with a comfortable home could fall ill or lose his job, and although the savings provided by the co-operative dividend were a vital support, we know from Guildswomen's personal stories that the wife's wages from casual work were often an essential backstop when times were hard.

One such account comes from Mrs Layton, a leading Guildswoman, who was one of fourteen children. Mrs Layton's mother had died young, her health broken by financial worries and 'the continual grinding away at work for her own family and working outside the home'. Like many in the Guild, she herself started work at the age of ten. Later, married to an ailing husband who was often laid up, she took in washing and sometimes other work too: '... I was very poor, but no one outside my door ever knew how often I was hungry or how I had to scheme to get my husband nourishment.'[91] For women like Mrs Layton, any paid work had to be fitted in somehow around their home duties. A wife had sole responsibility for managing family finances, running the home and looking after husband and children; struggling in cramped and often substandard accommodation with the never-ending cycle of shopping, cooking, washing and housework, and without running hot water, washing machine, or any of the domestic appliances we take for granted today.

By 1911, Mrs Layton was a leading Guildswoman and part of a Guild deputation to the Attorney General, demanding a state maternity grant. She explained to him that a woman might go short of food even when pregnant or breast-feeding, because 'the man had to be kept going for the work's sake, and it would break her heart to starve her children'. Mrs Layton knew whereof she spoke. Years earlier, she had miscarried and nearly died, having regularly stayed up till four in the morning doing other people's washing – heavy work in those days – to save for her maternity expenses.

Although relations and good neighbours often helped, this could be a hard life. For some, it was also a lonely one. The Guild provided a welcome chance to get away from home and enjoy the company of other women.

Initially, the Guild faced hostility among co-operators. Some argued that it divided male and female co-operators into opposing camps, and many co-operative men were outraged by the very suggestion that their wives should get out of the house to meet one another – and in the evening, too! When a nervous group of Burnley women went to their local co-operative management committee, to propose setting up a Guild branch with similar educational advantages to 'the men', committee members were initially horrified, exclaiming '"Education for women!' 'Let them sat at whoam!'

'Who's to mind the chidder?'"[92]

So it is not surprising that early Guild leaders were defensive. At the inaugural meeting in 1883, Mrs Acland had declared, 'Our part in Co-operation is to be the sunbeams, the encouragers ... our motto [should be] "Study to be quiet and do your own business"'. A later article in *Woman's Corner* stressed that 'The Women's Guild does not lift up a banner with "Women's Rights" inscribed on it in large red letters, and forthwith proceed to make war upon co-operative mankind'.[93]

Whilst cautiously pushing at the boundaries, leading Guildswomen suggested that the organization might help to equip women for their traditional domestic role. As Annie Jones (an early leader always known as Mrs Ben Jones) argued, 'Some say that women's work is to stay at home; but we think that always to stay at home is to rust and become so useless that we are neither fit to be companions to our husbands nor nurses to our children.'[94]

It helped that education, traditionally a vital element in cooperation, was also generally seen as part of the woman's domestic sphere. Moreover women, as the shoppers, were especially well placed to increase their local co-operative societies' membership. Sympathetic men in the movement often justified supporting the Guild on this basis.

Did other women who joined the Guild agree with their leaders? Whatever they felt about venturing into the public sphere, many were proud of the domestic skills they had built up through years of heavy toil. Mrs Ben Jones was applauded when she told members in 1886 that, in working for the Guild, 'One thing they must guard against above all others was neglect of their household duties'.[95]

This did not mean that they were necessarily content with their lot. From the beginning, Guildswomen's opinions varied widely. Along with details of recipes and suggested methods of washing and cleaning, the letters column in *Woman's Corner* already contained occasional mutterings of dissatisfaction. As early as 1885, a lively discussion was triggered by an article which argued that a wife should have a right to a full share of 'the money value which accrues to the marriage firm.' It was even suggested that the Guild should hold a competition for a model prenuptial 'deed of partnership', providing for the wife's right to maintenance – though *Woman's Corner*'s editors, under pressure, were obliged to clarify that this was not Guild policy.[96] Five years later, several correspondents reacted furiously to an article which extolled traditional housewifely virtues. They attacked the 'present system of pampering and coddling men', instead comparing it to a mother's 'eternal round of drudgery'.[97]

Much later, Mrs Acland said of initial reactions to the Guild:

> People charged me with stirring up unrest and discontent among the women, but one knows now that one only voiced the unrest – the desire for a wider outlook – that was rising in the minds of all women.[98]

Guildswomen may not have identified themselves with the middle-class feminists who Margaret knew so well but, even in these early days, they were far from passive sunbeams in the home.

From Marylebone to the Central Committee

Margaret took up the Marylebone Guild branch with dynamic energy, spreading the co-operative word with remarkable success. Her progress report to *Woman's Corner* in summer 1887 showed that the branch already had 52 members. It regularly organized for Margaret, or another member, to meet small groups of potential recruits informally in their homes. Demonstrating her taste for terrible jokes, she described one 'highly satisfactory' meeting place on the roof of a housing block, 'encouraging broad and lofty views of things in general'.[99] Margaret was clearly enjoying herself – and it was paying off. In September, while she was away on holiday, her mother reported that that the Woolwich Guild branch (Mrs Lawrenson's, and one of the longest established) was jealous of Marylebone's progress: 'they have 4,000 members [of the co-operative society] + only forty women among them all this time – + you, in Marylebone have already sixty members. However did you do it?'[100] How indeed? Margaret's exceptional energy and organizing ability must have helped, along with the time she could put in as a single woman with few household responsibilities.

Like many other branches, Marylebone attracted members by its lively social activities; but it also emphasized education. A meeting might include singing and readings, but also discussions which gave members experience of speaking in front of others, or question and answer games to help them learn about co-operation. And there was the occasional outside speaker, including one on women's trade unions.

Margaret must have been tactful and a quick learner, but she also enjoyed using her persuasive powers, as shown in this revealing comment about her approach to women who appeared to agree with her but in the end refused to join: 'This seems rather discouraging, but a little judicious treatment will generally produce a cure after a time in these cases.'[101] Margaret was never one to take an initial no for an answer.

From the beginning, she was ambitious. In 1887, within months of starting out in the Marylebone branch, she stood for election to the Guild's governing Central Committee. Most of the other members were considerably older than she was, some perhaps only able to take up this work when they no longer had young children to cope with. Margaret was twenty-five.

As she was a newcomer, little known outside her own branch, it is not surprising that Margaret was unsuccessful. This initial setback was a salutary reminder that, unlike the charitable bodies she had worked in before, the Guild was run democratically. She might offer her services, but they might decide to reject her. Undaunted, Margaret continued to make herself known; publicizing her energetic approach to recruitment in her reports to *Woman's Corner*, speaking up at a joint meeting of branches, and writing a pamphlet for the Co-operative Central Board. As a result, when she stood for the Guild's Central Committee again in 1888, she gained more votes than any other candidate.

Even before that, the leadership had already singled Margaret out to speak at the Guild's national meeting, asking her to move a crucial resolution about a new district structure for the Guild, and also to give a paper on branch work. The latter showed her strong opinions, and her lack of inhibitions about expressing them. Indicative perhaps of her attitude to Guildswomen in these early days, its tone is didactic. Although she began with practical pointers about how to organize a branch and recruit members, Margaret went on to emphasize the need to spread co-operative ideals. Already, for her, this was vital. As she put it:

> Co-operation will never become the mighty regenerating force we wish to see it, unless it is fully recognized that the aim is to make people not only richer but better. A genuine sympathy must unite all ...

She went on to quote Walt Whitman – much admired by Edward Carpenter – on the 'lifelong love of comrades'.[102]

Margaret also put a feminist spin on the sense of responsibility attached to being a co-operator. Echoing ideas around at the time, aired, for example, in Olive Schreiner's acclaimed *Story of an African Farm*, she highlighted a woman's responsibility to herself, and not only, as convention had it, to others. So Guild meetings should allow time for 'some small amount of personal culture', through poetry, lectures, debates and readings. She suggested that lectures should include topics such as votes for women and women's trade unions, and argued against branches providing classes for children, on the basis that members' 'co-operative energy' could better be used in other ways.

All this may well have been challenging for some Guildswomen in the audience. Indeed, the member giving the vote of thanks for the paper openly disagreed, citing the long-held principle in the movement that 'co-operation should know neither politics nor religion'.[103]

Nevertheless, Margaret had put down a marker.

Within months of this meeting, Margaret's life was turned upside down. Towards the end of 1888, her father was abruptly informed that after over thirty years' service he could no longer continue as minister of Christ Church, Marylebone. Llewelyn was nothing if not outspoken, and it appears that at some point, when acting as honorary chaplain to the Queen, he may have preached a sermon which displeased Gladstone on theological or political grounds.[104] There is no hard evidence to show exactly what had happened. He himself gracefully attributed the enforced move to his age – he was 63 – but it is clear that there was more to it.

Although many thought he should have received it, Llewelyn had never sought promotion within the Church. His lack of advancement was attributed to his outspoken advocacy of social reform, along with theological views which did not find favour with the Church authorities. Nevertheless, he was popular and well-known, and his enforced move was seen as an unfair and uncalled for demotion. It was even mentioned fleetingly in a *Times* editorial as 'a reward … far from commensurate with his long services as a preacher and philanthropist'.[105]

When Llewelyn finally left his post at the beginning of 1889, nearly 700 people, including bishops, peers, MPs, judges, baronets and senior Churchmen, signed a public congratulatory address. At a leaving event in the parish, he was given a presentation of 1,000 guineas. After considerable searching, he had accepted a living in Kirkby Lonsdale, a small country town on the southern edge of the Lake District. In February 1889, aged 27, Margaret had no option but to accompany her parents and leave London for the north-west.

Section Two

GROWING

CHAPTER 4

Changes, 1889-1892

Little bigger than a village, with stone houses clustered around church, marketplace and the main street, Kirkby Lonsdale was pleasant enough; quaint and grey and clean, as Margaret's mother described it. Although smaller than Mary Davies would have preferred, the vicarage was, in fact, of a good size. What was more, it was beautifully situated, looking on to a large churchyard at the front and over the river Lune at the back to Ruskin's View – greatly admired by him and painted by Turner. Both parents soon came to love the countryside around. For Margaret's father, especially, who loved walking and climbing, the nearby fells of the Lake District were a major consolation.

However, the limited local social life available to the vicar's family was dominated by the local squire, the Conservative Earl of Bective, and his family. One visitor to the vicarage remembered Lady Bective acting like the 'feudal lady' of the area, and her relations with the Llewelyn Davieses were evidently lukewarm. The family nevertheless did their best to participate in Kirkby Lonsdale life, and reports of concerts and other entertainments to which they contributed feature regularly in the parish magazine. Margaret herself, a gifted singer, sometimes took part, and visiting friends were liable to find themselves enlisted to help.

The family also organised a series of lectures at the working men's club. The first session, an illustrated lecture on botany, would have been unremarkable had it not been delivered by a woman, Margaret's Girton friend Ethel Sargant. The lectures finished with Aunt Emily Davies, whose speech on women's suffrage attracted a large audience. Interestingly, there was a unanimous vote in favour at the end; though perhaps a desire not to offend the vicar by opposing his sister played a part here.

For Margaret, the move was a huge wrench. At a stroke, she had been cut off from her closest friends, her stimulating social life, and her work in the youth club and the Marylebone Guild. Her brothers had already decamped and, although they and other relatives and friends visited regularly, she was often alone with her parents in the vicarage. Rosalind remembered that her friend's feeling of 'banishment' lingered for many years. Contemplating life in Kirkby Lonsdale, Margaret must have felt that the outlook was bleak.

More evidence of her unhappiness comes from a Girton friend who came to stay six months or so after the move north. Meta Muir wrote home describing a pleasant and peaceful routine at the vicarage, with Margaret writing in the mornings and the rest of the time spent reading, walking and sitting in the garden. But although Margaret's old warmth and vivacity still shone through, Meta felt that she was not content. In her eyes, Margaret's anxious concern about social problems was over-exaggerated and was not doing her any good. As we shall see, Meta was not the only one to feel this way.[106]

The new General Secretary

There was one positive development for Margaret during these early months at Kirkby Lonsdale. In spring 1889, a new opportunity came out of the blue. Mrs Lawrenson, the Women's Co-operative Guild's General Secretary, tendered her resignation and the Central Committee invited Margaret to stand for election as her replacement.

Mrs Lawrenson's resignation had clearly not been of her choosing. A remarkable and energetic woman, she had been devoted to the Guild ever since she helped to get it off the ground six years before. She was an inspiring speaker and popular with Guildswomen, who, it is said, referred to her as 'Mother'. But she clashed with some women on the Central Committee, of which Margaret had been a member since the previous summer. There were disagreements about the direction that the Guild should take, and complaints about her allegedly erratic administrative work. Matters seem to have come to a head in January and February 1889, when the *Woman's Corner* editor had to retract statements which appeared in an article Mrs Lawrenson had written. A month later, she abruptly announced her resignation.[107]

There was clearly some personal enmity. Never one to take a perceived slight lying down, working-class Mrs Lawrenson had crossed swords with a couple of middle-class committee members who had criticised her work in patronising terms. She reacted fiercely, 'I appreciate as highly as it is possible to do the presence of educated women amongst us, but I am not disposed to place myself in the position of your humble obedient servant'.[108] Not long after her resignation, she wrote in *Woman's Corner* of her hope that members would be 'determined to think, vote and act for themselves', stressing that the Guild was 'an association of working women' who needed to see that 'real progress will be attained only by their own efforts'.[109]

This is a rare and interesting instance of overtly expressed class antagonism within the Guild at this time. As we have seen, in these early years middle-class women were certainly prominent in the leadership and some seem to have viewed this much as a kind of charity work. It is difficult to assess how far Mrs Lawrenson's views were reflected in the Guild more generally. While class differences must have had some impact, the other six Central Committee members who pushed her to resign included at least two women with impeccable working-class, co-operative antecedents: the president, ex-mill worker Mrs Ben Jones, and Emilie Holyoake, daughter of the venerated co-operator, G.J. Holyoake. The situation was not straightforward.

Although her earlier relations with Margaret had been cordial enough, Mrs Lawrenson was evidently bitter about the committee's backing for this inexperienced and privileged newcomer. This was not the easiest situation to inherit but, after initially hesitating, Margaret made up her mind. Early in April, *Woman's Corner* announced that she had agreed to be nominated by the Central Committee as General Secretary.

Margaret must have seemed like a godsend to the Committee. They knew what she was like to work with, as she was already a member. Both there and in Marylebone she had more than proved her energy and her persuasive skills. Her father's connection with Christian Socialism would also have recommended her as a safe pair of hands. And, as a single woman who did not need to earn her own living, she could offer not only ability and energy but also, crucially, time.

Different worlds

The move to Kirkby Lonsdale proved to have one major advantage; it brought Margaret within reach of the northern industrial towns which were the heartland of the co-operative movement. While the Guild grew more slowly here than in the south, perhaps because it faced greater hostility from male co-operators, there was also great potential. This was particularly true in Lancashire where there was a tradition of married women retaining independence by continuing their mill work.

Once General Secretary, Margaret began to travel around, seeing the conditions in the industrial towns with her own eyes and getting to know Guildswomen and local co-operators. Towards the end of 1889 she spent several days promoting the Guild in Yorkshire, speaking at three meetings in the course of three days. Mrs Knott, secretary of a Sheffield Guild branch and wife of a railway worker, reported in glowing terms to *Woman's Corner*. She described the enthusiastic reaction which Margaret received; although one local councillor, faced with the incursion of a well-bred southern female onto a co-operative platform, declared in the course of his congratulatory speech that 'He was very glad she had come into the north and to Sheffield to finish her education'. Mrs Knott, certainly, was bowled over: 'Those of you who have had the pleasure of listening to Miss Davies, and catching her sunny smile, will not be surprised to hear that she won all hearts.'[110]

Margaret struggled to reconcile these new experiences with the world of her family and friends. Early on, when she went to Castle Howard as bridesmaid to her good friend Mary, daughter of the Earl of Carlisle, there was no doubt a serious undertone to her mother's joking admonition: 'be happy + enjoy everything. Don't give *all* yr sympathies to the working classes. The poor rich want a little also. They too are human!'[111] [original emphasis and abbreviations]

Later, around the time Margaret made such an impression on Mrs Knott, Lady Maude Parry visited the vicarage with her daughters for some weeks. By this time, Margaret was beginning to get into the swing of Guild work. Lady Maude (wife of the composer Sir Hubert Parry), kept a diary which makes very interesting reading. She was a sympathetic listener, and often an acute observer – although not without a tendency to exaggeration. She evidently got on well with Margaret, although she did not really share or understand her preoccupations.

Margaret's boisterous vigour still survived; her mother described her as messing around 'like a crazy thing' with the teenage Parry girls.[112] Nevertheless, Lady Maude recorded that Mary Davies had confided 'how trying Margaret often was – how she ... made herself ill, + wd have working men to stay with her who called her "Margaret" when talking of her, or "that girl".'[113] [original abbreviation] Even if this were an exaggeration – there is no other evidence that working men actually stayed at the vicarage – the story does show that Margaret was definitely making waves.

Lady Maude also wrote that Margaret was 'very low' when she returned one day from a trip on Guild business. 'She wants now to live in Lancaster [the nearest city]. Says it is of no use living unless you are working from morning till night.' According to her, Margaret refused to play *God Save the Queen* when asked to do so at a local temperance concert, and confided that she 'always sang "God save Mr Gladstone" or something else'.[114]

Some eighteen months later, when Margaret called on the Parrys while on a visit to London, Lady Maude reported that she clearly found a conversation about clothes 'very frivolous'. Daughter Dolly was more forthright, complaining that while she was amusing the assembled company with impressions, assisted by Kitty Maxse (formerly Kitty Lushington, and an old friend of Margaret), 'Margaret sat on the sofa and scowled at Mrs Maxse and glared at me, and never laughed and never spoke, except once to say "Fool"'.[115]

Starting off in the Guild

Meanwhile, Margaret had become a senior official in a national organisation with up to 1,800 members. Scattered around the country and often coping with home responsibilities, the other six Central Committee members only met face to face a few times a year; though they corresponded in between times, when necessary. Margaret would have the main responsibility for administration and also, following Mrs Lawrenson's example, would be expected to take a central part in promoting and supporting the Guild across the country.

Furthermore, though Margaret may not have realised the implications at the time, new rules were about to put her in a particularly powerful position. It had recently been decided that Central Committee members should stand down after three consecutive years' service, although they could stand for election again a year later. This was a good way of keeping the Guild's democracy alive and of training up new leaders. When the proposed rule was discussed shortly before Mrs Lawrenson's resignation, Margaret herself suggested that the General Secretary should be exempted. The Committee was initially doubtful but, a few months later, when she herself had become General Secretary, it agreed.[116]

This meant that if – and it was potentially a big if – Margaret continued to stand and be re-elected, she would be the Committee's only long-term official, and thus in a powerful position to steer the Guild's direction. At the time, she may simply have been thinking about the need for administrative continuity, but this rule proved to be crucial to her long-term leadership.

Margaret found herself working alongside a formidable Central Committee, most of them considerably older than herself and with much more experience. As we know, Mrs Ben Jones, the well-known and much-loved president of the Guild for some years, was a former factory worker, a mother of four and wife of a prominent co-operator. Several other Committee members had also served previously, and among the newly elected figures was Sarah Reddish from Bolton, of whom we shall hear more.

Her inexperience seems not to have fazed Margaret in the least, and she confidently assumed her leading role. In a graceful speech accepting the post of General Secretary, she spelt out the two aims she thought most important for the Guild: 'More unity, more education.' To promote the former, the Central Committee had already proposed a new organisational system. Modelled on the Co-operative Union structure, this grouped branches into districts, and districts into regional sections, with elected secretaries at each level, and branch subscriptions to support the central office.[117] This idea may actually have originated with Mrs Lawrenson, and Margaret had already drafted the first version of the new rules for the Committee.[118] But it was Margaret's forceful emphasis on education which immediately put her personal stamp on the Guild. As she insisted, 'Guild meetings must not descend into being mere "mothers' meetings". There must be some educational work connected with them, or they might as well ... not [be] co-operative at all.'[119]

Margaret still had something to learn about putting her ideas into practice. Early on, she produced the Central Committee's first annual *Winter Circular* recommending topics for branches to discuss, and also arranged a series of six open lectures on economics and co-operation by her Girton friend Adelaide Anderson. The circular included a major proposal for branches to study *The Laws of Every-day Life*, a textbook on topics such as prices, wages and co-operation being used in the movement.[120]

It's fair to say that this idea was misjudged. Only sixteen out of over fifty branches eventually read *The Laws of Every-day Life*, and only nineteen members entered for an examination which Margaret had arranged. Even the most committed and enthusiastic of branches found itself struggling: 'we really worked hard ... asking ourselves questions as we read, to see if we fully grasped the meaning; making familiar examples to illustrate long high-sounding words'.[121]

Initially, Margaret took the response badly, writing severely in her Annual Report:

'One of the most common difficulties is found in trying to arouse the interest of members in anything of at all a serious character. They have a great distaste for what they consider dull and dry. We have to face the fact that co-operation and all economic subjects are difficult, and require thought and attention. To give women a knowledge of co-operation is one of the first objects of the Guild, and we must not shrink from trying to realise it.'[122]

This was hardly the best way to persuade members. But then, these were early days.

Outside the Guild: co-operation and more

For most women, the job of General Secretary would have been quite enough to cope with. Not so for the ever-energetic Margaret. For some time after she was elected, she continued to cast around for other ways to make sense of her new life.

Even while she was making her first contacts with Guildswomen in the industrial towns, Margaret was hoping to set up a part-time project in London. Towards the end of 1889, she took a flat with her friend Rosalind Shore Smith in Jubilee Buildings, a working-class block near Waterloo Station. Margaret still needed her parents' backing, if only because she depended on them financially. Like the remarkable parents they were, they gave it with relative goodwill. Her mother wrote, 'Well you cant wish me to be very enthusiastic at the idea of losing you for ½ the year!", continuing gamely, 'I suppose it will be endurable, + I can easily understand your great and increasing interest in all you are doing …'[123] [original abbreviations] Unfortunately, information about this fledgling venture is sketchy. There are suggestions that Margaret and Rosalind were planning to set up profit-sharing workshops – being promoted in parts of the co-operative movement at the time. In the event, though, it was not long before Margaret was back at Kirkby Lonsdale, holding the fort while her mother was away looking after Aunt Emily Beesly during her final illness. She was definitely staying in Jubilee Buildings in May 1890, but after that the project disappears from view.

Around the same time, clearly already ambitious to take part in wider debates within the movement, Margaret also entered a competition for a prize paper to be read at the annual Co-operative Congress in 1890. Only one woman had ever done this before and, despite her normal self-confidence, Margaret was anxious about it, drafting and redrafting the paper and sending it to brothers Crompton and Theodore at Cambridge, for comment.

She had chosen the most contentious subject on offer: 'The relations between co-operation and socialistic aspirations.' Margaret argued that socialism and co-operation had the same aim, to replace competition by association and that the difference lay only in their methods: socialists believed in state reforms, while co-operators relied on voluntary association.[124] She claimed that co-operation could not achieve its aim alone and that the two approaches need not be exclusive or antagonistic. Indeed, co-operators and socialists should draw closer together. Referring to the influential *Fabian Essays* which had been published the previous year, she now argued for state intervention as part of the solution. This was a change of emphasis from the paper she had given to the Guild in 1888, which had highlighted co-operative action and the importance of the quality of personal relationships.

Margaret won the competition and presented her paper at the Co-operative Congress in Glasgow in May 1890. Shortly before the event, she was in quite a state about it, though she would also have been concerned about her first Guild annual meeting as General Secretary, which took place at the same time as the Congress.

The overwhelmingly male audience at the Co-operative Congress was likely to be unsympathetic to Margaret's message. There had been some bad blood between organised socialists and co-operators, and many of the latter were bitterly opposed to what they saw as socialists' reliance on state control. Appropriately then, Margaret's tone was conciliatory; indeed, she stressed that she did not claim to be an 'apologist' for socialism. Despite her earlier worries, she rose to the occasion and spoke with 'grace of expression and delivery', replying with vigour and clarity in the ensuing discussion.[125]

Beatrice Webb (still Miss Potter at this stage) was at the Congress, and her diary illustrates the gulf between Margaret and the more conservative elements of the movement:

> The event of the day was the sudden springing on a congress of hard-headed co-operators of advanced socialist theories. Margaret Davies' paper, literary and thoughtful, was listened to with respectful perplexity; then Ben Jones came forward and in his sonorous tones announced the conversion of socialists to a due appreciation of co-operators, and the "new compact" whereby socialists and co-operators should work together as far as they could go, and then separate in good will.[126]

Margaret had yet another iron in the fire, too. Like many other feminists and socialists she was a strong supporter of temperance. Soon after arriving in Kirkby Lonsdale, she became secretary of a local temperance group.[127]

There was not such a gulf between this and her Guild work as might be imagined. Quarrying and tunnelling for major water works was taking place locally, and the nearby villages of Lupton and Hutton Roof temporarily hosted hundreds of labourers, referred to as 'navvies', some accompanied by their families. Living conditions were grim, and there was not always enough room for all the navvies in the huts thrown up to house them. They were often partly paid in 'drink tickets' and, at least once, fierce fighting broke out between Irish and English on payday. The temperance mission which Margaret helped to set up did something, however small, to make the navvies' lives a little more comfortable, providing a 'mission room' – at least somewhere warm and dry – where she regularly sang at entertainments.

From what we know, it seems that Margaret only continued this work for two years or so, and after that the Guild took over completely. Long term, the most important thing about Margaret's temperance involvement was that it brought Lilian Harris into her world. Highly intelligent and the daughter of a wealthy local banker, Lilian had received little education. Now like Margaret a single daughter living with her parents, she was chafing against their restrictions and spending much of her time 'sitting at home … trying to occupy herself with carving and embroidery'.[128]

Lilian became a frequent visitor to the vicarage, providing companionship for Mary Davies when Margaret was away and gradually helping Margaret with the Guild work. Mary Davies described to Margaret how Lilian had confided that 'it was impossible to tell what we all were to her – her life was quite changed since we came – specially you no doubt'.[129]

Early progress

The Guild's membership continued to grow, and by spring 1892 it had mushroomed to over 4,000. The new sectional and district structure was up and running, and members were gaining experience and confidence.

As membership expanded, so did Margaret's administrative work, and it soon became clear that she needed an office. Her parents obliged by donating a spacious room on the vicarage's first floor, from where she did the routine paperwork, conducted correspondence, sent out mass mailings (on one occasion, said to be large enough to require a wheelbarrow) and received visitors on co-operative and Guild business. Early 1892 was a particularly busy time, when a round of district and branch visits in late March included Richmond, Cheltenham, Gloucester, Doncaster, Nelson and Carlisle. Members reacted very positively and, for her part, the more Margaret got to know Guildswomen and find out about their hard lives, the more she admired them.[130] A mutual bond was being forged.

On top of all this, Margaret began to experiment with campaigning. In the summer of 1891, Tom Mann, the fiery socialist and trade union leader at the forefront of the famous 1889 dock strike, spoke at a co-operative festival in favour of links between co-operators and trade unionists, arguing that co-operators should only buy goods which had been produced according to union principles, by workers paid union rates. For this to happen, prices as well as wages would have to go up – and working-class women, the family shoppers, needed to understand why. Tom Mann's approach struck a chord with both Margaret and Rosalind, with whom she worked out many of her ideas. The two women increasingly saw co-operation and trade unions as 'two halves of the same circle', that could together become 'a complete movement for the emancipation of labour'.[131]

Ready to look for a new Guild project, Margaret now decided to focus on links with trade unions. A predictable course would have been for Guildswomen to help unionise low-paid women workers, as reform-minded middle-class women were already doing. Instead, she decided on a campaign to bring co-operation and trade unionism together, along the lines Tom Mann had suggested. Against the background of some ill feeling between the two movements, together with the rise of the militant 'new unionism' among unskilled workers, this was a bold and potentially radical move.

This was Margaret's personal initiative, and when a discussion started in Tom Mann's paper, the *Trade Unionist*, she saw her opportunity. She wrote in reiterating the arguments for linking the two movements, and stressing the advantage for unionists of joining their local co-operative societies. Not only would they benefit financially from the dividend on purchases, but they would also be able to influence conditions in co-operative workshops, and persuade co-operative societies to buy goods from 'union houses'. Like Tom Mann, Margaret stressed that women's support was essential, and she proposed that the Guild was the way to get this.[132]

A lively correspondence followed, in which some contributors criticised poor quality and high prices at co-operative stores, or reacted against what seemed like patronising advice from those praising the virtues of co-operation. One letter demanded whether the newspaper's editor 'ever had to go out on a Saturday or a Friday night with eighteen shillings in your pocket … And with six children who must be fed out of that …?'[133]

Margaret went on to obtain backing for a series of meetings in different parts of London, advertised with the slogans, 'How Trade Unionists can help Co-operators, How Co-operators can help Trade Unionists, and how Women can help both'.[134] The message was simple: unionists should become co-operators, co-operators should become unionists, and women should join the Guild. Speakers included Tom Mann and Ben Tillett from the Dockers' Union, and co-operative officials such as Ben Jones. Margaret persuaded Guild Central Committee colleagues to speak as well, including Mrs Ben Jones, who had earlier been wary about women speaking in public at all. Picking up on an idea from America which was ahead of its time, the organisers proposed a 'trade union label' which would show that goods had been produced under fair conditions, for fair wages.[135]

The Guild was now actively collaborating with militant male trade unionists, an unheard of departure. Margaret's enthusiasm for trade unions did not mean that her feminist convictions had taken a back seat. Now that she was beginning to learn from Guildswomen about their hard lives, she made no bones about claiming in her speeches that working-class family life would be improved if women were not seen as 'mere penny-in-the-slot machines – wages being dropped in, and puddings and shirts being expected to come out'.[136] There was laughter and applause when she declared, while committing the Guild to press for boycotting non-union goods, that 'Each woman was now "a man and a brother", they were no longer playthings or doormats, and they must act accordingly'.[137]

In the event the campaign failed to get much support, but Margaret still had the bit between her teeth. Early in 1892, she and Lilian decamped temporarily to lodgings in London's East End, planning to organise co-operative meetings and canvass locally to recruit women to come.[138] But early on, after leafleting all day in a blizzard, Lilian fell dangerously ill with peritonitis. Margaret had to drop everything to look after her, and the scheme fizzled out.[139]

Even though this project did not get anywhere, it was an important first step. As well as creating new personal links between trade unionists and co-operators, it illustrates Margaret's proactive approach; identifying potential opportunities as they came up and acting swiftly on them. It highlighted working with unions and ethical co-operative trading, both issues which she and the Guild would take up later on. Also, it pointed up for the first time the influence which Guildswomen could exercise as consumers – which Margaret came to call their 'basket power'.[140]

Coda: friendship, love and marriage

Although spring 1892 was a very busy time, Margaret somehow found a way to spend time with her Aunt Carrie (Caroline Croom Robertson), to whom she had always been particularly close. Carrie died at the end of May, after a long illness.

Hot on the heels of the loss of Aunt Carrie came what must have been another wrench when Rosalind Shore Smith married Vaughan Nash, a young journalist. Nash shared many of the two women's political ideas. Having spent time at the Toynbee Hall Settlement, he had supported the 1889 dock strike and had also been involved in Margaret's recent trade union campaign. Although Margaret had told her mother when the engagement was announced that she liked Nash, and approved of Rosalind's choice, Mary Davies acutely observed, 'I know it [the engagement] must be hard in some ways for you – almost like a third person stepping in between a happily married pair!'[141]

Rosalind and Margaret had been the closest of friends since Girton days. She had followed Margaret into the Guild, volunteering as secretary of a new branch in her local area and beginning to speak at Guild meetings elsewhere. She was nominated for General Secretary in 1889, but hastily withdrew in favour of her friend. We don't have their own letters or diaries to tell us about their relationship; instead, we see it mostly through the prism of Margaret's mother's letters. Mary Davies recognised Rosalind as particularly important, writing to a worried Margaret when she was due to give her acceptance speech as the new General Secretary,

> How often I have been thankful to know you have your closest friend with you. ... I wanted to say 'take care of her' to R [Rosalind] but no words would come ...[142]

In 1887, the two young women had travelled to Italy together for several weeks. Unusually for her, Margaret preserved a memento of the trip, a gift from Rosalind of a tiny volume of Michaelangelo sonnets on themes of beauty and love, exquisitely bound in leather. Rosalind's handwritten translations of a couple of the sonnets were folded inside, and the book was inscribed 'R to M April 1887' and '(Till next time)'.[143]

This hints at a romantic element in their friendship. It was not at all unusual at this time for middle-class women who ventured into the public world to form loving, even romantic, partnerships with other women, which sustained them in and outside work.[144] But such relationships did not necessarily have a sexual component, and we have no way of knowing about this in relation to Margaret and Rosalind.

Certainly, Rosalind continued to be involved with the Guild. The same year that she got engaged, Rosalind delivered a paper at a London Guild conference, and within weeks of her marriage she travelled to Manchester to support Margaret in her next big project. A talented journalist, she edited *Woman's Corner* for some years from 1896, went on giving occasional papers to Guild meetings and worked closely with Margaret in the suffrage movement. In 1904, Margaret described them as 'inseparably associated ... during the whole of their Co-operative life'.[145] As we shall see, the two women remained close friends into old age.

While she had good men friends and enjoyed male company, Margaret herself never married, although she certainly received her share of male admiration. Throughout her life her most intimate relationships were with women, and there was only one marriage proposal that we know of. This was in the summer of 1889 while Margaret was staying temporarily in London. Undecided, she consulted her mother. Displaying a rare sensitivity for the time, Mary Davies accepted that Margaret did not necessarily want to get married:

> ... it is you + only you who can decide such a matter ... I believe matrimony was more in my line than it is in yours. I have no fear of your venturing on it unless your heart moves very certainly in that direction.[146]

Frustratingly, there is no information about the man in question except that Margaret thought well of him. He may have been a co-operative contact, as Margaret had been at the movement's Congress shortly before. It certainly does not sound as if she were passionately in love, but at the age of 27, she might well have thought that this was likely to be her last proposal and so should not be turned down out of hand. However, it is not surprising that, after taking a few days to decide, she refused. Putting aside any feelings about this particular man, Margaret was already dedicated to work and an independent life. Marriage and children would have meant major sacrifices.

The gentleman apparently behaved 'beautifully' when rejected. And that was that.

CHAPTER 5

Public Success, Private Grief, 1892-1895

The Manchester Festival

By early 1892, the trade union campaign was tailing off. With typical energy Margaret began to plot something new – and something big. Early in March, while still nursing Lilian in London, she came up with the idea of a national Guild festival, lasting three days. She set her sights high, hoping that the festival would put the organisation on the map, give members a feeling of unity and success and, crucially, provide a mandate for her ideas about its future direction. The Guild's Central Committee promptly agreed, and it was all fixed to take place in Manchester in July.

The festival was very much Margaret's baby, and she took on the main responsibility for making it work, even turning up at the railway station to give delegates a 'smiling welcome'. The atmosphere was buzzing from day one. 120 delegates turned up, from 77 of the Guild's hundred branches; and including the many visitors, there were sometimes two to three hundred people in attendance. The large meeting hall was bedecked with plants and flowers, along with Guild banners displaying mottoes such as 'Co-operation improves social conditions', 'United we stand, divided we fall', and 'A woman's influence begins at home: who can say where it ends?'[147]

Margaret had planned it all carefully. At each session, a speaker read a paper which had been provided to delegates in advance. This was followed by discussion, and voting on resolutions. Speaking up in such a large meeting and in such imposing surroundings must have been daunting to many delegates, but they were gently encouraged to 'take advantage of every opportunity of speaking … and point out anything in the papers and subjects under discussion which may puzzle you, or upon which you can offer any useful suggestion'.[148]

Clearly, Margaret's approach hit the spot. One observer commented on how delegates 'seized hold of all tracts, and how they [jotted] down the remarks of the speakers, to tell other folks back home'. Another wrote:

> The wives, the older ones especially, had not had outings of this kind, having experienced only mothers' meetings and treats; but this affair seemed to show them that they were of importance, and some of the older women marvelled at it.[149]

Delegates enthusiastically passed resolutions urging branches to help their local co-operative societies recruit more members, to equip themselves to take part in the committees which managed the societies, and to recruit for the Guild among co-operative employees and their families. They also resolved that branches should lobby for trade union pay and conditions for those employees, and after a speech by Clementina Black of the Women's Trade Union Association, followed by an impassioned discussion of the hardships suffered by low paid women workers, a resolution for the Guild to encourage women's trade unions was carried by acclamation.

Another resolution, potentially much more controversial, was central to Margaret's plans. It proposed that branches should study 'municipal questions' and support 'women and labour candidates' in local elections. Crucially, it also touched on votes for women, resolving that 'all property and sex qualifications should be abolished both as regards voters and candidates'. Margaret had persuaded the respected leader Mrs Ben Jones to introduce the resolution, and in the event surprisingly little discussion was recorded. It was carried 'unanimously and with much applause'. She had the backing she wanted.

Although she herself did not speak at the festival, Margaret was definitely the power behind the scenes, and made good use of her considerable tactical skills. For example, she dropped a draft resolution about co-operative production after Mrs Lawrenson had objected to it in the Central Committee.[150] It also has to be said that when a couple of resolutions were passed which she and the majority of the Committee did not support – urging branches to set up classes for children and sickness benefit clubs – Margaret failed to ensure they were picked up on afterwards. With other more major issues now on the Guild's agenda, there appear to have been no complaints.

As *Woman's Corner* reported, the festival was much more than a business meeting:

There was ... a kind of happy holiday look about all these delegates, as if now that they had got away they had made their minds up to have a thoroughly good time of it.[151]

Margaret enthusiastically adopted the Guild's traditions of sociability, organising a day's outing and an informal evening 'conversazione' with speeches and music, all as part of the festival. On another evening, a delegates-only get together included a mock ceremony in which Margaret introduced each of the elected officials in the Guild's new sections and districts in turn. There was music and dancing – Margaret's rendition of *Molly Malone* proved to be a popular favourite – along with opportunities for individual delegates to arrange to meet up: 'we hope that many lasting friendships were begun in this way.'[152]

Evidently primed in advance, the *Manchester Guardian* gave the festival two lengthy reports and it was also covered in the *Daily Chronicle*. *Co-operative News* reported the proceedings in full in a lengthy supplement. Plainly, it was a huge success.

Most importantly, Margaret now had members' backing for political and social action, and support from leading Guildswomen – a huge change from the Guild's earlier days. The shift was underlined when Mrs Acland and Mrs Jones, both previously associated with a more conservative approach, explicitly approved the resolution about the Guild taking up public work. To applause, Mrs Acland declared:

> We have often been told how great is the influence of women upon our [co-operative] stores, but their influence may extend wider than that, and be made in municipal and even in parliamentary life.

She went on to declare that 'all we have to do is to decide what we want and then unite to get it'.[153]

The Manchester Festival was a major milestone. Only three years after Margaret had taken over as General Secretary it showed that her ideas already struck a chord with many Guildswomen. She may have opened the door, but they were more than ready to stride through.

Progress, 1892-94

Within a year of the Festival, Margaret signalled the Guild's shift of emphasis from 'domestic economy' to 'co-operative and labour matters'. Membership continued to grow, reaching over 6,000 by spring 1893, and the new sections and districts were increasingly active; organising conferences which discussed topics put forward by Margaret and the Central Committee in their annual winter circulars.[154]

The leadership also made practical suggestions about equipping members to take part effectively in the hitherto all male management committees of the local co-operative societies. Guildswomen began to stand for these committees, and some were elected, though in fewer numbers than to the societies' less powerful education committees. Standing for election required courage: one activist remembered, even years later, that when she first stood for a management committee, her husband was sent 'dreadful' postcards: 'When a woman stood for any position ... the abuse they met with was awful.'[155]

But once on management committees, women were active, and particularly took up the cudgels for store employees, many of whom were female. As one branch secretary reported on a management committee meeting, '[the] women carried the earlier closing resolution, despite the grumbling and protestations of a considerable number of the male members'.[156]

Guildswomen also worked with other groups to support women's unionisation, and Margaret spoke out on the national stage on issues affecting women workers, both at the Trade Union Congress and at the Co-operative Congress. During the bitter 'Coal War' strike of 1893, the Guild set up a special fund for miners' families.[157]

In 1894 the law changed, and women were for the first time permitted to stand as, and vote for, Poor Law Guardians. The locally elected Guardians were responsible for interviewing applicants for poor relief, who were often women – predominantly widows, unwed mothers or deserted wives – and also oversaw local workhouses and other kinds of relief. Up until then, the all-male Boards of Guardians had been dominated by middle- and upper-class local worthies. Margaret pushed for Guildswomen to take advantage of this new opportunity for women to take some power. In the event, a number were successful in these first elections – a small beginning which would be built on in later years. Reporting this, the *Daily Chronicle* was full of praise for the Guild, describing it as, 'one of the most strenuous and democratic of organizations' and declaring that 'these results ... show what can be done where there is the right spirit, and a vigorous organisation to give women a voice in civic affairs'.[158]

And it was not all serious work. On the last evening of the 1894 Annual Meeting, Margaret instigated a 'high carnival' in which she insisted that the other officials 'cast aside the last remaining vestiges of formality, and ... run wild for once'. When the evening ended, 'nothing but cheers, loud hip! hip! hurrahs!! ... followed by Auld Lang Syne would content the meeting as giving expression to their appreciation of a perfectly happy time'.[159]

The Guild was beginning to change lives. Take Mrs Dickenson, a local Guild official and the wife of a miner, who travelled from Leeds to London to speak at a mass meeting of women in support of the 1893 miners' strike. It is difficult now to imagine how daunting this must have been. Yet her rousing, defiant contribution was a great success. Mrs Dickenson recalled:

> It was at that time that I understood the true meaning of Co-operation, and especially the Women's Co-operative Guild. When I got to St James' Hall, and saw so many faces I knew ... and the kindly welcome they each and all gave me, I felt no longer frightened and nervous. It was then I fully understood the power of our Guild, how we could make each other feel at home away from home.[160]

How to describe what the Guild provided for members, especially those who became activists? Yes, it offered education, experience and practical training, but much more; a very special sort of friendship, support and solidarity. Perhaps 'empowerment' comes nearest.

Problems

Inevitably, though, there were difficulties. Despite a small grant from the Co-operative Union, the governing body of the movement, the Guild was chronically short of money and still had to struggle for recognition. Early attitudes were forcibly illustrated in 1892, when Beatrice Potter (later Webb) criticised working-class women's 'inertia' and claimed the movement did not include any women's associations. Yet Margaret had spoken about the Guild at the very same meeting![161]

In the wake of the Manchester Festival, though, things were changing. Margaret will have been heartened when, two years later, the Co-operative Congress passed a resolution congratulating the Women's Guild. As her ally, Catherine Webb observed, for the first time it was possible to 'feel that the guild was no longer regarded with mere kindly tolerance by the men ... and – dare I say it? – patronised somewhat'. She concluded that 'the guild has ... won its footing'.[162]

Meanwhile, although Margaret was a quick learner, she still had some way to go. This is illustrated by her approach to the recruitment of women factory inspectors, officially appointed for the first time from 1893. At first, these were all educated middle-class women, including her Girton friend and erstwhile Guild lecturer, Adelaide Anderson. Margaret seems to have seen these appointments as an unqualified victory, and assumed that a high level of education was an essential qualification for the job. But trade unions had been lobbying for working-class factory inspectors, and there was pressure for this to apply to the new female inspectors, too. Mrs Ben Jones spoke out about this at the Co-operative Congress (that is, the Congress of the whole movement) insisting that the inspectors should be 'working women who understood the question, and could understand also the feelings and needs of the workers'.[163] Others in the Guild took the same line, and by autumn 1894 Margaret, appreciating the strength of feeling, and perhaps with a new understanding of the class issues involved, had changed her mind.[164]

Margaret under pressure

As we can see, Margaret had plunged into running the Guild with huge enthusiasm – but there was a downside. Her workload was increasing inexorably with the growth of the Guild. Not only was she responsible for a large amount of administration but, in the absence of modern communications, spreading the word was greatly dependent on personal contact. So Margaret continued to travel around the country, encouraging potential branches and supporting those already in place. Even for someone with her formidable energy, this was time-consuming and exhausting, involving cross-country train journeys from Kirkby Lonsdale, only then to have to find the venue, often some distance from the nearest station.

Margaret's workload was already a worry early in 1893, when her mother made an anonymous donation to fund a full-time organizer for two years, in the hope that this would take some of the pressure off. Sarah Reddish, who took the post, was an exceptional campaigner. A committed socialist, she was already a Guild stalwart, and went on to play a major part in the suffrage movement, as well as, later, in local public service. In her forties, unmarried, and from a family of working-class co-operators she was devoted to the movement, and especially the Guild. Sarah Reddish had been the president of the Guild's Bolton branch for some years, and had already done a stint on the Central Committee. With a calm, sympathetic manner, she had a gentle and tactful approach to differences of opinion within the Guild. Moreover, shared life experience – she had worked in the Bolton cotton mills for over twenty years – gave her a rapport with many members in the north, where her work definitely helped to grow the Guild.

Sarah proved to be a popular speaker and, like Margaret, worked unstintingly, attending over 120 meetings and conferences in different places during her first year's organising. Luckily, Bolton was not far from Kirkby Lonsdale, and she and Margaret seem to have worked well together. Margaret praised her work and, years later, recalled their discussions on trains and sitting by the fire in the Guild office. But there is no other evidence that they were particularly close.[165] Significantly, although she remained active in the Guild, Sarah did not take up the offer to stay on as organiser at the end of her two year stint, but moved on to other campaigning work, first with women's trade unions and later for the vote.[166]

The two women were both single, of a similar age, with similar political views, and both shared a devotion to the Guild. But the social gulf between them may have made it difficult for them to become personally close, especially with the Guild office being in Margaret's vicarage home. And it is indicative that – despite her real admiration and appreciation of Sarah Reddish and other working-class Guild leaders – from what we know it was Rosalind and Lilian, friends from her own background, to whom Margaret consistently turned for support and advice about the Guild.

Meanwhile, despite the extra help, Margaret was still under pressure. In late October 1893 *Woman's Corner* announced: 'Miss Davies – whose flagging health has been noticeable for some months past – [has] yielded to the pressure of her friends and consented to take a two months' holiday abroad.'[167]

This seems to have been a serious breakdown, and the family definitely blamed it on overwork.[168] They quickly rallied round, organising a lengthy holiday in Italy and Switzerland with brother Crompton, and Margaret seemed to recover well. By December she was strong enough to pen enthusiastic letters to *Woman's Corner* about her travels: the trip ended in Zurich, and she made a point of adding that the last International Socialist Congress had been held there.

When she came back to work in January 1894, Margaret admitted for the first time that she must make some limits. The Central Committee told *Woman's Corner*:

'[Miss Davies] is decidedly better, but still not so strong as she hoped the two months' rest would make her. She therefore hopes that if she declines some of the kind invitations of branches or [co-operative] societies to address meetings, they will understand that any refusal is not from want of will, which is as strong as ever, but want of power.'[169]

From now on, Margaret reduced her travelling, and it would seem that Sarah Reddish took on some of her speaking load. But the Guild was still expanding, producing more and more administrative work, and also taking on a more public profile in which she, as General Secretary, played a major part. Despite a short holiday in summer 1894 with her old friend Ethel Sargant, by October she was having to cancel planned commitments. As she had in the previous year, she consulted the pioneering woman doctor Elizabeth Garrett Anderson, who specialized in treating women and children and was a family friend. The advice remained the same: a long period of complete rest.

At the beginning of December 1894 there was another announcement in *Woman's Corner*. This time, Margaret would be out of action for at least six months.[170]

Ill and alone

Although overwork and exhaustion clearly played their part in Margaret's repeated illness, there was more to it. Her mother advised her to ask Elizabeth Garrett Anderson about her menstrual problems, and to tell the doctor 'just how you feel *before* + at those c – d times [ie when menstruating]', suggesting that she might be suffering 'by not saving yourself enough when they come on'.[171] Margaret was also suffering from back trouble and insomnia; perhaps, although only in her early thirties, she may have been experiencing an early menopause.

Whatever the cause of Margaret's condition, the family rallied round once again. The consensus was that a long trip abroad was the answer, and Mary Davies suggested various women friends and relations as possible companions. Brother Harry also affectionately offered to put his work plans on hold for a while and go to Germany with her if she preferred: 'remember what pleasure it would be to help you, my best girl.'[172]

Margaret however had other ideas. In November 1894 she took herself off to Reigate, where the family had the use of a cottage. Her mother, of course, wanted to come down: 'Last night ... I felt as if I was deserting you when perhaps you wanted me a little + when I could ... be a calm old soporific'. Although Margaret seems to have been suggesting she would only be away for a short time, her mother pointed out presciently that if she did come back, 'how could you ever keep yr finger out of Coop Pie, with letters coming + Lilian always longing to discuss?'[173] [original abbreviations]

In the event Margaret did not even go home for Christmas, although she was well enough to send presents, including a volume of Ibsen's plays – still considered shocking by many. At the end of December she moved again, still alone, to take up lodgings in Cadgwith, a remote Cornish fishing village. Once again, her mother wanted to join her. 'I can't help being anxious + petty.....It seems as if ...my place ought to be by you.' She went on, 'Shall I send anything? Potted meat? Tell me if you are *well fed.*'[174] [original emphasis]. But once again, Margaret put her off.

We know very little about Margaret's reasons. Perhaps she needed space from her mother's overwhelming affection and anxiety, and from her family's insistent, though loving, concern. Contrastingly, she was prepared to see her closest friends. Rosalind planned to visit her at Reigate but, possibly because she was heavily pregnant, did not make it, while Ethel Sargant arranged to visit her in mid-January.

Whatever was going on, Margaret soon began to feel better and her mother, no longer so anxious, seems to have accepted the situation. Mary Davies wrote frequently during the first weeks of 1895, relaying local gossip and passing on news about Lilian, Sarah Reddish and another friend, Mary Spooner, who were covering the Guild office in Margaret's absence.

Sarah Reddish figured particularly frequently in Mary Davies's letters. Social encounters between the judge's daughter and the ex-mill worker must have been awkward to start with. After all, Mary Davies usually came across working-class women either as servants or as recipients of charity. But this changed as the two women came to know one another in Margaret's absence, especially after Sarah's own much-loved mother died at the beginning of December. Overwhelmed with grief, she continued working in the red room office. Mary Davies responded sympathetically though her report to Margaret sounds slightly patronising when read today. On 6 February, she wrote,

> "You do take such care of me" she [Sarah Reddish] said today, when I made her stop her work + sit by the fire with a book, till tea ...What a good thing she is – More of a lady than many so by birth.[175]

Margaret inscribed this letter 'the very last'. The following day, three telegrams from her father arrived in quick succession, gradually breaking the news that her mother had suddenly died. The cause was recorded as heart failure. Mary Davies was sixty.

Coda: Mother and Daughter

Mary Davies was exceptionally close to all her children but, as we have seen, she depended a great deal on her only daughter. She scrupulously refrained from giving her views when Margaret asked for advice about the marriage proposal. But after the refusal she wrote confessing that it would have been 'hard work' for her if Margaret had accepted, and that 'those 2 or 3 days [while Margaret was deciding] were some of the worst of my life'.[176] While touchingly honest, this is a surprising reaction to the possibility of her daughter marrying.

Margaret's devotion to her work was also an issue. In principle, Mary Davies wholeheartedly backed her, providing practical help, accepting Guild visitors to the vicarage, and coming to the Guild's annual meetings. However, Dolly Ponsonby's memories of her 1889 visit to Kirkby Lonsdale, though possibly exaggerated with the passage of time, point up the difficulties. At a time when ideas about women's role were still highly restrictive, both mother and daughter were treading new ground. As Dolly Ponsonby recorded:

> At that period it was accepted as a matter of course that a daughter would help her mother. But so advanced and so unselfish was Margaret's mother, that I am sure she hardly breathed it to herself that she would have liked the feminine companionship of a daughter and her help. Margaret would attend meetings and Co-op parties nearly every evening – and her sitting-room downstairs was swamped with pamphlets on various progressive questions of the day.[177]

Mary Davies seems to have struggled valiantly with an underlying ambivalence. When Margaret was in London for the trade union campaign, beginning to get the measure of what she could achieve in the Guild, her mother wrote:

> You wont want me to say I can do perfectly well without you who are my great comfort + brightness (in spite of your queer unlike-me nature!) but I should do very well don't be afraid of that. I am proud of all you do *and of all you will do* – nothing would pain me more than to think I was any block in yr way, or that for me you gave up anything.[178] [original emphasis and abbreviations].

Although she left very little other personal correspondence, Margaret preserved hundreds of letters from her mother – though, frustratingly, her own side of the correspondence has not survived. Their relationship was one of the most important of her life, yet, despite their closeness, Margaret must at times have felt pulled in opposite directions by her work and her mother's needs. It is significant that during her illness, she insisted on keeping her mother at arm's length. As with many mother-daughter relationships, it was complicated.

Compared with other young single women from her background, Margaret was extremely lucky. Unusually for the time, her parents adapted, apparently uncomplainingly, to her independence, her frequent absences on Guild business, and its increasing domination of her life. Now her father had suddenly been widowed. Would all this have to change?

CHAPTER 6

Making a Mark, 1895-1904

Convalescent, alone and far from home, Margaret had to cope not only with her overwhelming shock and grief but also with the knowledge that she had refused to see her mother during what had turned out to be her final weeks. The journey from deep in rural Cornwall to Kirkby Lonsdale and home must have seemed interminable.

This was a terrible time for the whole family. For Llewelyn, who was probably the hardest hit, religious faith provided some consolation. Soon after his wife's death he wrote bravely, 'we have enjoyed a family of such rare felicity that we feel it would be a kind of baseness not to let thankfulness master and transfigure all our sorrow.'[179]

As for the effect on Margaret, we can only imagine. After *Woman's Corner* reported the death, she wrote thanking Guildswomen for their ready sympathy and stressing her mother's active support for the Guild: '... She was deeply sympathetic with all women's movements, and with an exquisite generosity never grudged that much of my time should be spent away from her.' Margaret added that Mary Davies not only came to the annual meetings but also sometimes helped with the mountain of administrative work, and explained that it was she who had funded Sarah Reddish's post.

Margaret could only hint at her grief and loss: 'Those friends who have stayed with us here will be able to realise, to some small extent, what a light has gone out of our home.' She ended, 'To me she was mother and sister in one'.[180]

Life and work at the vicarage

In the absence of Mary Davies's lively and perceptive observations, we have to rely mainly on *Woman's Corner* for a picture of Margaret's life over the next decade.

Firstly, she had to adjust to a very different home life. The unmarried daughter living alone with her father, now in his late sixties, she was suddenly responsible for running the household. As a well-known clergyman, active in local affairs and also in national debates, Llewelyn had regular visitors; for example, we find the local bishop staying at the time of the 1901 census. In any case, Mary Davies had always welcomed visitors to the vicarage and Margaret was expected to continue, organizing hospitality not only for her brothers, but, as time went on, also for their families and for other friends and relations. It might well have been assumed that from now on she would devote herself to running the home and looking after her father.

True to form, Margaret defied such expectations. Her way of coping with bereavement was to plunge herself into work. Barely a couple of months after her mother's death she was busy compiling the next Guild Annual Report. From May, she was back more or less at full throttle, writing a major paper on co-operative education, overseeing the Guild's annual meeting (which included managing a particularly sensitive debate) and more. Evidently, work would remain a central part of her life – and, indeed, as the Guild took off over the next few years, it increased.

Fortunately, whatever had caused Margaret's earlier ill health seems to have abated. Between 1895 and 1904 she had only one bout of sickness serious enough to affect her work, and even then did not have to give up completely.[181] Perhaps this was because she gradually found ways to control the ever-increasing workload. How did she do it? She must have been organized, though that may not have come easily, as she was said to be impatient with detail. Most importantly, she had help; and here, Lilian, who had a real talent for administration, came into her own. Initially the Guild cashier, Lilian was formally designated assistant secretary in 1901, and Margaret recruited Lucy Davenport, another Kirkby Lonsdale volunteer, to take over as cashier. Operating alongside the Guild's formal structure, with other occasional office helpers, they kept the expanding show on the road.

Meanwhile, for some years, a paid organizer took on much of the exhausting travelling around local branches. Although Sarah Reddish left in 1895, Catherine Mayo, a lively and enthusiastic socialist, successfully took over. And Rosalind Nash was also in the background. Although living in the south, married with young children, she was still involved, termed by Margaret her 'unseen friend and counsellor', and from 1896 editor of *Woman's Corner*.

Margaret could not have managed, however, without the three capable servants who kept the vicarage going, doing the housework, cooking and much more. The 1901 census records Annie Tandy, the housemaid, Isabel Bell, the parlour maid and Kate Jones, the cook. Kate stayed for over ten years, and Annie, who had been with the family since 1889 or earlier, was obviously a mainstay as both Llewelyn and Margaret remembered her in their wills. Although the vicarage was a large house to keep up, this was probably a good place from the servants' point of view. Provided they worked well together, they may have found life easier with a mistress who was often out, away from home, or preoccupied with her own work. And their length of service suggests that they and Margaret got on well.

Meanwhile Llewelyn had to get used to her regular absences. As Lucy Davenport reported in *Woman's Corner*, despite her efforts to reduce, Margaret was often on her travels, '... here, there and everywhere; sometimes all the office staff are away, and then the shutters are put up and Dr Davies has to send on the batch of letters'.[182]

Not surprisingly, it seems that Margaret rarely played the part of the vicar's hostess at parish events; although one of his projects, to set up a free public reading room and institute – at his insistence, open to the whole community regardless of religious affiliation – struck a chord. She took to it with enthusiasm, characteristically insisting on a William Morris design for the curtains.

It is worth remembering that Margaret was not the first woman campaigner in the family. Llewelyn had always been close to his redoubtable sister, Emily Davies, so perhaps it is not surprising that this Victorian clergyman accepted both his daughter's frequent trips away and her increasing colonization of the vicarage for the Guild. Even so, combining work and home as she did cannot always have been easy. As Rosalind Nash later concluded, 'for most of her life [Margaret] had to carry the double burden of woman'.[183]

While we know a great deal about Margaret's intense relationship with her mother, little survives about her and her father during these years. We do know, though, that Llewelyn was proud of Margaret. When the *Manchester Guardian* reported on the 1892 Festival, he proudly carried around a press cutting about her 'fine energy and dauntless enthusiasm' to show to his friends,[184] and on one occasion he even came to the Guild Congress and gave a short address. In turn, as we saw at the beginning of chapter one, Margaret admired her father's achievements. While she herself moved towards more radical politics over the years, we can see the continuing influence of his Christian Socialist ideals in her commitment to public duty and her belief in the moral importance of the quality of individual relationships across the class divide.

With Margaret in charge of the vicarage, the office inevitably spilled over from the 'red room' as the original Guild office was always known. In 1901, readers of *Woman's Corner* learned that the Guild had expanded to take up two and a half rooms, in one of which 'Miss Davies thinks in solitude'. This was not always uninterrupted; Margaret wrote at various times that Guild visitors were welcome, and evidently some took her at her word. When Mrs Wood and a friend turned up out of the blue, she told *Woman's Corner* that 'in her homely way' Margaret had made them very welcome, and gave each a bunch of flowers from the garden.[185] Occasionally, Margaret also had Guilders or other co-operators to stay; Lucy Davenport joked that the brothers sometimes had to sleep at neighbours' houses when they visited.

Margaret arranged for a photograph of her and Lilian at work in the thriving Guild office to be part of a slide show used at Guild meetings. To modern eyes, the picture presents a charming if slightly eccentric home office, complete with pictures, framed photos on the mantelpiece, overflowing papers in a basket on the floor and the family dog snoozing in front of the decorative fireplace. Margaret described it at length in *Woman's Corner*, stressing that it was a serious workplace:

> The three windows down one side of the long-shaped room look out on to a beautiful avenue of lime-trees, leading to the little town. Inside the walls are white-washed, as befits a 'factory', and books and pictures find places where the wall-spaces are not occupied by large cupboards and drawers, containing stocks of guild literature, account books, records of the guild, badges, brooches, stationery, blue books, &c.
>
> There are three tables now in daily use, covered with correspondence and papers. A great many of our members, by the aid of the lantern slide, will have seen the general secretary sitting at one and the cashier (Miss Harris) sitting at another; and recently we have secured a new helper in Miss Davenport who has been busy at the third table making out the innumerable lists needed for the annual meeting.[186]

A snapshot of the six months between January and June 1901 gives some idea of how hard Margaret worked. She travelled to three Central Committee meetings during this time, organizing them, taking minutes and as usual circularizing committee members when decisions were needed in between. One such example was whether the Guild should send a letter of condolence to the King on Queen Victoria's recent death. (Agreed by a majority, this will have grated on Margaret – according to Lady Maude Parry already a republican – who had to actually write and send the letter).[187]

The Guild's annual evening meeting had recently been replaced by a much more ambitious Congress, lasting three days. In preparation, as she did every year, Margaret wrote up the Annual Report – with its detailed figures on membership and branches, records of activity and campaigning both local and national, a report of the previous year's Guild Congress, lists of papers and books available, topics for discussion, accounts, and more. The final version had to be approved by the Central Committee and printed in time for the Congress in mid-June.

Margaret did manage a two week holiday in Holland but, typically, also used this to make contact with the Netherland Co-operative Women's Union. Also in May, she went to the Co-operative Congress, the annual gathering of the whole movement, as she did most years, and played a major part in one of the debates.

June was dominated by the Guild's own Congress. Margaret had to work out which resolutions would be discussed, suggest who might be asked to propose them, and get this discussed and approved by the Central Committee. There was a mountain of other administrative work to co-ordinate: arranging travel, accommodation and refreshments for the 340 attenders and planning the Congress programme.

While much of this was by now routine, there was also the specific work Margaret did on Guild campaigns that year, in which she worked particularly with the Women's Trade Union League to lobby against the tax on sugar.[188] Furthermore, she was still in demand to speak at local Guild meetings. Her 1901 diary began with a major address at Sarah Reddish's large branch in Bolton, which was reprinted in the local paper and then in *Woman's Corner*.[189] Over the next six months, she also spoke at six or seven other meetings around the country and, in between, produced the occasional report for the *Corner*.

The workload was still impressive, but now it seems to have been brought under control.

Progress in the Guild

In 1904, the occasion of the Guild's 'Coming of Age', the Central Committee tasked Margaret to write a formal history of its first 21 years. In this she paid lavish tribute to other Guild leaders, but while she was reticent about her personal role, she made no bones about promoting the campaigning policies she had introduced and the achievements that had resulted.

From its tiny beginnings, the Guild had now expanded to 18,500 members in 359 branches across England and Wales. What is more, despite earlier lack of support, even hostility, from conservative co-operators in the north, the Guild was now growing there, too.[190]

This success partly reflected a rapid growth in co-operation overall at this time, with increasing membership of co-operative societies providing a larger pool of potential Guildswomen. Furthermore, times were changing, for working-class as well as middle-class women. A growth in socialist activity, especially in northern industrial areas, and the advent of the Independent Labour Party (ILP), provided a fertile climate for the Guild and for Margaret's insistence that members should become a 'body of reformers'.

She firmly believed that they needed information, training and experience in order to make this happen. Papers and discussions on topics like 'How to start and work a branch' provided practical information about getting organised, but that was only the beginning. The system was soon operating smoothly and every year the Central Committee decided on a major topic for education and debate. It then published pamphlets, organised outside speakers, and made plans for members to read papers and discuss them at branch, district and sectional conferences, as well as at the annual meeting. From here, Guildswomen could go on to gather evidence, and to begin to campaign for change.

A crucial part of the programme was for women to gain experience of writing and, especially, speaking in public, first at branch meetings and then in larger settings. A good start was to read out a paper written by someone else, something often required when a new paper on a campaigning issue was being discussed throughout the Guild. But Margaret encouraged grass roots members to write and read their own papers, too, for discussion at all levels of the organization – and this soon took off.[191] Thus in 1901, *Woman's Corner* described a member who at first had not dared to speak in public, even at a branch meeting. After first writing a simple report and reading it aloud, and then taking part in discussions, she could now, in her own words, 'talk as bold as a lion'. Margaret quotes another member's powerful comment: 'Our Guild has turned out women who are capable of making speeches such as few men could beat – women who all our lives have worked hard in the factory and the home.'[192]

Guildswomen did not all see themselves as campaigners and throughout it remained a 'broad church' with some members and branches partly, or completely, opting out of this side of the organisation. However, as the increase in membership shows, Margaret's programme appealed to many other women. The Guild proved itself a training ground for women who, later, became impressive activists. One example was Selina Cooper, who joined the Guild while she was a winder in a cotton mill. Later, in 1898, she helped to set up a local branch in Brierfield, Lancashire and became its president. She went on to be elected a Poor Law Guardian on a socialist ticket, singlehandedly gathered 800 signatures for a suffrage petition, spoke to MPs at a deputation and argued for votes for women at a national Labour conference. A committed socialist, she became a local, and later a national, suffrage organizer, and a lifelong activist for women's and labour causes.[193]

An interesting tribute to this side of the Guild comes from an unexpected quarter: published some years later, D.H. Lawrence's semi-autobiographical novel *Sons and Lovers* offers a modest, but nevertheless powerful, demonstration of the impact of Margaret's policies. A central character is Mrs Morel, an ex-teacher married to a miner. In her old age, Margaret preserved a copy of Lawrence's description of Mrs Morel's Guild branch, 'a little club of women ... which met on Monday night in the long room over the grocery shop of the Bestwood co-op'. The story tells how the women discussed co-operation along with 'other social questions':

> Sometimes Mrs Morel read a paper. It seemed queer to the children to see their mother, who was always busy about the house, sitting writing in her rapid fashion, thinking, referring to books, + writing again. They felt for her on such occasions the deepest respect.
> ... they loved the Guild. It was the one thing to which they did not grudge their mother – and that partly because she enjoyed it, partly because of the treats they derived from it. ...The Guild was called by some hostile husbands, who found their wives getting too independent, the 'clatfart shop' – that is, the gossip-shop. It is true, from off the basis of the Guild, the women could look at their homes, at the conditions of their own lives, and find fault. So the colliers found their women had a new standard of their own, rather disconcerting.[194]

Margaret may have been a dedicated campaigner, but like other members she also loved the convivial side of Guild life. She wrote of the 'teas, social evenings and coffee suppers' which encouraged the 'friendliness and sense of brotherhood' in the movement. It is not surprising that Clementina Black compared the 'jolliness' of Guild meetings favourably to the 'sedateness' of debates at the middle-class National Union of Women Workers.[195]

Early campaigning

In practice, Margaret played the main part in determining the Guild's campaigning direction, though always with the agreement of the Central

Committee. Sometimes, for example on public health and housing, the aim was mainly to equip members to understand existing laws: once equipped with the information, they could begin to take action locally. *Woman's Corner* reported how this helped one Guildswoman: '"I was not going to stand any more smells, when I knew how to get rid of them," said a guilder after Miss Ravenhill's lecture on Public Health.' She immediately tackled the local sanitary inspector and, the next morning 'all the dustbins in her row of cottages were cleared'.[196] But Guildswomen were also prepared to think more broadly. There were lively discussions, for example, on developing co-operative housing – and even co-operative housework.[197]

As before, the struggle for equality within the co-operative movement continued. Margaret supported women in pushing for 'open membership': battling with those local co-operative societies which still excluded wives of existing members. Even where women could join, to carry any weight they had to overcome the hurdle of attending the quarterly members' meetings, frequently all male, which governed each society. Although daunting, this was a crucial first step towards women standing for education and management committees – and being elected. Margaret consistently encouraged them, and publicised successes in her Annual Reports. Progress was slow, but by 1904, women had gained places on twenty local management committees and many more on the less powerful education committees. Several gained national positions. A major triumph in 1904 saw Mary Spooner become the first woman to chair the United Board, the central body of the movement.

It was a hard slog but the rewards would be great. For Margaret, women's involvement in co-operation was not only about equality, but also about changing how it operated. This was also dear to the hearts of Guildswomen, who enthusiastically demanded that co-operative societies adopt business policies which were more in line with the movement's ideals. They continued to lobby locally for better conditions for co-operative employees, and for boycotting 'sweated' goods, demanding that co-operative stores should sell those produced under fair and safe conditions – preferably by co-operative producers – and for decent pay.[198] A popular cause with Guildswomen, some years later it would take centre stage.

It was from the early1890s that Margaret began to make her personal mark within the movement. From its early days, education had been a key aspect, and in principle at least local societies were enjoined to follow the Rochdale Pioneers' principle and allocate it a percentage of profits, to be administered by their education committees. Yet while many in the movement accepted that the Guild had an important educational role, branches often found it difficult or impossible to gain practical support of any kind from their local co-operative societies – even sometimes being blocked from using a meeting room.

Margaret wanted to look at co-operative education more broadly. Building on existing concerns about the need to improve it, she plunged in with a lengthy paper (written surprisingly soon after Mary's death) pointing out that education had been allowed to stagnate in recent years, and making various ambitious suggestions for change and expansion. Although the Guild approved the paper and sent it up the co-operative hierarchy, Margaret's proposals seem to have got nowhere. But she did achieve a result of sorts. Soon afterwards, she was invited onto the national Co-operative Education Committee (CEC), and is credited with securing a major enquiry into co-operative education, established in 1896.[199] But this was just a first step.

At the same time, Margaret continued to prioritize support for women workers and trade unions. Collaborating with the recently formed Women's Industrial Council, she encouraged Guildswomen to join campaigns for greater legal regulation of women's work. From 1897, Sarah Reddish regularly sent in returns to the government's Labour Department about women's work in the textile industry, obtaining her information from local correspondents, many of whom were Guildswomen.

However, not all members supported state regulation of women's work – or indeed that of children. In the summer of 1895, a contentious debate highlighted, perhaps for the first time, the potential for deeply felt divisions within the Guild. At that date, children aged eleven or over were allowed to work 'half time', attending school for the other half of the day. Plans were afoot to change the law, and the Central Committee agreed to Margaret's proposal for the Guild to back a current campaign to raise the age to twelve.

Margaret knew this would be controversial, especially in Lancashire and Yorkshire, where many families relied on children's earnings to make ends meet. Her first tactic was to test the opinion of the branches there. When they appeared divided, she set up a debate at the 1895 Annual Meeting. Margaret made the Central Committee position quite clear: it hoped that 'co-operative guild mothers will not allow self-interest to blind them to the true welfare of the children …'[200] The question touched a raw nerve for women from manufacturing areas, both those who had managed to avoid sending their children to work, and others who, having taken the opposite course, felt accused of being bad mothers.

Margaret and the Committee carefully chose a former factory worker, Mrs Rigby, to present the paper opposing the half time system. Women who had themselves worked in factories or mills were prominent in the debate, with passionate contributions on both sides. Among the more emollient contributions was a typically tactful intervention from Sarah Reddish who, whilst herself opposing half time, declared to applause that she sympathised very much with women who 'earned small wages, and having a large number of children, considered the raising of the age limit would be a great hardship'.[201]

In the event, Margaret's planning paid off and the Committee's resolution in favour of raising the minimum age was passed, with only five delegates openly declaring dissent. Judging by the fierceness of the debate, more might have agreed with them but were unwilling to break the Guild's tradition of consensus. This was in any case a significant moment. The debate reflected members' increasing empowerment and a willingness, if necessary, to question and oppose the leadership. We will hear more of this later on.

Margaret's other campaigning priority was what she termed 'citizenship', extending women's rights in public life. The initial step was to take up any local opportunities. After the first Guildswomen had been elected as Poor Law Guardians in 1894, Margaret aimed to double their number at the next elections in 1898. Once again, the systematic plan of campaign has her fingerprints all over it. Well in advance, the Central Committee produced pamphlets, arranged for current Guild Guardians to address branches and asked for new 'municipal secretaries' to encourage members to stand. There were regular discussions and articles in *Woman's Corner* and, as the elections drew near, Margaret urged Guildswomen to stand, or failing that, to canvass for other women candidates. All this paid off; 40 Guildswomen were successful in the elections with only five unsuccessful. From now on, Guildswomen would regularly be elected as Guardians.

Emboldened by their success, members now supported lobbying against women's exclusion from newly created London Councils, and from the local education committees which replaced School Boards, on which women had been able to sit. Margaret was aware that helping to run local poor law and education services, associated with women's traditional caring role, was less controversial than women voting and standing for parliament. She was sensitive to a current of disapproval about female suffrage within the Guild and was cautious about extending the campaign to include parliamentary votes for women.

There were signs, however, that, with regard to the latter, the climate both within and outside the Guild was changing. As early as 1893, the National Society for Women's Suffrage had initiated an ambitious new petition for the vote from 'women of all parties and all classes', and, significantly, asked for the Guild's help in collecting signatures.

As Margaret reported in her Guild history, suffragists in the north-west went on to organise a petition specifically from women textile workers, who responded enthusiastically. Campaigners travelled to mill towns and villages large and small; addressing union meetings, canvassing house to house, standing with the petition in mill yards, and holding open air meetings – even collecting signatures standing on orange boxes in the local market.[202] They quickly gathered an extraordinary 29 thousand signatures in Lancashire alone. The deputation which presented the petition to parliament in 1901 included Sarah Reddish, but also seventeen other members of the Guild.

While this was going on, in 1897 a private member's bill demanding women's suffrage succeeded in passing its second reading in the House of Commons. This emboldened Margaret to organise Guild discussions on 'Why working women need the vote', in which she argued that this was the only effective way in which they could influence legislation on subjects which directly affected them.

This 'political' topic was still controversial for some members and, whilst praising the Lancashire women's petition and the Guild members who worked for it, Margaret cautiously made it clear in her 1904 history of the Guild that they were acting as individuals rather than on behalf of the organisation. Nevertheless, she felt able to claim that members were beginning to support votes for women, 'not only from the point of view of justice, but also because they see how closely the actual needs in their lives are connected with it'. [203]

A notable event in July 1897 confirmed that the Guild had begun to achieve a national profile. Unexpectedly, Margaret was invited to a special dinner and reception organised by a 'committee of ladies' to commemorate Queen Victoria's Diamond Jubilee. The committee aimed to achieve attendance from women right across the 'notable' elements of society, and the press report described Margaret as 'Miss Llewelyn Davies, whose energetic advocacy has much to do with the progress of the Women's Co-operative Guild'.[204] Margaret's connections with the great and the good – in this case committee members Elizabeth Garrett Anderson and Millicent Fawcett, both family friends – no doubt played a part in her selection. Given her increasingly radical politics, we can imagine her ambivalence about such an invitation. But still, this constituted undoubted recognition. Another acknowledgment, this time of the Guild rather than of Margaret individually, came in 1901 when Mrs Gasson gave evidence to a House of Lords committee about its policy to limit shop workers' hours.

Meanwhile, from the mid-90s onward the Guild lobbied parliament on all sorts of policies and proposals, from taxation of land values to licensing reform. The co-operative movement, long wedded to a belief in a 'free breakfast table', particularly opposed the taxation of food. Guildswomen strongly supported this – after all, they had to manage household budgets. They campaigned first against the tax on sugar and then against taxation of bread and flour. As a resolution almost certainly written by Margaret 'indignantly protest[ed]', under such a system 'the food of the people is taxed while the monopolies of the wealthier classes are left untouched'.[205]

In 1903, the threat of protectionist tax changes at a time of rising living costs highlighted the issue. Up until now, the Guild's national campaigning had been relatively low profile, concentrating on gathering evidence, publicising its policies, contacting MPs and writing to ministers and the press. Now, Margaret moved up a gear. As well as contacting the Co-operative Union to arrange joint action, and encouraging branches to campaign locally,[206] she organised a national women's demonstration, hosted by the Guild and supported by a wide range of other organisations, appropriately in Manchester's Free Trade Hall.

Margaret called on members for support: 'Let us show that co-operative women can be roused, and let us make our voice heard throughout the length and breadth of the land.'[207] As was her wont at such public events, she herself did not speak on behalf of the Guild. Instead, Mrs Bury, currently Vice-President, chaired and also addressed the meeting. But Margaret probably drafted the resolution which was passed, linking free trade with votes for women: 'seeing that women, both as workers and as housewives, are so deeply concerned in this question, [the meeting] deplores that they cannot make their protest effective through being debarred from the parliamentary franchise.'[208]

The meeting was highly successful. Messages of support were read from Winston Churchill, Millicent Fawcett, John Bright and more. The *Manchester Guardian* headed its long report 'Women and Free Trade – A remarkable platform – Unionists, Liberals and Socialists,'[209] while *Co-operative News* praised the Guild as the only organisation which could have got such a meeting together.[210] The Guild Central Committee formally passed a vote of thanks to Margaret and Lilian for their hard work.

This was Margaret's first foray into political alliances on a high profile issue. The Guild was now a national player.

'Interpreting the needs of the workers'?

Margaret named a chapter in her history of the Guild 'A Democracy of Working Women'. Here she stressed that the crucial distinction between the Guild and other organisations such as the 'mothers meetings' organised by the Anglican Mothers' Union was its democratic character: 'The principle underlying the whole organization of the Guild, from top to bottom, is that *of self-government.*' [original emphasis]. She went on to make it clear how she saw the position of middle-class Guildswomen like herself,

> ... a few women who have had time – 'that commodity much needed by working women' – at their disposal, and whose sympathies attracted them to a working class organisation rather than to philanthropic work. But those who join the Guild take their place on an equality with all, standing for election with the rest, and winning their way if the members wish it. They must identify themselves with working class interests, and come as interpreters of the needs and wishes of the workers.[211]

This was a bold statement at the time. Inevitably, though, the issues involved were not so straightforward. Like other middle-class women who played leading roles in working-class organisations, such as Mary Macarthur of the National Federation of Women Workers and Margaret Macdonald of the Women's Labour League, Margaret was passionately committed, and certainly identified herself with working-class interests. But from today's vantage point her description of interpreting working-class needs and views for them raises more questions than it answers.

While the Guild's structure was indeed democratic, it gave considerable power to the leadership. Margaret saw the elected Central Committee's authority as directly derived from the annual Congress, writing: 'The object ... is healthy independence in local work, combined with response to the policy and suggestions coming from the centre.'[212] An accompanying diagram showed the Guild as a tree with the Central Committee as the trunk and the regional sections branching off it. Policies, usually initiated by Margaret, had to be approved by the Central Committee, which consisted of an elected representative from each section. They were then debated at the Annual Congress (until 1900 the Annual Meeting). The only long-term member of the Central Committee, she could and did steer the Guild, providing it very effectively with a clear direction.

While Margaret herself only occasionally contributed to Annual Meeting or Congress debates, she certainly never pretended to be impartial. An article by a visitor to the 1896 Annual Meeting described her reading out responses from branches that had objected to taking part in a Guild investigation into women's working conditions. Although the writer insisted that Margaret 'seeks to convince, not to dominate', this is hardly borne out in the report of Margaret in action: 'Her fine, musical voice assumed an indescribably effective intonation of contemptuous humour, that scourged while it ridiculed.'[213]

This was not, however, the whole story. Margaret's Guild work was based, above all, on a belief that grass roots Guildswomen must make their voices heard. Much as a result of her policies, by the mid to late 1890s women from working-class backgrounds, often experienced and determined local activists, routinely made up most if not all of the other Central Committee members: a major and essential change from the Guild's early years.

Margaret also insisted that, with Guild training, grass roots members did not need others to act for them. When an article in *Woman's Corner* suggested that branches might need to have educated women in leading positions, she immediately challenged it in no uncertain terms, declaring that 'our most flourishing branches are just those where all are working women together'.[214]

The social gulf was very real and, especially early on, Margaret sometimes displayed the top-down attitudes which came from her initial background in philanthropic work. But this changed as the Guild developed. Throughout her long service, Margaret was not only subject to annual re-election but also responsible to the Central Committee, which had to approve her policies and whose members changed every three years. Margaret knew and worked with these women and also, throughout her time in the Guild, travelled around meeting others in branches and regional sections. It is clear that, as time went on, a relationship of mutual respect and affection came into being.

Margaret's persuasive skill, and her ability to listen and encourage – part of her often-described personal charm – played a part in this. Rosalind Nash later remembered a characteristic scene at the end of a three-day Guild Congress. After the intense, unrelenting demands of planning and organising the event, Margaret was to be found leaning wearily against a table, responding to a queue of local Guild officials wanting help and advice. Rosalind was close enough to hear the 'constant kind solicitous notes of her voice', although she ruefully added that it was really too much for Margaret: 'The scene is too long, they don't stop coming.'[215]

CHAPTER 7

Reaching the Poorest, 1899-1905

Margaret's forty-first birthday, in October 1902, was very different from any other. She spent it not in the comfortable Kirkby Lonsdale vicarage but in the north east, living in a cramped flat above a co-operative shop in Sunderland. She was to stay for three months but the project which had brought her there would absorb her for much longer.

Like some others, Margaret was firmly of the belief that the poorest in society deserved access to the advantages of co-operation. It was not only that they would benefit from joining, but also that including them was central to the Owenite co-operative ideals which had brought her into the movement. In 1904, she would write of the 'faith that co-operation, if many sided and rightly directed, can prove a powerful lever for raising the poorest and most unfortunate among us'.[216]

But the co-operation of Margaret's time was far from well-disposed towards poor people. The main problem was the high prices often charged in co-operative shops. Unlike the very poor, co-operators came mostly from better off sections of the working class and so did not need to seek out cheap prices. More important for them was the magic 'divi', based on how much they spent at the co-operative store. This was a vital protection when hard times hit, and a way of saving for one-off expenses. Each local co-operative society could decide how much dividend to pay, and, by now, two thirds were paying members over two shillings for every pound they spent (10%), some even as much as five shillings (25%).

Such high dividends had to be paid for somehow, so they were often accompanied by high prices. As one Guildswoman put it, many co-operative shops were, effectively, operating like savings banks. She pointed out that whilst this appealed to those with steady, reasonably well-paid jobs, it kept out low-waged and casual workers.[217] Poor people had other hurdles to cope with, too. Whilst anyone could shop at the co-op, in order to qualify for the dividend you had to become a member – and this meant buying a share. Societies often charged entrance fees, and if hard times forced you to cash in your share but you later wanted to re-join, the fees had to be paid all over again, sometimes along with a fine.

Not surprisingly, then, there were few co-operative shops in really poor neighbourhoods. And in the movement, many blamed poor people themselves, accusing them of thriftlessness and drunkenness, and arguing that they too could become co-operators if they chose to mend their ways.

The campaign begins

Margaret first took up these questions in 1899, when she produced *Co-operation in Poor Neighbourhoods,* a comprehensive paper initially for discussion within the Guild, but aimed at a much wider audience.

She was not alone; there had been stirrings in the movement during the 1890s, as poverty was increasingly highlighted in public debates. It had been suggested at the 1890 Co-operative Congress that specially adapted branch stores should be set up in poor neighbourhoods, and Sidney Webb read a prize-winning essay about the problem at the following year's Congress. Some co-operative societies were sympathetic to change, indeed, the Guild worked with one such in London. Meanwhile the Co-operative Union floated something rather different, proposing that Guildswomen might act as 'district visitors' among the poor, with the implication that they would help poor families manage better.[218] As this indicates, discussions of extending co-operation to the poor had two potentially conflicting aims: on the one hand, changing co-operation to meet poor people's needs and, on the other, changing the 'feckless' poor into good co-operators.

Initially busy building up the Guild, Margaret first highlighted such questions in 1897, when she arranged for the annual meeting to discuss high dividends.[219] Two years later, *Co-operation in Poor Neighbourhoods* marked the beginning of what was to be a lengthy battle. Margaret did not mince her words, declaring that high dividends were 'a convenient form of saving for the well-to-do ... a means which the better-off, who are in possession, use to help themselves at the expense of the poorer'. In terms which must have been anathema to some, she argued that 'high dividends corrupt the morals of our movement, and lure men and women from the paths of true progress and reform'.

She went on to make a broader challenge:

> ... good steady trade, good quality, an educated taste, a well-to-do membership, are all excellent things ... But is this all that co-operation

can do? Are we not becoming dangerously respectable, in more ways than one? ... I sometimes wonder whether I can be in the right camp when I find we have dukes and bishops and royalties and *The Times* newspaper on our side.[220]

Drawing partly on suggestions which had already been tried by some local co-operative societies, Margaret made specific recommendations about special 'people's stores' in poor areas. Dividends would be low, and food would be sold cheaply and in small amounts. The store would also sell hot food, and there would be a department providing secured loans, along with a 'reformed pawnshop' to tide people over inevitable misfortunes. Drawing on examples from philanthropic work in poor areas, she also suggested a club room or settlement with resident workers. These would 'attract from the public-house ... bring personal help, and form a centre of co-operative activity in the district.'[221]

Enthused about tackling poverty, and angry with the lack-lustre approach of the co-operative mainstream, Margaret now initiated a flurry of activity both within and outside the Guild. She arranged for 3,500 copies of her pamphlet to be published, and within months, it had been discussed at ten Guild sectional conferences and at least 150 branches. Five articles in *Woman's Corner* had been reprinted as a pamphlet, and the issue had also been raised at nineteen district meetings between the Guild and the Co-operative Union. Meanwhile, Margaret had been speaking all over the country and making contacts with directors of sympathetic local co-operative societies.[222]

Reports of Guild discussions suggest that members did not feel as strongly about the campaign as Margaret did. Most Guildswomen agreed that bringing the poor into co-operation was morally desirable and scorned the 'divi-hunters' who just saw using the co-operative shop as a way of saving. Even those who blamed poverty on individual failings often believed co-operation could and should help the poor to change their ways. So there was support for many of her ideas, although her suggestion of a pawn shop caused consternation.[223]

A few years later, Margaret wrote, 'Co-operators as a whole, especially the men, did not take very kindly to the proposals'.[224] Certainly, reports of Guild discussions in autumn 1899, which like others were open to visitors, suggest it was men who were most vociferous in opposing the scheme. At a lively discussion in Huddersfield, several male speakers jumped in immediately after the paper had been read. The first claimed that poorer people could become co-operators if only they, like him, 'had grown up in the movement, and stuck to its principles, and had thus become well-to-do'. Another added, 'the great cause of [slum-dwellers'] misery was due to drink,' and a third, defending high dividends, declared, 'the working classes of the country must look to themselves for their own welfare'. After this, the Chair had to insist on calling women to speak next, most of whom supported Margaret's suggestions (as, to be fair, did several men).[225]

Not only were there strongly felt disagreements about the content of Margaret's proposals, but also, in making them she had gone beyond the Guild's traditional remit. Activist Guildswomen were already making waves in some co-operative societies, demanding better conditions for women employees and a boycott of 'sweated' goods. Now, with this new, national initiative, Margaret was proposing a major incursion into what had previously been the men's domain – and they were not pleased.

Undeterred, Margaret quickly produced another pamphlet which amplified her earlier proposals. This time, perhaps hoping to strike a chord with the many nonconformists within the movement, she drew on the quasi-religious language often used in public revelations about slum life. Entitled *A Co-operative Relief Column,* the pamphlet included the fervent hope for 'a movement within our movement', and for 'co-operative missionaries, both men and women' in poor areas.[226] But it also, significantly, denounced high dividends under the heading 'The greatest hindrance to the greatest number'.

Discussions within the Guild continued, and its 1900 Congress backed Margaret's call for the movement to set up a special association to promote the extension of co-operation to the poor. This had become her priority and, with the Guild on side and sympathetic local co-operative societies interested, she tried to obtain national backing. But, although a supportive resolution was passed at the 1900 Co-operative Congress, the movement's governing United Board refused to pursue the issue – either through Margaret's proposal for an association, or through a joint committee with the Guild. There seemed to be a stalemate.

Margaret now showed her mettle. In January 1901 she went public with a combative statement on behalf of the Guild Central Committee, significantly sent to the main part of *Co-operative News* rather than its *Woman's Corner* pages. This complained about the failure of the movement's leadership to take any action, and its refusal to work with the Guild on this issue. The Board did not relent, however. It dismissively reported that it had decided not to take up the Guild's proposal because '[co-operative] societies in large towns were quite able, if they were willing, to undertake this work for themselves'.[227]

Undaunted, Margaret continued pushing. In October, the United Board gave in and agreed to give the Guild a grant of £50 to pursue an enquiry into the topic. Perhaps they hoped this would make her go away. If so, they were to be disappointed.

During the 1890s, public debates about the causes of poverty had increasingly highlighted the importance of structural economic factors rather than concentrating only on perceived individual moral failings. Throughout the decade, Charles Booth (coincidentally, a distant relation of Margaret's) was publishing his ground-breaking studies of poverty in London. These showed that, contrary to his original expectations, nearly a third of the city's population was living in poverty. Seebohm Rowntree's study of York, published in 1901, produced similar results.

This was the background to the Guild enquiry, which took place early in 1902. Immediately, sparks began to fly: Margaret came up with a much more ambitious exercise than the co-operative officials had bargained for. Having absorbed the fact-finding social research approach of the 1880s and 1890s, and influenced both by Booth's findings and by Rowntree's recent study, she saw the enquiry as a full scale research job. Joined by Mrs Abbott, another middle-class Guildswoman,[228] she undertook a comprehensive investigation into co-operation and poverty which involved visits to Sheffield, Bury, York (where she spent several hours with Rowntree), Newcastle and Sunderland.

So Margaret and Mrs Abbott observed the impact of appalling housing conditions at first hand by accompanying women sanitary inspectors on their visits. They found out about disease, population density and mortality rates from Medical Officers of Health, they visited settlements, they gathered information on housing, shops and pubs in poor areas, and they talked to council staff, health visitors and local co-operative employees and officials. Margaret also undertook a survey of local co-operative policies on such things as pricing, deposits, and entrance fees.

Margaret maintained that the Guild had the right to decide how it used the £50, but evidently the committee which administered the grant did not agree. They complained that they had never contemplated that the Guild would send 'deputations' around the country and could not understand why 'Mrs Abbott should be brought all the way from Tunbridge Wells to investigate at Sheffield and other distant places' when the local Guild branches could provide the necessary information.[229] Margaret now had to defend herself against powerful critics – something she was not used to.

This all happened early in 1902, and Margaret speedily published her report in a series of articles in *Woman's Corner*. On the basis of what she had found, she recommended various measures to help co-operative societies reach the poor. These included abolition of entrance fees, reduced requirement for new members to make deposits towards shares, easier withdrawal of dividends, establishing 'penny banks', and stocking and advertising lower price goods.[230]

Although it did not produce new insights into the causes and nature of poverty, Margaret's enquiry provided important evidence for the movement to consider. Its detailed analysis of what local co-operative societies provided, how poor people shopped, and why they were often forced to adopt what seemed improvident habits such as buying in small amounts, turned the problem around, presenting poor people's failure to become co-operators from a new angle. The Co-operative Congress recommended that the report should be circulated within the movement, and the Guild sent out 4000 copies of a pamphlet focusing on the recommendations for local action.[231] Perhaps opinion was on the move.

Coronation Street

Margaret had made a point of meeting local co-operators during her enquiry visits. Visiting Sunderland, she found that leading officials in the local co-operative not only shared her views but had already opened three branches in poor areas. By the time she wrote her report, she had been hatching plans with them. The report explained that, in the very poorest of these areas, a slum district centred on Coronation Street, the Sunderland co-operative society planned to develop a group of buildings to include a grocery shop, a butcher's, a meeting hall, and rooms for resident workers above the shop. The report did not say so, but these workers would come from the Guild, and Margaret would be one of them.

Although Margaret had travelled around industrial towns for years for the Guild, she found the area around Coronation Street an eye-opener. She painted a grim picture: 'rows of houses with no sanitary conveniences, and no back yards – with imperfectly-paved open gutters down the passages in which milk and slops stagnated – with broken windows stuffed with rags.'[232] Jobs for men were mainly as labourers in the shipyards, while many women were fish-hawkers; and there were frequent crises of unemployment when trade was bad. Children had to pull their weight and contribute financially, too. Older girls often worked in the local brewery or in service, while smaller children sold oranges or winkles, or carried 'errands for neighbours for pennies'.[233] Sickness and premature death were everywhere. One settlement worker commented on how few old people were to be seen in the area. Baby and child deaths were common. Life was more than hard.

Against this background, the co-operative buildings made a splash when they opened in October 1902 with a celebratory public tea and concert. The new store went out of its way to attract custom. It sold cheaply, in small quantities, advertising milk sold in halfpennyworths, loaves from a penny, and 'splendid' potatoes. The cooked dishes on offer, 'hot bowls of soup, steaming pork chops, basins of nourishing pease pudding, first class sausages' were immediately popular in an area where home cooking facilities were limited to say the least.

Within ten days the new grocery store had more than doubled the takings of its predecessor. There was a penny bank for the children, and a savings club for adults. New members flooded in, and children flocked to the penny bank in their hundreds. Margaret ascribed the success to 'the price and quality of the goods, bright attractive premises, small quantities sold, obliging shop men, easy customs as regards entrance, dividend, etc., the support of committees and managers, and *active propaganda*'.[234] [original emphasis]

Propaganda – that is, recruiting members – figured prominently in discussions about extending co-operation to poor neighbourhoods and had long been seen as the province of local Guildswomen. Drawing on her father's Christian Socialist contacts, and indeed her own – Gertrude Toynbee, sister of Arnold of Toynbee Hall fame, was a friend from her youth – Margaret suggested that the Guild take a new approach: running something along the lines of a settlement at Coronation Street, but with a co-operative twist. The Sunderland society agreed. Resident workers would visit and get to know local people, encouraging them to join the co-operative store and smoothing over any difficulties they encountered in doing so.

Margaret took personal charge of this, and, indeed, covered the costs of a worker for a period. She also demonstrated her commitment by dropping everything to live in the settlement for its first three months. After she left, the Sunderland co-operative society paid for one worker, and Margaret herself contributed to cover a second. She also drew in volunteers from among her middle-class friends at various times. Among them for a short while was Lilian, whose New Woman clothes fascinated the local girls: 'She wears bloomers + no petticoats at aal!'[235] [original spelling]

A devotee of William Morris, Margaret believed that beautiful surroundings were crucial to health and happiness and previously had criticised the dinginess of many co-operative shops in poorer areas. In contrast, she proudly emphasised the attractive appearance of the Coronation Street shop, with its large window displays drawing in adults and children alike, its welcoming meeting hall, 'a picture of brightness', and the little settlement, with its kitchen – equipped of course with leadless glaze crockery – in which the resident workers could receive local people'.[236]

Typically, Margaret's plans were ambitious. But they were also sensitive to some of the realities of poverty. While in true co-operative tradition she was a keen temperance advocate, she also knew that, in areas like Coronation Street, pubs were the only comfortable public places for entertainment and socialising. So the settlement also operated as a kind of community centre, with facilities for reading and borrowing books, a sewing class, a club for young women which Margaret ran herself, another for young men, a branch of the Guild, discussion and debate meetings, and a weekly 'co-operative party' with concerts and lantern lectures.[237] Margaret also suggested processions and outdoor concerts.[238] One can sense her drawing on the youth club experience which she had so enjoyed decades earlier.

The settlement work included visiting homes in the area, partly to get to know the local women and persuade them to come to the store, and partly to gain a picture of local conditions. Margaret kept detailed notes, asking systematically about housing conditions, health and finance, but also, very much like a modern social worker, recording what women told her with the addition of her own assessments of them and their situations.[239] She also preserved notes of how well the shop was doing, and wrote a good deal about the local children who hung around the settlement rooms. Unusually for her, she kept some of their touching letters.

Margaret loved the work and seems to have built up a rapport with local women and children. A colleague reported that, after she left, a 'crowd of small children' complained, asking when she was coming back, while one of the shop managers reported that many people had come in with the same query. A local woman wrote to her, 'Our children declare, you were the best and sweetest lady in the little hall. I have heard people say myself that Miss Davies is the best among them.'

Margaret claimed that this experiment showed not only that co-operative societies could cater to the poorest communities, but also that the shop could be an effective base for reaching out to the poor, in which relationships could be 'unspoilt by the demoralising effects of charity and [poor] relief'.[240] This confusing blend of conventional philanthropy and co-operation seemed to work, at least initially. A glowing article in the *Daily News*, headed 'Good food cheap' presented a picture which seems too good to be true:

> The store ladies start out to induce the people to buy their bread, their tea, their sausage at the store. They show them how it is possible to keep

out of debt, spend even the halfpennies well, and lay by small deposits for boots and clothes, and out of the dividend even a little nest-egg against the worst of emergencies. There is ... no patronage, no church, no charity; but there is, on the other hand, a centre of real neighbourliness and absolute social equality.[241]

News spread. Keir Hardie visited at one point and was reported to have been particularly interested in the social work side.[242] By January 1904, one year and three months after it had opened, the Coronation Street store was sufficiently successful to pay a dividend and still cover the settlement costs. The Sunderland co-operative society, pleased with the resident workers, agreed to fund them on a permanent basis.[243] Margaret seemed to have found a way of putting her vision into practice.

Then it all went wrong. Just months later, in November 1904, she announced to *Woman's Corner* that the Sunderland society had voted to cut off funding, and the settlement had had to close. We do not really know why this happened, although it may have been the result of local co-operative politics rather than of any failure in the scheme itself.[244] At the Guild Congress the following year, Margaret explained that 'there were always wheels within wheels. There was always a small opposition, and then there came a change in the [local co-operative society] committee.'[245]

This was a blow at the time, although by now, nearly two years after her own stay at Coronation Street, Margaret was becoming engrossed in other campaigns. In any case, she insisted that the project had been experimental, and 'the more experiments we have, both in the shops and in organised propaganda, the better'. Getting back at critical co-operative officials and members, she added, 'The need is for co-operative societies to show greater enterprise, flexibility, and freedom from convention ... in their methods.' While she still maintained that the ideal approach was a store combined with a settlement, she stressed that the settlement was not indispensable.[246]

Bristol

Meanwhile, when the Guild set up a 'Coming of Age' Fund to celebrate its twenty-first birthday, Margaret saw her chance to set up another project similar to Coronation Street. Suggesting that Guildswomen did not all share her enthusiasm, Congress delegates were initially unconvinced, voting to add the money to the Guild's fund for convalescent members. However, Margaret stuck with the idea even after Coronation Street folded and, although some opposition persisted, the following year's Congress agreed.[247]

Margaret then worked quickly, arranging for the Guild to fund a worker attached to a branch in a poor area of Bristol. She would be temporary and non-resident, so this would be much more testing than Sunderland. The Guild funded the post for four months, and with voluntary help the organiser did some useful work, recruiting new members, setting up a penny savings bank and taking instalments on entrance fees. And as in Sunderland, she helped set up a new Guild branch for the district and organised teas and entertainments for adults and for children.

The project ran at a time when, as we shall see, Margaret was much preoccupied with family difficulties and the suffrage campaign. None the less, she managed to visit twice, gave detailed support by letter and kept regular tabs on it via her friend and experienced Guild activist Mary Spooner, who spent some time in Bristol supporting a new organiser. Ada Greener, in contrast to the previous settlement workers who had found the work difficult, was a lively young bicycle-riding socialist, from a working-class background.

Mary Spooner's letters provide some interesting sidelights on how class and gender affected the work. She reported that although Ada Greener still had problems, her approach and background helped. While local women had called the previous (middle-class) organiser, 'the lady', Mary Spooner reported that Ada Greener was 'much more homely and free ... and has already succeeded far better. She is called "Teacher"'. However, Mary concluded that, 'She [Ada] has the right way with the people, but is too young and unimportant-looking to cope with the [co-operative society's] committee and officials'.[248]

The correspondence also sheds light on Margaret's sympathetic way of working. In December 1905, while overloaded with work and at a very difficult time for her personally, she was supporting the Bristol project from a distance. When the work went badly, and Mary and Ada had been complaining about the difficulty of getting decent food, a surprise hamper suddenly appeared from Kirkby Lonsdale. They were astounded and delighted: 'You can't imagine how our sordid souls have been cheered ... We have just finished our tea, and eaten half of the chicken and many of Kate's good buns'. [Kate was the vicarage cook][249]

After Mary Spooner left, Ada Greener turned to Margaret for long-distance advice and support and, at one point, Margaret apparently exhorted her to make sure a forthcoming holiday was a real break. We have Ada's response, reassuring her that, as she was going with friends who were neither socialists nor co-operators, and was leaving her bike behind, she would be able to get a good rest![250]

In the event, once the grant for the paid worker ended the Bristol project fizzled out. Mary Spooner's verdict was that an ordinary Guild branch, however committed, could not effectively carry on such a project in the long term, partly because members were 'all married + busy' and could not offer continuity. She suggested that they needed to find 'some more educated person ... into whose hands the work might be safely entrusted.'[251] The boundaries between social work and co-operative activism were clearly becoming blurred.

Margaret nevertheless put the best possible spin on the outcome and reiterated that, with good premises, a stable dividend, low prices, suitable and varied goods and some propagandist work, her ideas could succeed even without the presence of a worker. She continued to give a high profile to the campaign, and there was still interest, both within the Guild and elsewhere. Margaret evidently decided to concentrate on getting local co-operative societies to take up her other suggestions; as late as 1907, she highlighted the need to abolish or reduce entrance fees, and she continued to mention such proposals regularly during the years that followed.

Coda

The Sunderland experiment had lasted just two years, and Margaret had only lived there for three months. It is tempting to see it as more important to the success of the campaign for co-operation in poor neighbourhoods than it was, simply because, unusually, she preserved a great deal of material about it, including diary notes, letters and photographs – all available in the archives.[252]

This material provides some welcome insights, both about the campaign and about Margaret herself. As we have seen, she loved the settlement work, and with Lilian's sterling support in Kirkby Lonsdale, she might well have decided to stay on for longer had her father, now nearing eighty, not been in poor health. Perhaps indicatively, she noted that Nelly, one of the children who haunted the settlement rooms, wrote a letter 'to Mr Davies, to set Miss Davies free'.[253]

Despite her shock at the appalling living conditions that the local people endured, Margaret was curiously exhilarated by her time at Sunderland. From the papers she left about Coronation Street, it seems that she relished her quasi-social work role. She enjoyed the contact with local people, and also the practical side of setting up a discrete project of this kind and making it work; so different from what she was used to.

In her regular, glowing progress reports for *Woman's Corner* – admittedly, very much for public consumption – Margaret wrote of the Coronation Street people she had lived among as friends and neighbours. She stressed that she and the other workers were in 'constant daily contact with the people, sharing the hourly events, sharing the same shop, smuts, sights, and noise, being within call whenever help were needed.' [254] Nevertheless, as Margaret was aware, in reality there was still a huge gulf between her and local people. She did not have to worry about money, she lived with other workers in a comfortable, if cramped, settlement flat, and she even had domestic help from a local Guildswoman.[255] She may have loved talking to the local children but she did not have to bring them up day after day in miserable poverty. Above all, she was safe in the knowledge that she was not trapped in Coronation Street for life.

While Margaret's work in the settlement sounds in some ways like a throwback to the personal service traditions with which she was brought up, she crucially had a broader vision of the changes that were needed. Her time in Sunderland opened her eyes to the realities of slum life, particularly for women. She became aware of domestic abuse, perhaps for the first time, and saw terrible ill-health and deprivation amongst mothers and children, both issues which she took up in later campaigning. [256]

The experience stayed with her. Twenty years later, a friend reported in her diary that Margaret still worried that saying to herself, 'I am not living in a slum in Sunderland, because it would do no good', was 'a sop to her conscience for living comfortably'.[257]

When G.D.H Cole commented on the failure of the Sunderland project, he suggested it came over as an attempt to mix running a shop with philanthropy or social service, '... it was not the sort of self-help they [co-operators] were used to; it savoured too much of soup and blankets even if the poor paid for the soup and blankets'.[258]

Yet, while individual self-help was part of co-operative tradition, so was solidarity and mutual aid. The settlement workers were important, as Margaret said, as 'propagandists and organisers', helping people in a practical way, for example, by collecting tiny instalments towards the shilling entrance fee.[259] Furthermore many co-operative societies ran reading rooms and provided entertainments and social activities: facilities proposed by Margaret and especially needed in overcrowded slum areas.

However, there were clearly problems with trying to combine co-operation with a Guild settlement. As we have seen, outside workers had to be parachuted in, and for practical reasons these were usually middle-class volunteers. With this, the project inevitably began to come adrift from its co-operative roots. One might argue that Margaret was setting herself up to fail.

She was certainly prepared to ditch the settlement idea when it did not work out. As well as her other proposals for adapting co-operation to poor areas, she also increasingly made a point of demanding state action to tackle the poverty, poor health, appalling sanitation and desperate housing conditions to be found in slum areas: 'Municipal and national reforms are necessary before stricken areas can be freed from all that trades on ignorance, poverty and misfortune'.[260] This confirmed a shift in her political thinking.

However, many co-operators still believed that poor people could solve their problems simply by adopting thrift, self-help and temperance. A Labour observer at the 1900 Co-operative Congress was struck by 'the solid unbending Toryism of the older men, and the meek acquiescence or flippant contempt of the younger ones, in relation to social affairs'.[261] Even if they paid lip service to the need to extend co-operation to the poor, such men would not be easily persuaded to do anything about it. True, there was a current in the movement which believed with Margaret and the Guild that the poor should benefit from the material and moral advantages of co-operation. The problem was that there was not sufficient backing either centrally or locally for it to be effective.

This campaign was a signal of Margaret's ambition of achieving far-reaching change in the co-operative movement. She had started by encouraging branches to lobby at a local level, but despite her one off intervention on education back in 1895, the campaign for co-operation in poor neighbourhoods was her first sustained, high profile challenge to the movement at national level – and her first open battle with the co-operative leadership.

CHAPTER 8

Entr'acte: Untimely Deaths, 1905-1910

Theodore

In the summer of 1905, when Margaret was in the middle of plans for the Bristol settlement, tragedy struck. It came completely out of the blue.

On 25 July, her thirty-four-year old brother Theodore drowned. His body was discovered at the bottom of a pool near Kirkby Lonsdale known locally as 'Job's Dub', a favourite spot where he had gone for a solitary swim. The inquest reported that the body had a deep cut in the head; he had slipped on a wet rock or misjudged a dive, hit his head, and then lost consciousness.

Theodore was the youngest, and perhaps the most outstanding, of Margaret's six brilliant brothers. Their mother doted on all the children, but possibly, particularly on Theodore, the baby of the family. As a boy he was lively and confident; on a journey by coach when he was twelve, he 'perched up on the box and amused the drivers by chatting all the time. He told one of them he was a Liberal and, he thought, rather a Republican.'[262]

Theodore went on to achieve great things. He won a Cambridge scholarship at sixteen and, after a first-class degree, was awarded a fellowship. With his brother Crompton, who was at the same college, he joined the Apostles, the elite discussion society which nurtured future members of the Bloomsbury group and was to provide both brothers with long-term friends. Later, Theodore rose rapidly in the Civil Service and by the time he died had already been in a top Treasury job for several years as Private Secretary to the Chancellor of the Exchequer.

According to the impressive obituary in *The Times*, Theodore Llewelyn Davies possessed

> many of the highest gifts of statesmanship: a calm temper, a cool judgement, a generous heart ... He won, in a rare degree, the trust as well as the love of all who came near him.[263]

Theodore was unusually loved and admired. Leonard Woolf remembered him as high minded and brilliant – but also good-looking and charming. Bertrand Russell, recalling the affection which he inspired, maintained that he only knew one woman who would not have been 'delighted' to marry Theodore. (Russell claimed that this was a distant relative, Meg Booth, adding that, unluckily for Theodore, Meg had been in love with Crompton, at least for a while).[264]

The family was devastated by Theodore's death. His father, now nearly eighty, mused sadly in the parish magazine on 'the mysterious Providence which removes the young from this world and leaves the old surviving'.[265] The hardest hit was Crompton. He and Theodore had been a pair from childhood onwards, and having shared rooms at Cambridge now lived in a little house in Westminster together with their oldest brother, Charles. When Theodore died, Crompton broke down completely.

It was Bertrand Russell who came to the rescue. He had been a very close friend of both brothers ever since they met at Cambridge nearly fifteen years earlier. Theodore's death, which came at an unhappy time in his own personal life, affected him deeply. However, he immediately made it his business to look after Crompton. As soon as Crompton had recovered enough to travel, Russell took him to France for a fortnight to look after him and give him a change of scene. He remained a rock of support. Some weeks after they returned, Crompton wrote, 'I cling to you with all my heart and bless you for loving and helping me.'[266]

Herself hard hit, Margaret not only needed to support her father but was also desperately worried about Crompton. Fortunately, while in France Russell reported faithfully on his progress, which made a huge difference. Margaret responded, 'Your love for Theodore and Crompton seems somehow to make gratitude out of place, but all the same for what you are doing for us I am ... truly grateful'.[267]

Tantalisingly, we have little detail about how Margaret coped otherwise. Friends rallied round – Rosalind left her young family to come up – and sympathy flooded in from Guildswomen. '... what touching and dear letters ... Margaret dear if loving sympathy can comfort and help you have that from hundreds, who are feeling ... that your sorrow is their sorrow', wrote Mary Spooner.[268]

To start with, Margaret cancelled her planned Guild meetings. But, as when her mother had died ten years earlier, she soon went back to work. This provided distraction and an anaesthetic of sorts, but it was only partially successful. Margaret's grief was still in full flood during the winter of 1905-6 when she and her father spent time in France with Bertrand Russell and his wife. According to Russell, Margaret was still terribly unhappy and needed a great deal of support. She wrote to him gratefully, 'your sympathy and patience have been very great, dear Bertie, and my trust in you, equally so. Forgive if they made me selfish.' Russell responded perfectly: 'Of course you have not been selfish towards me in the very slightest degree; and to let people give what help they can, when they wish it, is surely a kindness.'[269]

His sensitivity and emotional generosity towards Margaret and her family during this harrowing time are remarkable, given his reputation for coldness in more intimate relationships.[270] As we shall see, this was to become a long-term friendship, from which both Margaret and Bertrand Russell would gain a great deal.

Arthur[271]

In March 1906, Margaret wrote sadly to Russell of this first spring without Theodore. She was gradually getting over the worst of her grief, and although life would never be the same, some kind of normality was returning. She was excited by the advent of a reforming Liberal government, and, as summer approached, busy with campaigning for women's suffrage and with preparations for the Guild Annual Congress.

But there was soon to be a further, terrible, blow. At the end of May, Margaret's brother Arthur wrote to her that he had to have a small operation on his face. Initially, there appeared to be no cause for alarm, but within days he wrote that the doctors had discovered a sarcoma, a cancerous growth which in fact would require a major operation to remove part of his jaw and palate. He explained that he would be out of action for about six weeks, and although he would regain the ability to speak 'properly' after three or four months, he would be left with a significant speech impediment. With the operation due almost immediately, he begged Margaret to come and help the family.[272]

Margaret was just sixteen months older than Arthur, and they were emotionally very close. Tall and good looking, with a profile which admiring friends compared to a Greek coin, he gained scholarships and a first-class degree at Cambridge, going on to become a barrister. Arthur had married Sylvia, the beautiful and fascinating daughter of George du Maurier, the well-known cartoonist and novelist. They and their five lively boys, now aged between two and thirteen, lived in a large house in Berkhamsted.

Sylvia and Margaret could not have been more different. Margaret's single-minded passion for her work and her interest in politics were completely alien to the more worldly Sylvia. Although personally strong-minded and independent, Sylvia was no feminist. She was profoundly uninterested in social issues. Writing affectionately to his sister to announce his engagement, Arthur warned, 'I don't think she [Sylvia] would care for a vote'.[273]

Sylvia's light-hearted reaction to a major Guild meeting, which Margaret misguidedly persuaded her to attend, illustrates the difficulties that the two women faced in trying to bridge the gulf between them for Arthur's sake. Sylvia wrote:

> Dearest
> I enjoyed Essex Hall so much, and your part of it was splendid – I heard every word and you looked such a sweet.
>
> I wish I had been there in the morning, and I did not stay late this afternoon because I had to get back. I liked the old woman who got up on the chair near me, and threw her arms about! I do hope you are not too awfully tired. If there is a chance of my seeing you at Barton Street [Margaret's brothers' house, where she stayed when in London] any afternoon, do let me know and I would go in a moment!
>
> Dear love to you,
> Your Sylvia.[274]

Dolly Ponsonby, a close friend both of Sylvia and of the Llewelyn Davies family at this time, was amused by Sylvia's teasing of Margaret. But it clearly carried an edge. Dolly described how, when Margaret 'railed' against wealth, Sylvia teased her, saying '"I should love to have it. I should like to have gold stays + a scented bed and real lace pillows" and Margaret is shocked and swallows it all.'[275]

There were deeper differences, too. While Sylvia was lively, and sometimes enjoyed stirring things up, she kept her emotions private and was deeply reticent about expressing them. Margaret was the opposite. She entered into everything with boundless enthusiasm and ardent intensity which, while it was part of her considerable charm, could sometimes be exhausting.

The family memoir which Arthur and Sylvia's son Peter collated includes letters from this period which Margaret kept and eventually passed on to him. Thanks to this, we have more of a picture of Margaret's relations with Arthur, Sylvia and their boys than of other parts of her family life, though it's worth remembering that is selective; it is partly based on what Margaret chose to keep, and to send on.

Peter's account of his troubled childhood inevitably focuses a great deal on 'Uncle Jim', the rich and famous playwright J.M. Barrie. In a curious way, Barrie was in love with both Sylvia and the boys. Over a number of years, he made himself, effectively, part of the family, and for his part Arthur appeared to tolerate the situation.

When Arthur's sarcoma was diagnosed, Barrie dropped everything in order to help, including covering the large medical fees. Margaret went up to London with Arthur and Sylvia for the operation, which took place on 8 June. Later that night she left them and Barrie at the nursing home, to go back and hold the fort at Berkhamsted in their absence. She had hoped that a friend of Sylvia's might take over after a few days, as this was an especially busy time for her in the Guild and she was also concerned about her father, who was not well. But in the end she agreed to stay on, as 'Sylvia had been getting rather in a panic about my going.'[276]

Margaret stayed at Berkhamsted until Arthur and Sylvia returned on 27 June, missing the Guild's Annual Congress. It was a major sacrifice, but Arthur and his family came first.

Now in her mid-forties, Margaret apparently did not have much idea how to handle five uproarious little boys who were missing their parents. Peter, then aged nine, later remembered fondly, 'Poor Margaret! I fear she had the devil's own time looking after us as she so nobly did during those difficult days.' Of course, she was working with Mary Hodgson, their nurse, but Peter recalled that only Arthur could really keep the boys in order. '... we ragged [Margaret] mercilessly, and horrified her with the amount of potatoes we put away.'[277]

Margaret made sure she wrote to Arthur every day, and Sylvia asked her to prepare Mary and the boys for the change in his appearance, adding that she herself found it impossibly difficult to talk about. Arthur was, in fact, horribly disfigured. The surgeon had removed a cheekbone as well as part of his jaw and palate, affecting his voice, and he had to wear an eye patch because a tear duct had also been removed. Nevertheless, he recovered somewhat during July and August, and was fitted with a dental plate which enabled him to speak. He began to plan returning to work, and the family was able to take a holiday.

Sylvia confided to Dolly Ponsonby '... how Margaret's "luxury of woe" attitude nearly killed her, and her intensity about everything'. This stuck in Dolly's memory and years later, when he was pulling together his memoir, she wrote to Peter that Sylvia was 'very controlled and reticent – and minded so much poor Margaret's outpourings and desire to help her. She [Sylvia] felt much too much to talk about it in that way.'[278]

This was an agonising time, during which Sylvia's irritation with Margaret must have been hugely magnified. But although Margaret's emotional intensity grated, she was also an essential practical support, and

Sylvia trusted her implicitly. Peter remembered that, 'All the dirty work was nobly shouldered by Margaret, with Crompton in support, and J.M.B[arrie] powerfully in reserve'.[279] Like Arthur, Sylvia wrote effusively to thank her, '*How* I miss you and what you are to us – we can never never make you know'.[280]

In mid-September 1906 Arthur suffered a relapse and was told that he had between six months and a year to live. Margaret was due to visit Belgian co-operators with a Guild group, and Arthur initially told her not to cancel her plans. But, later the same day, he wrote again. He had changed his mind and stressed that Sylvia also wanted her to come and help. A letter to his father delicately acknowledged the ambivalent relationship between his sister and his wife:

> Sylvia will have many good friends, but scarcely anyone on whom she feels she can rely … I was a little doubtful about asking Margaret to come. Sylvia has broken and troubled nights, and I rather fear the effect of any breakdown caused by sympathy. We are not telling Mrs du Maurier [Sylvia's mother] at present. But I feel that Margaret's help will be invaluable.[281]

Once again, Margaret dropped everything. She abandoned the trip to Belgium and closed the Guild office for ten days, arranging for Lilian and others to keep it ticking over after that.

In October, Margaret told Bertrand Russell that over the previous month they had been 'face to face with death in a new and terrible way'. The outlook was temporarily much better, yet 'there is always the terrible background of uncertainty and fear'. Meanwhile she was thirsting to get back to work, and there were also other family commitments, including to her brother Maurice and family. Tragically, Maurice's wife May had died in childbirth four years earlier, leaving him with three young children. Margaret was busy: 'I came straight back [from Berkhamsted] last Tuesday and next week I am in Nelson, Manchester and Leeds, and Maurice and his three children come for their half term holiday.'[282]

Late in November 1906, Arthur relapsed. Llewelyn was also ill, and for a while Margaret again found herself shuttling between the two. She spent Christmas at Berkhamsted, and at Arthur's request took the children to see *Peter Pan* (though evidently it was not to her taste). Margaret spent long hours at Arthur's bedside, preserving her own poignant notes of some of their conversations. At one point in December he explained that Sylvia would want to live in London after his death, alluding obliquely to Barrie's likely future role, 'Her [Sylvia's] ways may not be quite understood by our family. Father would not understand. I told Crompton and he agreed all must be left to her to manage.'[283]

By January 1907, it was the beginning of the end. Margaret told Bertrand Russell that Arthur was not in pain thanks to morphine; 'Heroic is quite inadequate to describe what he is ... His mind is clear + he has faced all.'[284] She was at Berkhamsted regularly during his subsequent, agonisingly slow, decline.

The earlier friction with Sylvia seems to have disappeared. In a desperate letter about Arthur, she wrote to Dolly Ponsonby that 'Margaret is here + is dear + helpful + loving'.[285] Towards the end, when he could only communicate in written notes, Arthur, significantly, asked Barrie to 'remember that Margaret wants and will want help and comfort'.[286]

Margaret continued to work during this terrible time, especially on the suffrage campaign, managing to carry on with correspondence even while staying at Berkhamsted. As the harrowing ordeal ground on, this may have been a way to distract herself, and to keep work separate from the rest of her life. Nevertheless, she was often at Arthur's bedside.

A letter to Bertrand Russell at the end of March, less than three weeks before Arthur died, provides a rare glimpse of depression: 'I often shrink in a feeble way from seeing people, or asking them to come to stay – I seem to have so little to give or say – but it doesn't do.' Yet in the same letter, Margaret described how she managed to fit in going to observe a suffragette meeting while bringing one of the boys up to London for an exam. She continue with a lengthy and animated discussion of suffrage politics, and only at the end wrote of what must have been foremost in her mind, 'It is difficult to tell you how Arthur is – and writing is hard ... I cannot tell you how ill he looks ...'[287]

On 11 April, Margaret's brother Harry wrote:

Darling Meg,
I am trying to find you with this tonight, but don't know if I shall. Charley went down to Berkhamsted at 8.15 and Scrum [Crompton] followed on the next train. I have just been speaking to Scrum on the telephone. He says Arthur is unconscious + not expected to recover consciousness. We must pray that there will be no pain. My heart is bleeding for you – but there is no time for more if I am to catch you with this.

Agnes (Harry's wife) and I are going on the midnight train. How noble and beautiful he has been!
O my Margaret
Your own Harry[288]

Arthur lived on for another week. He died on 19 April 1907.

In her grief, Margaret was deeply moved by the courageous and selfless way in which Arthur dealt with his tragic illness. Much later, she wrote to Peter: 'To me, the knowledge of what Arthur was is one of my most precious possessions, showing one the rare beauty that happiness and suffering may bring out in a life ...'[289] Margaret may have felt the help she gave during Arthur's final illness was her duty to her family. But it is very clear that she also did what she did out of love.

Sylvia

After these terrible months Arthur's death, though devastating, must also have come as a merciful release. Margaret coped in the same way as before; her letters to Bertrand Russell at this time are full of ideas, discussion and accounts of her work, with only the occasional hint of underlying grief. At the end of May 1907, she reported on a visit to Sylvia and the boys, 'My dear Sylvia gets comfort from them – but the loss and emptiness'. In July, she went on holiday in Switzerland with her eighty-year-old father and some friends, but, although it provided temporary and welcome distraction, 'a thin covering when removed seems almost to make wounds sorer'.[290]

In the winter of 1907/8, Sylvia and the boys moved to London. J.M. Barrie was more and more involved in their lives, having taken them all on a long holiday that first summer, and he helped with the cost of the London house. As time went on, Sylvia became increasingly dependent on him. As for Arthur's family, Peter recalled that 'a fondness ... always remained between us and our Ll.D. [Llewelyn Davies] relatives, but there was a drift apart, most unfortunately'. He felt that Arthur's death exposed their underlying lack of rapport with Sylvia, and that they may also have found 'the curious position of J M B[arrie] ... rather hard to swallow'.[291]

Nevertheless, Margaret diligently kept in touch. In December 1907, she told Russell of her plans to go down to London and spend a day with each of the nephews, and she made a point of visiting George at Eton.[292] Peter remembered with affection how she 'played her part gallantly as a good aunt and link with the LlD element in our composition. She kept it up for many years, though possibly with decreasing satisfaction ...'[293]

Margaret did not always have a sure touch with children, but she did her best. Peter described how early on, when he seemed to respond to art, she brought him books about Greek architecture, and later about William Morris and 'similar edifying influences'. He added that, to his subsequent regret, he 'drifted away from it all'.

Auntly duty only went so far, however. Much later, nurse Mary Hodgson told Peter what she believed Arthur had agreed for the boys after his death:

> I understood that your Aunt Margaret had been asked by your Father – and could not see her way to accept the responsibility. That J.M.B. was put forward as being more than willing. Your Father acquiesced to the inevitable with astounding grace and fortitude. It would help your Mother – and further than that he neither desired nor was able to go.[294]

Mary Hodgson had only heard about this second-hand. It must have been Sylvia who 'put forward' Barrie, but was this before or after Margaret had declined? And what, exactly, had Arthur asked Margaret to do? It sounds as if he had asked her to take on joint responsibility for the boys, together with Sylvia. If so, her refusal seems entirely reasonable. Her relationship with Sylvia was not always easy, she was responsible for looking after her increasingly frail father, and, after all, devoted to her extremely demanding work. But it must have been very hard to say no to Arthur at such a time.

Less than two years after Arthur's death, there was the first sign of another tragedy. In January 1909 the family were on a skiing holiday in Switzerland, paid for, of course, by Barrie, when Sylvia had a sudden attack of severe pain. She appeared to recover at the time but was unwell over the following months, and that autumn she collapsed. The diagnosis was cancer. In consultation with Barrie and with her mother, the doctor decided not to tell Sylvia, though Margaret, at some point privy to these discussions, disagreed. Meanwhile, as Sylvia's condition worsened, she became even more dependent on Barrie for everyday support.[295]

In the summer of 1910, the final act of the tragedy unfolded. By now very ill, Sylvia decided to take the five boys on a lengthy holiday in Devon. Dolly Ponsonby, who had seen her a few days earlier, 'realised then that she was not going to live, and I remember going back and telling my husband, and weeping'.[296]

Sylvia's mother, very worried, travelled to Devon at the end of July. Looking back, Peter sadly considered whether another female relative should also have come down. He was probably thinking of his du Maurier aunts, Sylvia's sisters. He let Margaret off the hook by saying that she was tied to her 'enfeebled' father, but in any case, she was not the obvious person for Sylvia to turn to in extremis. In the event, Crompton was the only other relative who came. Staying with J.M. Barrie, and helping him to distract the boys, Crompton, 'was full of helpfulness and took us walks and climbed us to the top of the local mountain … in true Ll D fashion'.[297]

Sylvia was now fading fast. She died at the end of August 1910, with her mother, Barrie, the doctor and the nurse at her bedside.

In the immediate aftermath, J.M. Barrie and Mary Hodgson shared looking after the boys. But the relatives now had to make decisions about a long-term home for these five orphans, who ranged from Nico aged seven to George at seventeen. A crucial difficulty was that their mother had wanted them to stay together. The Llewelyn Davieses tried hard to think of possible options. Theodora, Maurice's daughter, was aged twelve at the time. She remembered that her father, a widower already bringing up three children, offered a home for two of the boys but could not take them all. The family agreed that it was more important for them to be kept together.[298] Within a month of Sylvia's death, Mrs du Maurier wrote that she, Crompton and J.M. Barrie were acting as guardians and that Barrie would almost certainly look after the boys.

In the end no-one else offered. The relatives could reassure themselves that, as Mrs du Maurier said, J.M. Barrie knew and loved the boys; and by and large they reciprocated. He was rich, and could devote himself to them.

So Barrie took over the boys.

Months later, he announced that he had discovered an informal will, probably written when Sylvia knew the end was very near. 'What I would like is if Jenny (Mary Hodgson's sister) would come to Mary, and that the two together would be looking after the boys ...' She wanted her mother, Barrie, Crompton and her brother Guy to be trustees and guardians, and her sister May and Margaret to provide 'advice and care'.[299] But in copying out the will for the family, Barrie substituted 'Jimmy' for 'Jenny', which clearly strengthened his claim to the boys. Not unnaturally, there has been speculation. Had he misread the will, or had he deliberately altered it? In any case, he had already, effectively, taken over full responsibility.

Much has been written about the consequences for the 'lost boys', as they are now known, and from a twenty-first century perspective the decision to let Barrie take them on might well be seen as questionable. Whatever the rights and wrongs, tragedy continued to haunt the family. George, the oldest of the brothers, was killed in the First World War, while Barrie's favourite, Michael, drowned at the age of twenty, possibly in a suicide pact. Many years later, Peter threw himself under an Underground train. Their sad story has continued to cast a spell, generations later.[300]

We cannot really know what Margaret thought of the decision for the boys to live with Barrie. Initially, a few months after Sylvia's death, she told

Dolly Ponsonby that he was 'quite wonderful' with them. But as time went on, she worried about the way he was bringing them up. One day in 1911, she and Dolly Ponsonby

> talked all morning of Sylvia + Arthur's boys – + Jimmie Barrie. M is very desperate at moments about them + I have felt too the pity of their easy luxurious lives ... in his desire to make up to the boys for all they have lost, he gives them every material pleasure – nothing is denied them in the way of amusement, clothes, toys, etc.
>
> It's very disheartening and when one thinks of Arthur, their Father – almost unbearable.[301]

Margaret made sure that she kept in touch with the boys over the years, and in his memoir Peter writes of her with considerable, if amused, affection. Inevitably, the boys sometimes gently joked about her. In 1914, George wrote what he described as 'a regular Aunt Margaret letter' to Peter – that is, one with a lot of questions – while the following year, Michael wrote to George from Eton, 'I feel that Aunt Margaret would approve of "gymnasia"'.[302]

In modern accounts of the story of Arthur, Sylvia and the 'lost boys', Margaret comes over as a shadowy figure. With the limelight on J.M. Barrie, the part she played during Arthur's illness has attracted little attention. Yet, as Peter later acknowledged, Margaret had a distinguished career in her own right, but was prepared to drop everything when she was needed. It is clear that Margaret and Arthur had a very strong bond, and her presence during his illness meant an enormous amount to both of them.

Information about the part she played after Arthur's death is tantalisingly patchy. But what we do know suggests that, over the years, Margaret remained a safe, consistent adult figure for the boys, albeit on the fringes of their troubled lives.

Mary Davies, Margaret's mother.
(Jane Wynne Willson)

John Llewelyn Davies,
('Llewelyn'), Margaret's father.
(Jane Wynne Willson)

The young Margaret.
(Jane Wynne Willson)

Margaret when older: the public face. (Reproduced from the Co-operative Women's Guild collection courtesy of Hull University Archives)

Kirkby Lonsdale vicarage, Llewelyn in the foreground. Margaret ran the Guild office from the vicarage for nearly 20 years. (Jane Wynne Willson)

Margaret and Lilian in the Guild office. (Jane Wynne Willson)

Rosalind Nash (née Shore Smith), Margaret's lifetime friend.
(M. Ll. Davies. 1904. Archives and Special Collections, Bishopsgate Institute)

Lilian Harris, Margaret's Guild colleague and life companion.
(Catherine Webb, 1927)

Section Three

FLYING

CHAPTER 9

In Their Prime: Margaret and the Guild, 1906-1914

Prelude – interesting times

The struggle for votes for women leapt to centre stage on the national scene from 1905 onward, and as we shall see, Margaret and the Guild became part of it. The movement was to be hugely significant even for women who, like many rank and file Guilders, did not personally take action. It forced women's rights and demands to the top of the agenda. Things could never be the same again.

This was an eventful time in other ways too. The Liberal Party gained a landslide victory in the general election of 1906, and for the first time a significant number of Labour MPs were also returned to parliament. With 'New Liberal' ideas dominating its social policies, the government introduced a series of ground-breaking reforms, marking the beginning of what would later become the modern welfare state. Laws were passed which enabled local authorities to set up school clinics, introduced the first state-provided old age pension, reformed the poor law, and more. There were also measures supporting trade union and employment rights, and minimum wages were fixed for selected trades.

Lloyd George, who was Chancellor of the Exchequer from 1908 onwards, needed extra taxation to fund such reforms, not to mention a growing arms race with Germany. In 1910, the House of Lords' refusal to pass tax increases led to a major constitutional and political crisis. In the end, the Liberal government survived, though with a much reduced majority and dependent on the Irish Nationalists. After forcing through legislation reducing the power of the House of Lords, Lloyd George was able to enact the 1911 Insurance Act which set up the first state-organised system of insurance-based social security benefits, mainly – but not only – covering the unemployed.

But there was also an explosion of industrial conflict. From 1911, a particularly sharp recession and a continuing rise in the cost of living led to a wave of highly militant, often unofficial, strike actions, soon dubbed the 'Great Unrest'. Dockers, seamen, railwaymen, miners and others all walked out. In 1913, a bitter transport strike in Dublin became a *cause célèbre*, and revolutionary ideas about using strike action as a weapon for changing society were spreading. In 1914, the miners, railway and transport unions agreed on a framework for collaboration which might have been a game changer had war not intervened. Margaret led the Guild in officially welcoming the strike movement, reiterating the need for an alliance between trade unionists and co-operators, and protesting against the imprisonment of Jim Larkin, leader of the Dublin strike.

Meanwhile, co-operative membership had continued to grow steadily. While the movement still adhered to the principle that party political links were not allowed, it could not fail to be affected by the ferment of these years. But while it supported striking workers, formal ties with the labour movement and the Labour Party, which many including Margaret demanded, were still a bridge too far. Even though the question came before the Co-operative Congress several times, it was consistently rejected.

In 1913, troubles boiled over when the industrial unrest coincided with a seemingly irresolvable confrontation between the government and the suffragettes, who had escalated their protests to include violent attacks on property. For its part, the government used the infamous 'Cat and Mouse Act' to release imprisoned suffragettes who were on hunger strike and dangerously ill, only to re-arrest them once they had recovered their health. At the same time, Ulster Protestants, rejecting the introduction of an Irish Home Rule bill, were actively threatening armed resistance; publicly supported by Bonar Law, the new leader of the Conservative Party. The Liberal government faced a perfect storm.

This was the political backdrop to what turned out to be, in many ways, a hugely positive time for Margaret and the Guild. We will go into their major campaigns of these years a little later. This chapter looks more generally at how they flourished, and indeed came into their own.

A new life for Margaret

Margaret was in her mid-forties in 1907, when Arthur died, still running the household for her father at the vicarage. She had never wanted to live in Kirkby Lonsdale in the first place, and over the years her feeling that this was a kind of exile did not lessen. Particularly as she became ever more engrossed in the politics of the struggle for votes for women, it must have been increasingly frustrating to be so isolated.

Nevertheless, Margaret seems to have accepted without argument her father's insistence on staying in Kirkby Lonsdale until he felt the time was right for him to retire from his church duties. Within months of Theodore's death, her hopes had been raised when they got as far as seriously considering moving to Barton Street, just behind Westminster Abbey, where Crompton and Charles still lived and Mary Sheepshanks, a fellow suffrage activist, was also a neighbour. But Llewelyn, by this time eighty years old, eventually decided he was still needed in Kirkby Lonsdale. Margaret's own plans had to go on hold.

The long drawn out ordeal of Arthur's illness and death then intervened, but father and daughter finally made the move to London in December 1908. After time-consuming house hunting, Margaret found a house in Hampstead, then still on the outskirts of London and retaining something of the flavour of a country village. While it had not yet developed its later artistic and intellectual reputation, there were already associations with figures such as Marie Stopes, who moved there soon after Margaret arrived, and, indeed, with Sylvia's literary and theatrical du Maurier family.

The house in Hampstead Square was handsome, though much smaller than the Kirkby Lonsdale vicarage. It was in a perfect location for Llewelyn, not too far from the Christian Socialist Working Men's College, with which he had been associated for many years, and where, for some time, he would still take a Bible class. Although she found the beauties of Hampstead Heath a major plus, more important for Margaret was that her close friends and confidantes Rosalind Nash and Janet Case both lived within ten minutes' walk. And it was perhaps a relief that, from now on, she no longer ran the considerably expanded Guild from home, but from a separate rented office nearby. After the hard years dominated by the losses of Theodore and Arthur, Margaret was gradually recovering; and her life began to open up.

A key element was her circle of close women friends. Virginia Woolf happened to coincide with Margaret one day when both were visiting Janet Case and her sister Emphie. She was considerably younger and, to her, these three unmarried, middle-aged friends seemed like schoolgirls, treating each other 'with the familiarity of a worn out glove'. Virginia Woolf described, with a tinge of scepticism but also of reluctant admiration, their shared preoccupation with such topics as the fight for the vote: 'I was struck by the conviction with which they spoke; a conviction that justice ought to be done, not to them or their children, but to the whole of womankind.'[303]

With Janet and Rosalind living nearby, Margaret now had much more day to day support and advice, and both took part in Guild work at various times. The circle was completed by Lilian, her indispensable right hand in the Guild, who was becoming increasingly important both in and outside work. Lilian moved down to Hampstead from Kirkby Lonsdale within a year of Margaret, taking lodgings in nearby Carlingford Road.

Margaret enjoyed an active social life back in London and relished the varied contacts she made through her campaigning, even when some of them were difficult. We also know that once she had moved from Kirkby Lonsdale she was able to socialise more with some of Theodore's friends, whom she had got to know after his death. These included Charles Trevelyan, a Liberal politician, and the philosopher Alfred North Whitehead. (Margaret already knew the Whiteheads well enough to have included their teenage daughter Jessie in a group holiday to Switzerland in 1907, a few months after Arthur's death.)

Margaret's friendship with Bertrand Russell was particularly important even before she moved to London. As we shall see, they corresponded frequently, especially about the women's suffrage movement, in which both were involved. Margaret wrote at length, not only about politics but also using the opportunity to consult or to offload about whatever was uppermost in her mind. Although Russell did not reply every time, the tone of the correspondence is warm, occasionally even intimate, on both sides. Thus at one point during Arthur's final decline, Russell wrote to Margaret openly about feeling tired and depressed: 'Generally, I try to live on the surface of things ... but the ache for something more real is sometimes overpowering.'[304] It is significant that Margaret felt sufficiently at ease with him to invite him to Kirkby Lonsdale within weeks of Arthur's death.

As we have seen, Russell had put himself out to help the family after Theodore died, and Margaret had apologised for taking him for granted like a brother. She probably continued to see him and his Cambridge contemporaries, however eminent they later became, as her little brothers' college friends. She certainly treated them quite freely; after one of Russell's visits to Kirkby Lonsdale, she teased him: 'One night was better than nothing – but it remains one night. You might try and realise that Kirkby is on the way to everywhere and just send a post card to announce your arrival.' (Russell responded in kind, 'I wish I could realise that Kirkby is on the way to everywhere. But I am afraid I should first have to adopt pragmatism, which teaches that truth is what it pays to believe.')[305]

Russell's relationship with his then wife Alys had broken down years earlier, and they were still living together in great unhappiness. Margaret knew Alys partly through her involvement with suffrage, and was obviously aware of the couple's problems. When they finally separated in 1911 she wrote to Russell that she had admired them both 'through these hard years'.[306] Otherwise, their correspondence reveals nothing of this, and, though Margaret occasionally included 'love to Alys' at the end of her letters, her friendship with Russell seems to have been quite separate.

Was there a hint of romantic interest? Russell described the young Margaret, whom he first met in his Cambridge days, as very beautiful, insisting that although he later felt 'strong friendship' for her, 'there was never even a faint hint of anything beyond friendship'.[307] His last wife, Edith, is said to have thought – though no-one else did – that Russell might at one time have cherished unrequited feelings for Margaret.[308] However, she was over ten years his senior, and by the time they became friends, in her forties and happily single. Even if Margaret were sexually attracted to Russell, she is likely not to have admitted it to herself because he was married.

Meanwhile, as well as doing her best to be a good aunt to Arthur and Sylvia's orphaned sons, Margaret tried to do the same for her brother Maurice's family. After the tragedy of his wife May's death, her sister had joined the household to help Maurice with the three children. Margaret stepped in sometimes as back-up, and the children seem to have come to stay occasionally. She was not necessarily the ideal person; Theodora, Maurice's daughter, remembered her as 'fearfully kind, but she didn't know how to talk to children'.[309] However, Margaret did try.

As the years went by, her increasing preoccupation was her father's health. For some years now, Llewelyn had had occasional bouts of serious illness when, although there were trusted servants to look after him, Margaret either worried about leaving him or felt obliged to abandon important work commitments.

Then, in the autumn of 1911, a crisis changed everything. Llewelyn was suddenly struck down, probably by a stroke, and lost most of his sight. He could not read or write or go out alone. At the beginning of 1912, Margaret told Dolly Ponsonby that he was still affected, and 'very dependent on companionship'.[310]

Unsurprisingly, once the immediate crisis was over Margaret's own health suffered. In early March 1912 she had to give up Guild work completely for a couple of months and spent some time in a nursing home. Lilian, as ever, valiantly stepped into the breach but, with Llewelyn now in his mid-eighties and severely disabled, something had to give. In August, Margaret told the Guild Central Committee that she could not keep up her previous level of work. She proposed setting up a small Citizenship Sub-Committee for national campaigning, which would, 'watch and initiate legislation and administration in the interests of working-women'.[311] There would be a paid part-time secretary and, as she sometimes did when developing a project, Margaret had already secured donations to cover the cost.

Her suggestion for secretary was Margaret Bondfield, an ex-shop worker and trade unionist whom she already knew as a campaigning colleague, prominent in the Independent Labour Party and the Women's Labour League. This was contentious. Mrs Wimhurst, the new Guild President, was not happy, suggesting that a new post of this kind should have been put to the Guild Congress. However, Margaret prevailed. She argued that there would not be another Congress for nearly a year, and something had to be done as soon as possible. Miss Bondfield's undoubted campaigning experience would be a definite plus.[312]

From what we already know, it is not surprising that, despite what she had said to the Central Committee, in practice Margaret does not seem to have eased up on work. Perhaps Llewelyn's state of health improved, perhaps she recovered from the initial trauma, or perhaps she was able to employ an extra pair of hands to help the servants care for him. Whatever happened, she took on a huge amount of work the following year. As we shall see, with Margaret Bondfield's assistance, she was able to move the Guild's campaigns to a new level.

Thanks to her correspondence with Bertrand Russell and, later, with Leonard Woolf, we know something of how Margaret's ideas, and her life both in and outside politics, were developing at this time. She had a lively interest in the arts – she had always loved music – and once back in London was delighted to be able to go to concerts and the theatre regularly. Her wide reading ranged from Tom Paine to Bakunin to Santayana, and she wrote appreciatively of Gorky, Wells and Ibsen.[313] By now, her political horizons extended much further than the Guild and the British co-operative movement. She followed co-operative developments in Europe, and enthused particularly about what was going on in Belgium, which she described as an example of the 'socialistic form of Co-operation that is gaining everywhere'.[314]

Margaret's unwavering commitment to the Guild and the movement continued, but for her, co-operation was increasingly linked with the need to achieve socialism. In 1908, she wrote jokingly to Russell, who had been venting his irritation with the suffrage leader Millicent Fawcett, 'I agree with you that long advocacy of a cause does seem to destroy judgement. Is it time for me to give up Co-opn? But I think I am safe as a Co-operator, by being a socialist.'[315] [original abbreviations] She took a keen interest in European socialist politics, and admired the great French socialist leader Jean Jaurès, a powerful orator and also a pacifist, who was to be assassinated on the eve of the First World War; she complained about the quality of British labour leaders in comparison. She regularly read *L'Humanité,* the paper Jaurès founded, (presumably in French), and offered to lend it to Bertrand Russell.

Margaret was no hardline revolutionary Marxist, and wrote approvingly of the German social democrat Eduard Bernstein and his reformist version of socialism. Yet she was never a supporter of the Fabians. Instead, her humanistic approach fitted with that of the Independent Labour Party (ILP), which she is said to have joined around 1908 or 1909.[316] She was a faithful reader of the ILP paper, the *Labour Leader.*

Margaret's feminism also moved on during this period. She read the Swedish writer Ellen Key, who stressed that women's subordination was founded on their economic dependence, and kept up with current British debates around equal pay, the family wage, and state payment for mothers. As we shall see, this fed into her campaigning, and she began to develop increasingly radical views on the position of working-class women, both inside and outside the home.

In 1912, Margaret began a new and significant friendship with Leonard and Virginia Woolf. Their huge volume of meticulously preserved papers tells us a great deal, not only about their friendship but also about Margaret and her work.

Margaret already knew Virginia Stephen slightly, both through their mutual friend Janet Case and through family contacts. But it was not until 1912 that she met Virginia's new fiancé, Leonard Woolf, who had recently resigned from the colonial civil service. Temporarily without work and looking to get into political journalism, Leonard soon shared Margaret's enthusiasm for co-operation and they hit it off from the first. She quickly realised that he was a find, and she encouraged him to write for *Co-operative News,* provided him with co-operative and labour movement contacts, and, in early 1913, arranged for him to tour the country, visiting co-operative organisations.

That June, at Margaret's invitation, the Woolfs came to the Guild's Annual Congress. When Leonard wrote to say how much it had impressed him, Margaret's heartfelt reaction was telling:

I can't quite tell you what it is to have you + Virginia understanding, + helping these women to come to their own ... You wd have to have known all the opposition, contempt, desire to keep them in their places ... that we have gone through all these years − + still constantly experience − to understand the deep gladness they should at last be getting recognition.

She went on: 'To be at a discount has such a de-vitalising effect.'[317] [original abbreviations]

After nearly twenty-five years' hard slog, she must have been thinking personally, as well as of Guildswomen generally.

Margaret wrote as if Virginia Woolf shared Leonard's unqualified enthusiasm, but as she was to confess later on, Virginia's respect for Guildswomen and the Congress was offset by significant unease. She also had reservations about Margaret's role in the Guild. As she wrote to a friend, 'nothing − except perhaps novel-writing − can compare with the excitement of controlling the masses ... I see now why Margaret and even Mary Macarthur [a pioneer of women's trade unions, from a middle-class background] get their Imperial tread.'[318]

Just months after the Guild Congress, and as the publication of her first novel loomed, Virginia's fragile mental health gave way. That September, she had a breakdown and attempted suicide. Margaret seems to have recognised that she could not help directly, as when she sent a lavender bag for Virginia's pillow and suggested that Leonard might say it was from him. But although she was juggling Guild work and her responsibility for Llewelyn, she immediately moved to support Leonard, seeing him every few days, and writing in between. To help distract him, she mingled her sympathy with enthusiastic comments about work, and nagged him gently about keeping his strength up, 'an egg beaten up in milk at 11, + hot milk when you go to bed, and you must take them!'[319]

When Virginia Woolf's mental stability once more broke down in 1915, Margaret supported Leonard in the same way. As his biographer Victoria Glendinning concluded, she played a vital part at this time.[320]

Although the crisis of Virginia Woolf's illness brought Margaret and Leonard together, he was already, also, becoming a kindred spirit in the co-operative movement. Early on, Margaret exclaimed 'I can't get over the wonder and pleasure of having such a sympathetic supporter of the work and cause.'[321] Leonard shared her despair at the conservatism of the dominant male leadership of the co-operative movement; her emphasis on the importance of political education and advocacy of a Co-operative College; her support for an alliance with trade unions and the Labour Party; and her belief in co-operation as a basis for eventual socialism.

Leonard quickly became a valued ally, providing advice, active support and the opportunity for Margaret to offload. She wrote to him, 'I can't imagine how it is you always think + feel just what I wanted + express it so infinitely better'.[322] They did not always agree, however. Leonard went on to do a considerable amount of work for the Fabian Society, about which Margaret – who cordially disliked the 'Webberies', as she called them – was not entirely happy. Nevertheless, he continued to work with Margaret, both in the Guild and the wider co-operative movement, and both he and Virginia actively supported some of her campaigns.

In relation to the Woolfs, Margaret is often either discounted, or seen mainly as a work-driven campaigner who made relentless demands on Leonard. Little attention has been paid to her support for him during Virginia's breakdowns. Virginia may have been exaggerating when she complained that Margaret was on the phone almost every other day with new proposals, but in any case Leonard does not seem to have minded. Indeed, he often asked Margaret for comments on his work.

In his autobiography, he conceded that 'like all fanatics', she could be a bore. But he still paid tribute to her as a 'born leader', one of the most eminent women he had ever met. More than this, he affectionately recalled Margaret's

> immense energy and enthusiasm ... her laugh which was so characteristically Margaret, a deep, contralto spontaneous laugh ... her feminine charm which was also so spontaneous and unconscious, and sometimes amid her regiment of working women, her blue books and Co-operative Stores so endearingly incongruous.[323]

On the other hand, Margaret often irritated Virginia. This was partly a matter of mutual chemistry, but there was the added twist of Margaret's close working relationship with Leonard, which could make Virginia feel inferior and excluded.[324] In a letter to Janet Case, she exclaimed, 'Do you ever take that side of politics into account – the inhuman side, and how all the best feelings are shrivelled? ... I saw Miss Ll. Davies at a lighted window in Barton Street with all the conspirators around her, and cursed under my breath.'[325] [original abbreviation]

While Margaret was a natural extrovert, to whom activism was second nature, Virginia Woolf was very different. It is not surprising that Margaret, so intense and single-minded about her causes, could both intimidate and annoy her. Yet Virginia Woolf was by no means indifferent to social and political commitment.[326] She had already volunteered to teach working-class students at Morley College, and did some voluntary work for the People's Suffrage Federation, which Margaret had helped to found. She was indeed often irritated by Margaret, but combined this, frequently, with respect and affection. As we shall see, she went on to support the Guild in her own way.

These personal considerations aside, Virginia Woolf had put her finger on something when she wrote of Margaret's 'Imperial tread'. Of course, Margaret's personal authority in the Guild was greatly due to her remarkable skills, energy and vision, along with the indefinable charisma which led Leonard Woolf to describe her as a born leader. It was also made possible by the self-confidence which she drew from her background and education. And as we have seen, the Guild's structure and rules put Margaret, as General Secretary, in a powerful position, one which she appears to have taken for granted.

Progress in the Guild

In 1908, the Guild's Congress marked its twenty-fifth birthday, and Margaret's nineteen years as General Secretary. They had both come a long way. A lengthy Congress report in the *Manchester Guardian* by journalist and suffragette Evelyn Sharp paid tribute to the quality of the discussion and decision-making, and to the Guild's 'splendid democracy'.[327] Underlining this, Margaret reported to Bertrand Russell that a Congress visitor from Hungary was impressed by Guildswomen's, 'fine, fearless expression of their opinions'.

Margaret was moved and excited:

I never saw them [Guildswomen] more determined, or afterwards, fuller of the inspiration the whole gathering had been to them. Their speaking is like nothing else, because their views are so close to experience – it gives a stronger sense of reality than any other I know – And there is such spontaneity and unselfconsciousness + unfailing humour.

She went on to muse, 'If such results can be got in 25 yrs from things as they were 25 years ago, one wonders what and where women will be in the next 25 years'.[328]

The Guild went on from strength to strength, and membership rose to over 32,000 in 1914. It was at this time that Alexandra Kollontai praised its achievements. Leonard Woolf, who lectured regularly to Guildswomen at this time, remembered members as, 'a unique and even exciting regiment of women whose energy and vitality were exhilarating'.[329] He was impressed with their commitment to co-operative ideals and social change, contrasting these with the parochialism of the male-run co-operative mainstream.

Margaret continued to do everything she could to encourage and support the pioneering Guildswomen who put themselves forward to take up elected positions in the movement. It was a long, slow grind, however, for women to gain any significant presence. In 1905, out of nearly 1,500 local co-operative societies, only sixteen had elected women on to their management committees. By 1914, with a similar number of local societies, the number had only gone up to fifty-six – hardly earth-shaking.[330] Women were rarely elected on to higher level regional and national committees. Occasionally they gained positions on the sectional [regional] boards, but in the industrial northwest, where the barriers to women seem to have been greatest, even the impressive and experienced Sarah Reddish tried and failed several times.

Margaret stressed the importance of education, and suggested that the Guild needed to become a 'sort of training college' for activists. As before, there were programmes to train members in such things as public speaking and how to read a balance sheet, the latter vital for those members who had managed to get on to local management committees. But Margaret also wanted to equip Guildswomen themselves to lecture their fellow members about campaigning topics, rather than have outside experts come in; she began to plan advanced courses with this in mind. Already, in 1911, Margaret was circulating district secretaries asking them to find speakers for branch meetings on campaigning topics, including women's suffrage.

Guildswomen were coming of age. As Margaret Bondfield put it, they were 'determined to be citizens in the widest sense'.[331] Leonard Woolf, too, recalled the passionate desire for self-education, which went alongside their devotion to the Guild.[332] A fellow lecturer, Margaret's Girton friend Helena Swanwick, summed Guildswomen up as:

> ... shrewd, indomitably kind, humorous, tolerant and public–spirited beyond anything I have ever known ... To see their competence in taking the chair or introducing a motion; to delight in their unegoistic self-assurance, their fairness in debate, their orderliness under provocation; to note that the arguments which move them most are those which appeal to the common good – often the good of people very far away and remote from their lives; to observe the rapid, efficient and economical way in which they advertise meetings, prepare vast refreshments, raise

money and help the afflicted; all this and much more was to make me marvel at these modest heroines who do so much in addition to all the insistent and never-ending toil of a working-woman's home.[333]

Guildswomen were, indeed, motivated by a deep-rooted commitment to making life better for others as much as for themselves. Like Margaret, they often spoke of the co-operative ideals which united them. And it was not only a matter of ideals, but of putting them into practice. As we saw earlier, education and experience gained in the Guild equipped members to take part both in public life, for example as Poor Law Guardians, and in the burgeoning women's and socialist movements of the time.

Shared ideals did not necessarily translate into shared politics, however, and at times vigorous divisions on social and political issues came to the fore. Margaret was beginning to promote the idea of state-provided welfare services, but while she had considerable backing, there were some women in the Guild who strongly opposed this. They drew on the more conservative co-operative traditions which gave pride of place to individual responsibility and self-help. At the other end of the spectrum, some labour and socialist-oriented Guildswomen were suspicious of state welfare for opposite reasons, seeing it as a ruling-class initiative likely to create dependence and weaken working-class self-organisation.

The divisions were graphically illustrated in 1905 and 1906 Guild debates over proposals for the medical inspection and feeding of school children. Margaret and the Central Committee wanted the Guild to support campaigns for local authorities to be obliged both to carry out medical inspections in elementary (primary) schools and to provide food for any child for whom the medical inspection deemed it necessary. The Congress reports document furious disagreements. Supporters of the leadership claimed that parents often could not afford to feed their children adequately, and that hungry children could not learn. Opponents argued that such provision was not needed; it would only undermine parental responsibility and pile unfair costs on ratepayers.

In a heated debate in 1906, Miss Whitby, a Poor Law Guardian and 'qualified medical woman', argued that even medical inspection was unnecessary. Mrs Abbott, a well-known Guild activist, declared herself 'astonished at the words fallen from the lips of a medical woman. Were they blind to the fact that there were children half starved?' An amendment was put forward to remove the resolution's demand for children to be fed. Proposer Mrs Haworth said that it was 'in opposition to parental responsibility, and would open the floodgates of abuse. Parents were well able to feed their children themselves.' Others joined in: 'If the State undertook feeding, the people would be demoralised,' and 'they had no right to put taxes on hard-working parents.'[334] Despite some opposition, this amendment was eventually passed by 24 votes. Most unusually, Margaret and the leadership had been defeated.

The following year, however, the reforming Liberal government which had recently come to power passed an act requiring local authorities to organise medical inspections, and some branches began to lobby for this to be implemented locally. More discussion followed, and at the Guild's 1909 Congress Margaret and the Central Committee put forward a fresh resolution, demanding that clinics in poor areas should be funded by the exchequer rather than locally, and insisting that feeding of needy school children should be compulsory. This time there was little opposition, and both parts of the resolution passed easily. Harriet Kidd, of whom we shall hear more later, was greeted by cries of 'hear hear', when she declaimed, 'what had been done by philanthropy in the past should be done by the state. Philanthropy had been tried, and had failed.'[335] Guild opinion, perhaps affected by changes in government policy and public debate, had definitely shifted. But the divisions in the membership had been exposed.

Another example came up in 1913. During industrial tumult which emerged in the 1910s, the Guild Congress agreed to support what it termed 'labour uprisings', and advocated that all co-operative employees should be union members. There were fierce arguments, therefore, when Miss Gration, a recent Guild president and a director of her local co-operative society, took the place of striking employees to serve behind the counter at a co-operative shop. As Mrs Robinson from Halifax put it, 'As guildswomen ... we pass resolutions asking trade unionists to be co-operators, and yet one of our speakers ... goes and serves as a blackleg.'[336]

As with the school clinics issue, Margaret sometimes faced outright challenges to the policies which she put forward. Although she generally tailored her approach to be acceptable to Central Committee members, during this period she came into direct conflict with two conservative-minded presidents, Mrs Bury (1908-9) and Miss Gration (1909-10), and another, Mrs Wimhurst (1912-13), was also occasionally critical.

The general political turmoil in the later years of this period was reflected in increasingly divergent currents of opinion with the Guild. Margaret usually operated pragmatically, managing to craft policies which commanded the support of the elected leadership and a majority of activist grass roots members. The fact that she began to face division and challenge was partly a sign of success rather than failure, suggesting a healthy democracy at work.

Despite the Guild's overall vibrancy, though, some branches still refused to get involved with campaigning. Even others, which were more sympathetic, sometimes felt there was an overwhelming barrage of demands emanating from the centre. In 1912, a Lancashire official plaintively asked how to approach those branches that did not want to hear about campaigns, which said, 'We have had enough of school clinics,' and, 'On no account must you mention suffrage or credit trading [another campaign] in your speech'. Another reported that some branches were 'sick to death of the minimum wage'.[337]

In 1909 and 1910, the usual membership increase stalled. A 1910 piece in the main section of the *Co-operative News* (i.e. not the *Woman's Corner* pages) suggested that the Guild was active on too many fronts to be effective and should beware of neglecting co-operative issues.[338] This covert attack on the Guild's public work, which as we shall see included campaigning on some controversial issues, would come up again.

The setback might have come about because Margaret was particularly taken up with external campaigning at the time, and had devoted less energy to internal co-operative matters. But it may also reflect the continuing unhappiness in some quarters of the Guild.[339] Whatever the reason, membership soon began to grow again and, in 1913/14, a special push resulted in a 12 per cent increase over a single year. All in all, the Guild was still thriving.

CHAPTER 10

Votes for Which Women? 1904-1914

Introduction: Who's Who

Suffrage players

Radical suffragists	Modern shorthand for the Lancashire and Cheshire Women Textile and Other Workers Representation Committee and sister organisations of northern working women. Committed to legal protest.	Organizers included Guildswoman **Sarah Reddish,** who had previously worked closely with Margaret.
National Union of Women's Suffrage Societies (NUWSS)	Founded in 1897, bringing together local suffrage groups. Committed to legal protest, supporters known as 'suffragists' or 'constitutionalists'.	Led by **Millicent Fawcett**, friend of Margaret's family. Margaret's aunt Emily Davies also involved.
Women's Social and Political Union (WSPU)	Founded in 1903. Carried out direct action protests which broke the law. Supporters known as 'suffragettes' or 'militants'.	Led by **Emmeline Pankhurst** and her daughter, **Christabel**.
East London Federation of Suffragettes	Founded in 1913, breakaway from WSPU.	Set up by Christabel's socialist sister, **Sylvia**.

| People's Suffrage Federation (PSF) | Founded in 1909, aiming to gain support for 'adult suffrage' – votes for all adult men and women. | Margaret helped to set it up and was a leading light. |

(There were other suffrage organisations, but they don't appear in this particular suffrage story)

Politicians

Sir Henry Campbell-Bannerman	Prime Minister, 1906-1908.
W. H. Dickinson	Liberal MP and supporter of women's suffrage.
Herbert Henry Asquith	Prime Minister 1908-1916, opposed women's suffrage.
David Lloyd George	Liberal Chancellor of the Exchequer 1908-1915, played a part in suffrage negotiations.

Part One, 1904-1909

Women were nervous, emotional and had very little sense of proportion. Every man knew what it was to argue with a woman (Laughter). A woman would lay down her views, and though it were conclusively proved to her that she was wrong, she would continue to repeat her arguments. (Laughter)[340]

This report of a speech in a 1905 Parliamentary debate reminds us what campaigners for votes for women were up against.

One might say that Margaret had been born into the women's suffrage movement. Her parents already supported it, leading campaigner Millicent Fawcett was a family friend, and her aunt Emily Davies had helped to deliver the historic 1866 petition to Parliament organised by J.S Mill. All this was not lost on Margaret, and even in her early days in the Guild she had raised the issue. Now, as the women's suffrage movement came to the fore, it became a key element in her campaigning.

Much later, Margaret wrote that her aunt wanted the vote principally because 'she thought it infra dig for an employing lady not to have a vote when her gardener did'.[341] But for Margaret, as for so many other women, the suffrage struggle was not only about equality between the sexes but, crucially, about changing society and achieving social justice.

The labour movement and votes for women, 1904-5

It was in July 1904 that Margaret successfully swung the Guild behind a revived suffrage movement. Over the past few years, more and more members had come to support votes for women. Many in the north-west had become active in what is now known as the 'radical suffragist' movement of working-class women who, as we have seen in chapter 6, had gathered an extraordinary 29,000 signatures on their petition for the vote.[342] In 1903, they had set up a Lancashire and Cheshire Textile and Other Workers' Representation Committee, its cumbersome name belying its groundbreaking efforts to bring working-class women into the suffrage movement. The Guild was strong in this part of the country, and Guildswomen made up a third of the Committee's twenty-nine strong organising group.

The suffrage movement was gaining ground nationally, too, and in this changing climate, Margaret hoped to gain a firm commitment from the Guild to campaign actively for votes for women. When a private member's bill proposing limited suffrage reform was expected to come before Parliament, she saw her opportunity. She arranged for a full-scale Congress debate in July 1904, with her aunt as guest speaker. But then, as happened several times during these years, the demands of family took precedence. At the last minute, her father fell ill. The crucial debate took place without her.

At the Congress in Gloucester's hot, overcrowded Corn Exchange, the audience of over 300 listened intently as Sarah Reddish rose to move a resolution demanding the Parliamentary vote for women. Well known and loved in the Guild, and now a leading light among the radical suffragists, she must have seemed to Margaret the ideal choice to win over the conference.

However, it proved to be a bumpy ride. The resolution being discussed demanded the vote for women on the same terms 'as it is, or may be, granted to men' – the standard form of words used by suffrage campaigners and included in the upcoming private member's bill. Often referred to as the 'limited' or 'same terms' demand, this did not sound controversial. But there was one huge problem. At this time, because there was a property qualification, only 60 per cent of men were entitled to vote. In practice, the limited demand meant votes for better off women only.

As the conference discussion continued into the afternoon, deep-rooted disagreements emerged. Several delegates sprang up to express their opposition to a proposal which, they claimed, would not help working-class women. They argued that the proposed bill would only give more power to 'the property-owning classes'. Others, however, claimed that it was a crucial first step. Women 'ought to take what they could get, and after ... they could ask for more'.[343]

Up to now, such disagreements had not come to the fore. But now there was increasing fury among labour movement activists that four out of ten men were still voteless. Many labour men, and indeed some women, suspected that the predominantly middle-class women who campaigned for the limited demand were only interested in obtaining votes for themselves. Instead, labour critics argued, the demand should be for what they termed 'adult' – that is, universal – suffrage.

For their part, the women suffrage campaigners for limited reform had their own suspicions. Although they had their labour supporters, for example Keir Hardie, they knew that many other labour men either actively disapproved of votes for women or did not regard it as a priority. The fear was that while they might *call* for universal 'adult suffrage', labour activists actually only wanted to achieve the vote for all *men* – especially as the government was much more likely to grant this than votes for women.[344]

Back at the Guild Congress, in the end delegates overwhelmingly backed Sarah Reddish and the limited demand, despite the divisions. However, the discussion raged on in *Woman's Corner* over the following months. Margaret herself wrote in, claiming like others that, if women could first of all gain the vote on the same terms as men, when it was extended to *all* men that would make votes for all women almost a certainty. The vociferous disagreements which had been exposed hinted that more trouble was likely to come.

The Guild discussions also fed into fierce battles about whether the Labour Representation Committee (LRC, shortly to be renamed the Labour Party) should back the private member's suffrage bill when it came before parliament. A crucial conference in January 1905 would decide, and in the run-up, Margaret worked hand in hand with the radical suffragists to find a compromise form of words which might persuade the LRC to support the bill.

At this stage, Margaret believed – as did others, including Keir Hardie – that the limited demand might in fact enfranchise many working-class women.[345] So she organized a Guild manifesto in favour of 'Womanhood (or Adult) Suffrage', but with the crucial compromise that it would support 'any bill which would not exclude married women ... and which would include a large proportion of working women among those enfranchised'.[346] Margaret published this in the socialist *Clarion* newspaper alongside a very similar piece from the radical suffragists, which again used the term 'womanhood suffrage', but highlighted the specific needs of women wage earners.

But despite their efforts, the LRC conference voted against supporting the limited bill and committed itself to adult suffrage only. This led to bitter recriminations in the labour press, on both sides. As one woman put it:

> Some advocates of adult suffrage accuse the women's enfranchisers of wire pulling and intriguing. Not to be outdone, some advocates of the Women's Enfranchisement Bill accuse adult suffragists of not being sincere, and of really being opposed to women having the franchise at the bottom of their black hearts.[347]

Margaret saw the disagreement as being about tactics. But it went much deeper for many women, arousing passionate emotions and competing loyalties. Should their primary allegiance be to other women, of whatever class, or to the working class and its organizations?

For example Hannah Mitchell, a self-educated socialist from a poor family, was deeply unimpressed by those labour men who expected women to campaign for adult suffrage. Men should do their own work, she said. Women did not want to 'get our heads broken, as women did at Peterloo, in order to get more votes for men'. But Ada Nield Chew, another working-class socialist, thought otherwise. 'As a working woman, I would sooner place my interests in the hands of working men than in the hands of a class, whether men or women, who live by the labour of the workers.'[348]

This was Margaret's first experience of the bitter gender and class antagonisms surrounding suffrage politics. It would not be the last.

Setbacks, 1905-6

In May 1905, when the limited suffrage bill had its second reading in the Commons, a hundred and twenty Guild members – Margaret almost certainly among them – joined other women who crowded into the House of Commons lobby to await the result. Inside the chamber, the debate was outrageous. There were guffaws at comments like 'Now, would it really be desirable to turn this venerable and respectable Parliament into an arena with a promiscuity of sexes,' and at an MP's claims that 'he had seen in the lobbies all sorts of political flirtations going on to get their vote'.[349] One Guildswoman, lucky enough to get into the Ladies' Gallery, saw MPs falling asleep. The result was a foregone conclusion; MPs deliberately 'talked out' the bill so that there was no time for a vote. The campaigners, Margaret included, were furious.

A couple of months later there came the terrible shock of Theodore's sudden death, and then its aftermath. But, although Margaret was still in the depths of grief well into the following year, she was soon back at work; and the suffrage campaign was now a priority.

When the Conservative government called a general election in December 1905, she rapidly gained backing from a whole range of women's organisations for a manifesto which called on candidates to declare their support for votes for working-class women. She was beginning to pull together a network that would serve her well in the future.

Then, early in 1906, the Liberals had their landslide election victory. A large majority of MPs was now said to support women's suffrage. Thrilled, Margaret wrote to *Woman's Corner* with typical enthusiasm, 'Votes for women. A strong pull and a pull all together.'[350]

Almost immediately, though, hopes were dashed. In May 1906, Margaret joined the three hundred-strong Guild contingent in a huge suffrage procession organised to back up a delegation to Sir Henry Campbell-Bannerman, the new Prime Minister. But while supposedly personally sympathetic, he refused to make any commitment; 'He had only one thing to preach to them, and that was the virtue of patience'.[351]

Reporting back to the Guild, Vice-President Mrs Hodgett was furious. Why, she demanded, should women be patient while men were passing unjust laws?

> I think we must have impatience, and plenty of it ... until we have equal standing before the law for men and women; until women have a living wage, and until flesh and blood are not so cheap.[352]

The suffrage movement takes off, 1906 onwards

The Liberal Government had now been revealed in its true colours. What no-one had anticipated was the extraordinary strength of women's response. As Ray Strachey put it in her early history of the movement, thousands of them

> read into the Cause ... all the discontents which they, as women, were suffering ... The meetings which multiplied in halls and drawing rooms, in schools and chapels, at street corners, and on village greens, did not seem like the dull and solemn stuff of politics; they were missionary meetings, filled with the fervour of a gospel, and each one brought new enthusiasts to the ranks.[353]

There was now a whole new suffrage landscape. Hitherto, the main organisation country-wide had been the law-abiding National Union of Women's Suffrage Societies (NUWSS), an umbrella group led from 1907 onward by the impressive Millicent Fawcett. This focused mainly on achieving parliamentary support and had strong Liberal party links.

But from 1906, with the Liberal government refusing to move on votes for women, the Women's Social and Political Union (WSPU) came to the fore. Led by elegant, charismatic Emmeline Pankhurst, the WSPU rejected the NUWSS's methods as ineffective. Instead, it took to militant confrontation with the powers that be, including breaking the law. Famously, this had started in late 1905 when Emmeline's daughter Christabel, having disrupted a Liberal meeting, made sure of being arrested by spitting on a policeman.

The WSPU's daring and imaginative exploits certainly made both politicians and the press take notice. They were dubbed 'suffragettes' (as opposed to the law-abiding suffragists of the NUWSS) and the label stuck. WSPU militants now brought publicity to the cause as never before, 'They sprang out of organ lofts, they peered through roof windows, and leapt out of innocent-looking furniture vans ... they harangued ... the House [of Commons] from the river ...'[354] Membership mushroomed. The WSPU organised huge, dramatic processions, and battled with police in demonstrations at parliament. Many were imprisoned.

In these early years, especially, there was collaboration between the militant suffragettes and the constitutional suffragists, and women often moved between the two wings of the movement. When a number of suffragettes were imprisoned after demonstrating at the opening of Parliament in 1906, Millicent Fawcett of the law abiding NUWSS wrote to *The Times* supporting them. Margaret wrote to the *Manchester Guardian* on behalf of the Guild in similar terms. She argued that the WSPU action was not in any way unreasonable or hysterical, but aimed to 'bring home the fact that women have no voice in making or administering the laws they are expected to obey ...' She added that as a result, press and politicians were finally taking notice: 'opinion is ripening on the subject in a way which revives hope in the oldest agitators.'[355] (Margaret was now in her mid-forties.)

Although the Guild always worked with the law-abiding suffragists rather than the suffragettes, and Margaret had little time for the Pankhursts on a personal level, she did have a degree of sympathy with the WSPU. After attending one of their meetings in March 1907, she told Bertrand Russell in surprise that she was so impressed that 'I might have to join, and take all the consequences. ... It seemed as if the rise of women for their freedom had begun.'[356] This was just a momentary impulse, but at this stage, when the WSPU had not yet escalated from non-violent protest to attacking property, her sympathy was shared by others in the Guild.[357] A few weeks later she made a point of paying tribute in *Woman's Corner* to four Guildswomen who had been imprisoned. And as late as 1913, when anti-suffragette opinion in the Guild and the country had hardened thanks to their increasingly violent tactics, she insisted to Leonard Woolf that she had always regarded the claim that militancy harmed the movement as 'nonsense'.

Meanwhile the respectable NUWSS, much larger than the WSPU, also increased its membership. It, too, began to campaign in new ways. For the first time it organised mass street demonstrations, starting with the 'Mud March' of three thousand women on a wet February day in 1907. Action spread around the country; in one year alone, Margaret's friend Helena Swanwick spoke at 150 public meetings, with average audiences of six hundred.[358] Ignoring rules about how respectable Edwardian ladies should behave, these law-abiding suffragists campaigned all over the country, in all weathers. They 'chalked the pavements and sold their newspapers ... walked the gutters in sandwich boards and toiled from house to house canvassing'. When they set up stalls in marketplaces they braved threats and abuse, and were targeted with everything from pepper to mice, rotten eggs, fish and oranges.[359]

Votes for married women? 1906-7

Meanwhile, between June 1906 and April 1907 Margaret was juggling her Guild responsibilities with helping her dying brother, Arthur, and his family. Somehow, she still managed to keep on top of work, especially about suffrage. For example, at the end of October 1906 she wrote a long letter on behalf of the Guild to the Chancellor of the Exchequer, Asquith, expounding, among other things, the specific needs of married working-class women who did not earn a wage.[360]

As this suggests, Margaret was more concerned about which women would get the vote than about the rights and wrongs of militant WSPU protest. She had initially believed that the limited demand – for women to have votes on the same terms as men – was the best tactic. But it was increasingly clear that this would not help most of the working-class wives in the Guild. Currently, a man could gain the vote on the basis of occupying property of a certain value. As leading Guildswoman Mrs Gasson had argued back in 1904, even if the limited demand succeeded most working-class married women would not qualify. In a couple, the husband would always count as the householder – not his wife.

How could this circle be squared? For the first time, Margaret decided to act in a personal capacity rather than on behalf of the Guild, with backup from her closest friends. In December 1906, after Rosalind and Lilian had both written to the press preparing the ground, she wrote asking suffrage campaigners to consider extending the limited demand to include married women whose husbands qualified to vote.

Once again Margaret was looking to unite votes for women campaigners with supporters of adult suffrage. She claimed this would be welcomed by 'the great mass of married working women who have now joined the suffrage army' – in other words, the Guild.[361]

Her proposal was greeted with consternation. The NUWSS, which she had clearly not consulted in advance, issued a speedy and frosty rejection. Nor was there support from the radical suffragists. The proposal even failed to get through the Guild's Congress. In introducing a new and controversial idea without securing advance support, Margaret seems to have lost her normally sure tactical instincts.

We must remember, though, that this was the time when she was juggling the demands of the suffrage campaign with her need to be with her dying brother; she can be forgiven her uncharacteristically poor judgement. In any case, it was not all bad news. Margaret persuaded a sympathetic MP, W.H. Dickinson, to use her idea in two private member's suffrage bills (like their predecessors, these did not get far). And it had one immediate, positive spin-off.

In mid-1907, co-operative leaders refused to allow suffrage to be discussed at the annual Co-operative Congress. Margaret pointedly retaliated by inviting two well-known suffragettes, both prison veterans, to speak at a Guild meeting linked to the Congress. Then she found an ally in Thomas Tweddell, the powerful chair of the Co-operative Parliamentary Committee, who persuaded the following year's Co-operative Congress to back Dickinson's second bill. Margaret was delighted, '... To have got the old Co-ops to move – + that they shd support D[ickinson]'s Bill (*their own wives!!*) is so good.'[original emphasis and abbreviations] This was not only important for the suffrage movement, but 'a little victory for Justice'.[362]

Although Margaret's proposal did not get very far, it usefully publicised the specific disadvantages of working-class wives, and was taken up at various times during later suffrage negotiations. But as time passed, and the political environment shifted, her thinking was moving on.

Meanwhile, Margaret continued with the Guild's suffrage campaigning. They worked particularly closely with the radical suffragists, jointly organising a large demonstration in Manchester in autumn 1907 which aimed to put pressure on Labour MPs. The Guild collaborated with the NUWSS too, contributing in 1908 to huge marches and meetings in London and Manchester. Margaret was on the platform at both.

She worked particularly hard on one NUWSS event in 1909. This was a 'pageant of trades', a lamp-lit procession through London of a thousand selected women, representing sixty trades and professions, and carrying symbols of their work. The Guild supplied eight such groups, including weavers with 'shawls on their shoulders, and plain straw hats' and, significantly, housewives carrying 'the model of a fire, and hearth, and a broom and dustpan': reflecting its contention that, for a working-class woman, running a home and bringing up children was a job in its own right. Reporting that Margaret and Lilian marched with the secretaries, *Woman's Corner* teasingly commented on 'Miss Davies's office coat of light blue linen … An ink-blot on the elbow gave it the proper professional touch'.[363]

Towards adult suffrage, 1907-9

Bertrand Russell actively supported votes for women, and for several years he and Margaret used their correspondence as a sounding board about the ups and downs of suffrage politics. In the early days, while Arthur was dying, she seems to have found this – and, indeed, work in general – a welcome distraction. With the Liberals in power from 1906, and opinion among their MPs gradually shifting away from the limited demand, Margaret was becoming convinced that the time was now ripe to push for full-scale adult suffrage. As early as Easter 1907, she wrote to Russell, 'The "limited" bills belong to another regime and other conditions.'[364]

Now on the NUWSS executive, Russell supported full scale adult suffrage in principle, but was worried that it could only be achieved through long-term campaigning. If women insisted on it at this stage, they might find themselves excluded from a more immediate voting reform. But Margaret, whose long-term aim had always been votes for all, disagreed. Even if parliament granted votes to all men, '… it would not in any way make our position worse. I cant help fearing that the "limited" bill would prove a stumbling block to adult'.[365] She was increasingly scathing about Millicent Fawcett and the older generation of NUWSS leaders, who clung to the limited demand.

Early in 1908, these arguments took on new significance. The fortunes of the suffrage campaign nose-dived when Herbert Asquith – soon dubbed by the WSPU, 'The right dishonourable double-face Asquith' – took over as prime minister. Obdurately opposed to votes for women, he speedily announced plans for a government reform bill to enfranchise all men. Later, he craftily added that he would not oppose a women's suffrage amendment, provided it was framed 'democratically', and the majority of women could be shown to support it.

This immediately changed the political landscape. The limited demand could now be seen as an obstacle to more democratic reform, and Lloyd George and other prominent Liberal supporters of women's suffrage were no longer prepared to back it. There was a real risk that both Liberal and Labour MPs would support Asquith's manhood suffrage bill without including a women's amendment.

Suffrage supporters of all stripes were livid, and the WSPU escalated its militant actions, for the first time breaking windows and attacking property. For her part, Margaret organised a joint letter to Asquith from a range of organisations, demanding that women be included in the bill in some form. He failed to reply, and the press ignored it. In a fury, Margaret dashed off a note to Bertrand Russell, '... I hope politicians and newspapers will realize that it is they who are driving women into revolution ...'.[366]

Thanks to Asquith's bombshell, the limited demand now seemed increasingly irrelevant.

Part Two, 1909-1914

The People's Suffrage Federation

Recovered, at least in part, from Arthur's illness and death, and having managed the move back to London, Margaret now leapt into national suffrage politics with enormous gusto.

There was an initial blip when Liberal MP Geoffrey Howard proposed a private member's bill for universal adult suffrage in order to test the government's attitude. He had not consulted either the NUWSS or the WSPU, and both strongly objected. However Margaret, again acting in a personal capacity, persuaded twenty-three women, mostly prominent socialists or trade unionists, to sign an open letter welcoming the bill.[367] *The Times* published it – directly below another from Millicent Fawcett in opposition. Once again, Margaret was at odds with the NUWSS; but she was also cementing other important alliances.

Then, one spring evening in 1909, she hosted a dinner party. She had invited Rosalind and Janet, along with Vaughan Nash, Rosalind's husband, and Dolly and Arthur Ponsonby, to discuss the idea of a new adult suffrage organisation. Margaret and Rosalind seem to have operated as a double act. Dolly mused in her diary that Margaret

> looked + was splendid – fiery, keen + amusing as ever. She is more unreasonable than Mrs Nash + less practical but she has the inspiration and most of the enthusiasm. Mrs Nash sets things into shape.[368]

Unsurprisingly, Dolly recorded that Vaughan Nash was 'very silent and amused'; after all, as a senior civil servant, indeed Asquith's principal private secretary, he needed to be discreet. But this was more than just a dinner-table pipe dream. Over the summer, Margaret and Rosalind were among the key players in a new organisation and by the end of October 1909 it was ready to launch. The People's Suffrage Federation had a pithy slogan, 'One man, one vote; one woman, one vote', and a straightforward policy; universal adult suffrage on the basis of a short residential qualification.

From the beginning, the PSF hoped to unite women's suffragists and sympathetic Liberals with Labour MPs and the wider labour movement. The chair was Liberal Emily Hobhouse, well known for her campaign against the concentration camps set up by the British during the Boer War. Margaret shared the job of honorary secretary with Mary Macarthur, prominent in the Independent Labour Party (ILP) and a dedicated organiser of women's trade unions. A leading Labour MP, Arthur Henderson, was honorary treasurer.

The PSF hit the ground running, and within three months of the launch had gathered support from over seventy MPs. Although the radical suffragists do not seem to have been involved, local Women's Liberal Associations rapidly affiliated, along with Mary Macarthur's National Federation of Women Workers, the Women's Labour League, the Independent Labour Party and a number of individual union branches. While the socialist-oriented Adult Suffrage Society rejected the PSF, its one-time chair Margaret Bondfield, later to become a co-worker in the Guild, joined and became chair of the executive committee.[369]

In a conciliatory letter to the suffragist paper *The Common Cause*, Margaret explained that the PSF's aim was to, '… combine the splendid uprising of women against their subordinate position, with the democratic demand that the Suffrage should be placed on a human and not a property basis'.[370] She claimed that a majority of Liberals now opposed the limited demand and that, instead, the idea of broader electoral reform was widely accepted. Stressing that demanding adult suffrage posed no risk to gaining votes for women, she urged those she termed 'democratic suffragists' to join the PSF while still remaining in their existing organisations.

Once again, the NUWSS and WSPU were implacably opposed. There were bitter recriminations, with some suffrage supporters labelling the PSF's success among Liberal MPs 'a proof of treason on the part of Parliamentary friends.'[371] Margaret's hopes of building an alliance were in tatters.

Nevertheless, having gained the support of some leading trade unionists and of the ILP, the PSF was able to highlight the suffrage issue in the labour movement. Liberals and suffragists, though less well represented than labour figures, were also in evidence. And it tapped into a significant strand of intellectual opinion. Prominent supporters included Beatrice and Sidney Webb; the economist J.M. Keynes; the novelist John Galsworthy; and the poet John Masefield.

Margaret's wide range of personal contacts undoubtedly helped. The names of her relatives and friends leap out regularly from lists of PSF committee members and supporters. Bertrand Russell left the NUWSS and joined the PSF, as did his wife Alys. Russell later recalled how he had been converted to adult suffrage 'largely as a result of Margaret Davies' arguments'.[372] PSF activists and supporters included two of Margaret's brothers and numerous personal and family friends in Liberal and academic circles. Margaret had also recruited labour and co-operative allies including Mrs Gasson and Mrs Brown, both prominent Guildswomen. In 1910, when the young Virginia Woolf (then Virginia Stephen) volunteered to help the suffrage cause, Janet Case steered her towards the PSF. Margaret even managed to reel in J.M. Barrie, not otherwise known as an advocate of votes for women: a tribute perhaps not so much to her persuasive powers as to his desire to stay on the good side of the Llewelyn Davies family.

On a personal level, the PSF was the perfect suffrage home for Margaret. She was working alongside like-minded allies, without the constraints of representing the Guild, and with her closest confidantes, Lilian, Rosalind and Janet. She showed the strength of her commitment by backing it with a donation of £100, nearly £8,000 in today's money.

While the PSF's parliamentary work was central, it also worked hard to influence opinion more widely. It provided speakers, articles in the press and a stream of pamphlets and leaflets aimed variously at its prime constituencies: Liberals, suffragists, and the labour movement. Tantalisingly, not many of its papers have survived, and it is hard to estimate its overall impact. But by bringing prominent labour movement figures into suffrage campaigning, it must have played a significant part in shifting labour opinion towards votes for women.[373]

Guild disputes, 1909-10

While Margaret was helping to set up the PSF, sparks began to fly.

As we have seen, there had already been discord in 1907 when the Guild Congress failed to support the 'married women' proposal; though there was success the following year. Some Guild members remained opposed to campaigning for the vote, and opposition increased when the WSPU militants began to break windows and attack property. Margaret had to appeal to Guildswomen not to be put off by this; she later blamed the violence for an increasing reluctance to discuss suffrage in some sections of the Guild.

More significantly, while Margaret was busy helping to set up the PSF, there was serious trouble at the Guild's 1909 Congress. The old arguments about adult versus limited suffrage came up again, and for the first time she and Sarah Reddish found themselves on opposite sides.

Speaking on behalf of her fellow radical suffragists, Sarah Reddish still argued for the limited demand. Margaret responded that, to ensure women were included in the manhood suffrage bill which Asquith planned, 'the time had come for a new agitation – for working women to unite and demand the vote for women without any class distinction at all'.[374] As soon as she had finished, the Guild President, Mrs Bury, vacated the chair so that she could contribute to the debate.

Margaret had earlier described Mrs Bury as one of the Guild's 'foremost generals'; a surviving photograph shows her looking shrewd, severe, and formidably capable.[375] Her home was Darwen, Lancashire, and after starting half-time mill work at the age of eleven, she had educated herself at night school. By 1892, when she had several children, her husband had worked his way up to be manager of the mill. Now in her early forties, Mrs Bury could give up working there.

Although constrained for a long time by the demands of work and home, Mrs Bury was clearly a born public woman. In 1893, aged 43, she discovered the Guild and helped to set up a local branch. When she got to the Annual Meeting, she was ecstatic:

> ... here was the very opportunity I had always been seeking, but never put into words .... At the close of the meetings I felt as I imagine a warhorse must feel when he hears the beat of the drum.[376]

Mrs Bury quickly showed herself an impressive activist. Within the Guild, she was President of Darwen's large branch, had served on the Central Committee and was currently on her third stint as national president.

Locally, she was also a Poor Law Guardian, secretary of the Women's Suffrage Society, and alongside her husband, a mainstay of the local Congregational Church. A persuasive speaker and writer, she strongly advocated women's participation in public life; although, like many Guildswomen, she rejected the term 'woman's rights' and criticised the 'so-called New Woman and her vagaries'. She had little sympathy for socialist ideas either, declaring herself a 'conservative of the old school'.[377]

Despite their differences, Mrs Bury and Margaret had worked together amicably up till now – but no longer. Opposing the Central Committee's adult suffrage resolution, Mrs Bury stoutly argued that there was no justification for the Guild to abandon its existing policy. Other speakers, too, were suspicious of adult suffrage arguments. As one complained, 'They had been told that the men would do all they possibly could for them [women]. They had simply done all they could for themselves.' In the course of a lively debate, Margaret reiterated that as the government was promising to give the vote to all men imminently, it was vital to campaign for all women to be included.

When it came to a vote, numbers were nail-bitingly close. There had to be a recount. The adult suffrage resolution eventually declared passed, but only by six votes. As Mrs Bury was later to stress, this was hardly a mandate: a third of the delegates had failed to vote and simply sat on their hands.

So the Guild was split.

This might have dashed any hope that it might join the PSF, but Margaret was not easily dissuaded. Within weeks a newly elected Central Committee met, as normal after a Congress, and thanks to the rule that members had to stand down after three consecutive years' service, Mrs Bury was no longer on it. The Committee agreed to affiliate itself – not the Guild as a whole – to the PSF, and stressed that the individual branches could choose for themselves.

Another battle then ensued, ignited at the end of October by a newspaper interview with Margaret which had been reprinted in *Woman's Corner*. This stated not only that the Central Committee had affiliated, but that the PSF 'hoped to gain the support of the full membership'. Mrs Bury was outraged, questioning the right of the Central Committee to affiliate and suggesting that in the interview Margaret had implied that the Guild as a whole backed the PSF. A ding-dong argument ensued. Mrs Bury termed the Central Committee's action 'impertinent autocracy', while Margaret insisted that it was perfectly proper, and that the PSF sought affiliation from executives and branches of organisations.[378]

The adult versus limited arguments were now raised all over again, in

Guild discussions and in letters to *Woman's Corner*. Some members were convinced that women must fight their own battles and could not trust campaigners who promised votes for both men *and* women: 'How much longer are [women] to be humbugged by politicians and wire-pullers, only to be paid for their work by specious promises, which may or may not be like pie-crusts ...'[379]

The dispute widened into a more general attack on the leadership, with suggestions that its actions were undermining the Guild's democratic structure. One Guildswoman paid tribute to Mrs Bury for 'rousing Co-operative women to think before they are coolly handed over without even being consulted to a new suffrage policy'. Mrs Bury herself claimed that she had been asked to lead an opposition – though she had refused.[380] Helena Swanwick, who knew some Guildswomen in the north-west, wrote to Bertrand Russell that the *Woman's Corner* correspondence 'at last expresses what these women have so often said to me about the Guild. I don't say they're right but I'm glad they're speaking out'.[381]

Such bitter conflict in the Guild was unprecedented and must have been very painful for Margaret. This damaging muddle was certainly not her finest hour. She usually gauged members' mood with care and, while leading from the front, made sure to observe the Guild's democratic rules scrupulously. This time, faced with a rare split on a major issue, she seems to have been carried away by her conviction that her cause was right. By persuading the Central Committee to affiliate to the PSF, and by a newspaper statement which could easily be misinterpreted, she had exacerbated an already difficult situation.

Fortunately, it seems that after a few months the dispute had run its course. Ever pragmatic, Margaret confirmed that, despite its commitment to adult suffrage, the Guild would support a more limited measure if it became 'practical politics'. In any case, as time went on and the political context changed, the balance of opinion in the Guild shifted. By 1912, although only 83 branches had joined the PSF, the Annual Congress unequivocally supported adult suffrage. Once again, however, we need to remember that the conflicts about suffrage tactics played out between activists. Although many individuals and branches took up the struggle with enthusiasm, as always in the Guild, there were others who were just not interested.

Labour changes its mind, 1912

Back in Westminster, 1910 and 1911 saw compromise 'Conciliation Bills' presented twice to Parliament; as with previous suffrage bills, the government refused it time to proceed.

Committed to full adult suffrage, Margaret and the PSF did not actively promote these, although she appears to have taken part in some of the backroom negotiations that went on; writing to Bertrand Russell, she enthusiastically described a breakfast meeting with Lloyd George.[382]

Eventually, Lloyd George suggested a government manhood suffrage bill, this time specifically framed so as to allow an amendment to include all women. If this were not passed, the promise was that the Government would give time to a third Conciliation Bill. This meant there would be a guarantee of some measure of votes for women, and informally the NUWSS gave a positive response.

But in November 1911, Prime Minister Asquith once again put a spanner in the works, publicly announcing to a PSF deputation his immediate plans for a bill giving all men the vote. It was not clear whether or not this meant he was implementing Lloyd George's proposal, especially as there were rumours that Asquith would resign rather than accept women's suffrage. The PSF quickly decided to press for the government to introduce a bill guaranteeing votes for all women as well as all men.

In the light of Asquith's plans, it was time for the Labour Party to stand up and be counted. At the party conference in January 1912, Arthur Henderson of the PSF proposed a crucial resolution affirming that the Party was not in favour of any voting reform which excluded women. An impassioned speech by the PSF's Mary Macarthur, carried the day: 'We have often been told that we women adult suffrage supporters were being misled ... If this resolution is not carried, will not those who condemned us have spoken the truth?'[383] Amid great excitement, the resolution passed. This must have been music to Margaret's ears.

Alas, weeks after this momentous decision, there was a major blow. Lloyd George failed to deliver on his earlier promise, and Asquith's manhood suffrage bill was postponed. And there was worse to come. When the Conciliation Bill came before Parliament again in March 1912, it was rejected – even though, twice before, it had passed with large majorities. There are various explanations for this, but redoubled WSPU violence, in protest against both Asquith's planned manhood suffrage reform and the Conciliation Bill, certainly played a part.

For some time, adult suffrage sympathisers within the NUWSS leadership had been working hard behind the scenes for closer relations with labour forces. The Labour Party's new commitment to votes for women now provided a stark contrast to the Liberal Government's failure to deliver on its promises. In May 1912, the NUWSS committed itself to a ground-breaking electoral alliance with the Labour Party, which included providing financial help for Labour candidates.

The main immediate hope, however, was to get women included in the Asquith manhood suffrage bill. Margaret worked enthusiastically with the NUWSS and other groups planning women's suffrage amendments, including one based on the married women proposal. Reporting on a large demonstration in December 1912, a jubilant article in *Woman's Corner*, headed 'Enfranchisement of women: victory in sight', urged Guild branches to lobby their MPs.[384]

There was great excitement as the time drew near for the amendments to be discussed in Parliament. With just over a week to go, Margaret pleaded with co-operative men to contact their MPs in support of 'the greatest opportunity there has ever been to secure the enfranchisement of women'.[385] On the crucial day in January 1913, she and Lilian joined the Guild section of a sandwich board procession marching round and round Parliament Square.

Then followed a bombshell. Against all expectations, the Speaker of the House of Commons ruled the suffrage amendments out of order, deciding that they would mean altering the bill so completely that a new one would be necessary. In fury, the WSPU escalated their protests still further. The government retaliated with the Cat and Mouse Act, under which hunger-striking suffragettes who became gravely ill after being force fed could be released from prison, only to be re-arrested once their health recovered. And tragedy ensued when Emily Davison ran out in front of the King's horse on Derby Day and died of her injuries.

Although by now bitterly opposed to the WSPU militants, the constitutional suffragists of the NUWSS also took action. In the summer of 1913, they organised a huge, nationwide 'pilgrimage' in which some Guildswomen took part. Eight marches from the regions converged on London for a 50,000 strong mass meeting in Hyde Park.

Meanwhile, days after the Speaker's ruling, women's suffrage once again came up at the Labour Party conference. In the run-up, Margaret wrote in the socialist paper, *Labour Leader,* urging the party to keep the faith. On the day a stronger resolution than before, committing the party and its MPs actively to oppose any franchise bill which excluded women, was passed with a massive majority. The reaction showed how much the party had changed over the years: 'delegates sprang to their chairs, hats were waved, women in the gallery clasped hands, and their cheers were again and again renewed.'[386]

Four years earlier, when she helped to set up the PSF, Margaret had hoped for unity between suffragists and the labour movement. Now, the Labour Party had allied with the NUWSS and was finally lined up in support of votes for women. This seemed truly to be a game-changer.

Margaret's work in the PSF seems now to have faded into the background. Within the Guild, too, suffrage took a back seat. At the 1914 Guild Congress, for the first time in ten years there was no Central Committee resolution demanding votes for women.

Then, the outbreak of war in August 1914 changed everything for the suffrage movement.

Coda

The movement that burst into life at this time was life-changing for thousands of women. 'The cause', to which both constitutional suffragists and militants devoted themselves single-mindedly, had a significance which went far beyond ordinary politics. The WSPU, in particular, had an extraordinary appeal which, as Helena Swanwick suggested, was in many ways profoundly religious. Even Margaret, by no means an acolyte, recognised its emotional power.

Nevertheless, while Margaret worked for suffrage with passion and dedication, for her it was never the only cause. It is not surprising that she admired the socialist Sylvia Pankhurst, who broke away from the WSPU. Margaret wrote enthusiastically, 'I think the East End Fedn with S Pank and Lansbury is the best one going – East End workers, adult suff, men + women – + I'm going to write + subscribe'.[387] [original abbreviations]

Margaret had always linked votes for women with equality and social justice, and especially with the needs of the working-class married women in the Guild. As time went on, campaigns directly about these needs began to take over.

CHAPTER 11

Better Wages and More, 1906-1913

With fingers weary and worn
With eyelids heavy and red,
A woman sat, in unwomanly rags,
Plying her needle and thread ...

Stitch! stitch! stitch!
In poverty, hunger, and dirt,
Sewing at once, with a double thread,
A Shroud as well as a Shirt.[388]

Minimum wage, living wage or equal pay?

For the first part of this story, we return to May and June 1906.[389]

Sweated labour – that is, insecure, sub-contracted work, mainly carried out by women at home for appallingly low pay, had been a scandal for many years. Now, it was making headlines. Crowds flocked to large exhibitions about it in London and Manchester; an Anti-Sweating League was formed; and there were demands for legislation to fix minimum wages.

Margaret arranged for an exhibition and lecture about sweating at the Guild's Congress, but evidently it was not at the top of her agenda. Rather than her and the Central Committee, it was a local branch that submitted a resolution to the Congress in favour of state-regulated minimum wages for women. Then Arthur's cancer was diagnosed, only weeks before the Congress, and at the last minute Margaret had to rush to Berkhamsted to be with him and his family, missing the Congress and the fiery debate that took place.

When it began, heartfelt applause greeted Mrs Bury's declaration that 'women were still making shrouds as well as shirts'. Delegates enthusiastically clapped Mrs Fidkin, too, when she insisted that women working in sweated trades were 'part of us, and it was the duty of ... co-operative women to see that life was made worth living to them'.[390] In an electric atmosphere, the resolution was passed unanimously.

Although most Guildswomen had given up regular paid work on their marriage, this debate illustrates their deep sense of solidarity with women workers. With Margaret in the lead, for years they had supported trade unions and demanded that co-operative shops should boycott sweated products. Now, the issue was centre stage – and about to come much closer to home.

In principle, co-operators believed that they ought to provide the best possible pay and conditions for their employees. However, this often did not apply in practice. Back in 1893, prominent co-operator William Maxwell had already attacked the 'appalling' hours and 'disgraceful' conditions which many workers in Co-operative shops and factories had to endure; highlighting the plight of women workers, whose wages were considerably lower than men's.

The Guild investigated this in the 1890s and produced some damning evidence. On average, women working in co-operative shops were paid little more than women in similar jobs elsewhere, and certainly not a living wage.[391] Working hours were long, and conditions left much to be desired; Guild branches often had to lobby hard for such things as seats for tired shop assistants, or what were euphemistically dubbed 'issues of sanitation' (lavatories for female staff).

The question of minimum wages only came to the fore in the movement nationally after years of pressure from the Amalgamated Union of Co-operative Employees (AUCE). In 1906 the Co-operative Congress, the annual meeting of the whole movement, finally endorsed an AUCE proposal for a minimum pay scale, increasing with age up to full pay at twenty-one. Although this was only a recommendation – wages were fixed locally – it appeared to be a real trade union victory. But, and it was a huge but, the scale had been designed and agreed for male workers only.

During the months which followed, although Margaret was under pressure elsewhere, struggling to keep up with suffrage work during Arthur's terrible illness, the men-only minimum wage scale could not be ignored. She arranged for Guild discussions in the autumn, and negotiations with the AUCE, previously uninterested in recruiting female employees, slowly developed. In May 1907, the union agreed on a joint committee with Margaret and Mrs Bury to sort out the issue.

A big question was whether to demand a separate pay scale for women or to insist on equal pay. Although in principle she was all for the latter, Margaret believed that it was unrealistic as an immediate demand. When all was said and done, she thought, it was wrong to treat co-operative societies like capitalist employers. The immediate, large, wage increases involved would cause them real difficulties, especially as they had to compete with commercial retailers. She was also concerned that if adult female workers' wages were set too high, co-operative managers might sack them in favour of their younger and cheaper sisters.

So Margaret initially agreed that the AUCE should devise a lower minimum wage scale for women, and arranged to put it to the Guild's 1907 Congress for approval. Although a branch's proposal for equal pay gave her considerable pause for thought, in the end she stuck to her guns. In the final Central Committee resolution she proposed that 'while desiring that women should be paid the same as men for equal work', the Guild should work with the AUCE to win its suggested scale for women. This provided ten shillings per week for an eighteen-year-old, and sixteen shillings for a twenty-one-year-old. Yet the men's scale provided fifteen shillings at eighteen, and twenty-four shillings at twenty-one. Quite a difference.

In the event, it was Lilian who proposed the resolution; Margaret was elsewhere. The debate turned out to be unexpectedly heated. Many women lined up to denounce the suggested scale as far too low. Co-operative employers, some argued, had a special obligation to pay at the very least a living wage. There were arguments, too, for equal pay as the only solution.

Even Margaret's allies like Margaret Macdonald, Ramsay Macdonald's wife and a leading light in the Women's Industrial Council and the Women's Labour League, opposed the proposal. So did Catherine Webb, usually Margaret's devoted supporter. Although now a notable writer and lecturer – indeed, a national co-operative figure – Catherine had begun her working life behind the counter in a co-operative shop. For her, this was personal. She was furious:

> Men at 21 earned 24s. a week, and women were now asking for one third less. Why? Simply for the sake of custom and commercialism; they were exploiting women's labour, just as was done in the past.[392]

An equal pay amendment from Toxteth branch was only narrowly defeated, and although Margaret's proposal went through it only gained active support from less than half the delegates present. She had won, but by a tiny margin.

What lay behind this unexpected setback? Clearly, a major reason was the low level at which the scale was fixed. But also, some Guildswomen will have shared fears in the labour movement that a minimum wage could undermine trade union bargaining power and effectively become the maximum that the employers would pay.

Over-committed at work and struggling with grief, Margaret had not given this issue enough attention. She had been in a hurry; there had been relatively little time for joint work with the AUCE before Congress, and she had simply gone along with the union's proposals without considering their adequacy. Clearly, though, that minimum scale had to be adequate. Despite all she had learned from her contact with Guildswomen, she had not appreciated that, in fact, what was being proposed did not provide a living wage for women.

Realising her mistake, Margaret swiftly decided to compromise. Later that year she gave the issue more time, working both with the AUCE and on *A Co-operative Standard for Women Workers*: a detailed paper which put forward a higher minimum scale.

Just weeks before this was due to be discussed at the 1908 Guild Congress, the full Co-operative Congress demonstrated that the collaboration with the AUCE had paid off. This time, the union proposed a minimum scale for women very similar to that in '*A Co-operative Standard*' – and the Congress approved it. In a rousing contribution to the debate, Margaret insisted that co-operative societies could well afford the increase in their wage bill. More fundamentally, she appealed to the movement's ethical traditions: 'Co-operators had a co-operative conscience, … profits [should] be given the second, not the first, place to good conditions of labour.'[393]

Margaret's paper gave some shocking examples of low wages paid to women employed in the movement. There were areas where half the Co-operative societies paid women less than thirteen shillings per week.[394] In one place, a whole drapery department was staffed by assistants receiving ten shillings per week or less. Teenagers were paid less than adult women, and Margaret urged Guildswomen to educate their daughters not to accept 'mere pocket money wages'. Stressing that 'The emancipation of the workers was the ideal of the Rochdale Pioneers', she entreated current co-operators to ensure that 'none of our workers should be without the means of a worthy human life'.

Although Margaret's revised scale was still significantly lower than the men's (19s. at twenty-one-years-old for women, compared with 24s. for men), it was a distinct improvement on the previous year's proposal. And there was a subtle shift of emphasis in her wording of the resolution for the 1908 Guild Congress. This endorsed her revised scale, but only as 'a step towards the adoption of equal pay for equal work'.[395] All this convinced the delegates. After an amicable debate focusing on the general iniquities of low pay, the resolution was passed unanimously. From now on Guildswomen were united – and determined to get results.

The campaign gets underway

With official backing both from the Guild and from the co-operative movement as a whole, it might seem that victory was in sight. However, achieving better wages for women was easier said than done.

Whatever went on at the Co-operative Congress, individual co-operative societies were free to make their own decisions about wages. Often under pressure to pay out high dividends, they were faced with increasing competition from large scale retailers, and from their point of view, the cheap labour provided by women and girls definitely helped. High-minded resolutions were one thing, and local practice quite another. Just as in the campaign to extend co-operation to the poor, the Guild's demand for ethical policies conflicted with what many saw as business necessity.

It is not surprising that, despite the success at the Co-operative Congress, the movement's leadership was not keen to push for implementation of the minimum scale. As time went on, ripples of tension emerged. The ruling United Board refused to promote the scale by endorsing a model rule for local co-operative societies, which was demanded by the Guild; or even to organise another debate at the next Co-operative Congress.

Margaret could see that victory would mainly depend on local action. The minimum wage now rose up her agenda. When she wrote the annual circular outlining winter work for 1908-9, she put it top of the list, hailing it as 'our great work this year'. The circular pledged that leading Guildswomen would come and speak to local co-operators if required, but also stressed that alliance with the AUCE was essential; urging branches to collaborate with the union locally in lobbying for the scale and recruiting women workers. Meanwhile, Margaret continued to work with AUCE's national officials, and to speak and write about the campaign.

In a paper for Guild discussion, she provided detailed advice for branches about how to recruit women workers into the AUCE, especially the younger ones. 'The Guild is giving to married women a sense of solidarity and power. Our aim must be to foster in younger women the feeling that they must stand shoulder to shoulder as fellow workers.'[396]

Margaret described this as perhaps the Guild's 'most important and far-reaching agitation' to date, and it certainly struck a chord with members, with greater action than usual from branches. In February 1909, under the heading 'Honour to Enfield Highway', the Guild announced the first co-operative society to come onside, publicly committing itself to paying the Guild's minimum scale in full. Margaret gave the campaign great prominence over the next few years, with page after page in each year's Annual Report praising individual branches' achievements, however small, and listing the societies that had granted the scale in a 'roll of honour'.

It proved to be slow work, though. By the summer of 1910, only thirty-four co-operative societies had adopted the women's scale, compared with five hundred paying the men's. Over the ensuing years more joined them, but even by 1914 the number had only increased to 240: roughly one local Co-operative society in six. While this was progress, taken on its own it was not the success they had hoped for.

Fortunately, there was more to come.

Battling with the CWS

The Co-operative Wholesale Society (CWS), a national body running factories, workshops and farms producing goods for co-operative stores, was a huge and powerful organisation. It is said that by the mid-1900s it had become one of the largest businesses in the world, employing between five thousand and seven thousand girls and women – the majority of its workers. The CWS had already agreed to pay the minimum scale for men. Would it do the same for women?

By early 1910 the PSF was securely established and the subsequent rows in the Guild were dying down. Margaret had more time than before to tackle the CWS, in what would clearly be a major piece of work.

The campaign started well. In March she organised a twelve-strong deputation which presented a petition in favour of the minimum scale to the CWS directors. Demonstrating the strong feeling among large numbers of Guildswomen, it had been signed individually by thirteen thousand women – half the Guild's membership. The directors appeared to receive the deputation sympathetically. But when the decision finally came in June, it proved to be a bald refusal.

If the CWS directors thought that would be the end of it, they were wrong. Margaret speedily arranged a discussion at the Guild's forthcoming 1910 Congress, which demonstrated beyond the shadow of a doubt that Guildswomen did not intend to give in. Two men from the CWS were present and attempted to justify their decision, but completely misjudged the audience. Their claim that they had employees' best interests at heart only provoked hostile laughter, and they then left before the full minimum wage debate took place – another bad move. Mrs Clantman was applauded when she criticised their absence from the platform, pointing out that *they* didn't have to manage on a minimum wage.

Speaker after speaker rose to support Margaret's proposed scale, at least as a first step towards equal pay, and the delegates unanimously backed the resolution; also approving the demand that co-operative women workers be unionised, and that the AUCE employ a woman organiser. Another resolution supported Mrs Hodgett, ex-President of the Guild and a seasoned campaigner, as a candidate for the CWS board of directors. The Guild was in fighting mood.

Margaret went on to write a chilly letter to the directors, demanding an explanation of their decision. She received a curt response. It was 'not practicable to enter into a discussion of all the points of detail which formed the … basis of this decision'. After referring to the varied trades and circumstances which the CWS had to deal with, the letter ended 'These cannot well be thrust on one side without involving us in complications and difficulties which we are not prepared to encounter'.[397]

Undaunted, Margaret published the correspondence in *Woman's Corner*, and made it clear that the campaign would continue.

Although there were other urgent campaigns, fighting for the women's minimum scale continued to be a central commitment for the whole Guild. While branches pressurised their local co-operators, Margaret concentrated on the CWS centrally. Now blocked by the directors, she found another way to get results. The CWS's governing structure included a system of regional meetings, held every quarter and made up of delegates from the co-operative societies that were members of the organisation. If these meetings agreed the scale, the campaign would be won.

Working with the AUCE, Margaret and local Guilders now mobilised sympathetic co-operative societies to demand that the question be brought to these 'quarterly meetings', as they were known. This was due to take place in June 1911, but the directors played it cleverly and obtained a last-minute adjournment. With the debates then definitely scheduled for the December meetings, the Guild's campaign began in earnest. Margaret recruited leading co-operators to write to *Co-operative News* in support, stressing in particular that implementing the minimum wage would not necessarily lead to a reduction in dividends. She circulated a Guild statement to all co-operative societies that were members of the CWS, and offered to organise special deputations from the Guild Central Committee.

Guild branches played a crucial part. In a *Woman's Corner* article headed, 'Not words but deeds' (echoing the well-known suffragette slogan, 'Deeds not words'), Margaret urged them to leaflet their local co-operative societies' management committees, and to persuade them to appoint women delegates to the CWS meetings. In a final appeal, immediately before the December meetings, she exhorted members once more:

> Every delegate from every Society to the CWS meeting should be seen personally ... Guildswomen should assemble in force outside the [meeting] halls ... Our latest leaflets should be distributed, and the delegates impressed with the Guild's enthusiasm and determination.

Margaret was determined to win: 'Our agitation has now been going on for three years ... The time has gone by for waiting.'[398]

Lobbying in this way would once have been unheard of for Guildswomen. True, times had changed; after all, some already had experience in the suffrage movement. Nevertheless, speaking up at local meetings, demonstrating in the street, handing out leaflets and arguing with male co-operators must have been daunting for some. On the other hand, some of the men may have been equally unnerved when confronted by groups of determined middle-aged women, who could have been, and indeed perhaps were, their own wives.

In any case, Guildswomen responded enthusiastically to Margaret's call, with deputations, petitions, resolutions and more. The Guild was proving itself a force to be reckoned with. But in the event, the resolutions at the regional meetings were lost by 545 votes out of a total of 2,500 cast. The disappointment must have been hard to take, although Margaret, ever the optimist, described the discussions as excellent and the level of support as encouraging.

This setback seems only to have made Margaret and the Guild still more determined.

At the beginning of 1912, she drew up a carefully organised plan of campaign for the subsequent CWS meetings, co-ordinating even more closely than before with the AUCE, like-minded local co-operative societies, and sympathetic outsiders.

When the discussion was due once more, over 350 Guild branches took action, and the CWS Directors wavered for the first time. They agreed to grant the scale to women working in their distributive department – about a thousand packers – and on this basis asked for the resolution backing the scale to be withdrawn. But this left out thousands of other women workers. The Guild and its allies refused to give in.

In a last push, Margaret deployed her formidable network, persuading Margaret Bondfield and Labour MP Philip Snowden to support the campaign publicly, along with Maud Pember Reeves of the Fabian Women's Group and others. In the summer of 1912, too, the Co-operative Congress reiterated its earlier backing for the minimum scale.

Margaret also discovered another way to influence the CWS decision, once again using the co-operative movement's democratic structure. She urged each Guild branch to demand that members of its local co-operative society should have the opportunity to vote on the minimum scale. Then, the society should mandate its representative to vote the same way at the CWS quarterly meeting.

Once again, Guildswomen took up Margaret's suggestions, and lobbied locally as well as at the CWS meetings. When decision time finally came in December 1912, the Guild was on tenterhooks. At the office, there were, 'thrilling moments ... as telegrams came in with the results'.[399] These finally showed that the quarterly meetings had resolved to back the minimum wage resolution by an overall majority of 139. Margaret, delighted, claimed that the whole movement had been roused.

Unusually, the Guild Central Committee formally congratulated her personally. There was press publicity too, and a leading article in the *Manchester Guardian* hailed the decision as 'a triumph for the progressive power of democratic organisation and a vindication of women's capacity for politics'.[400]

In a quid pro quo, the Guild immediately undertook a 'Push the sales' campaign, encouraging branches to push local Co-operative societies to sell CWS goods. As Margaret put it, they now could do so 'with a clear conscience and invincible arguments'.[401]

Margaret tried to work with the AUCE in this campaign, but it had not always been easy. Until the Guild became involved, the union had conspicuously failed to recruit women workers, and ignored them in its negotiations. It was only with the Guild's campaign that this changed. In response, girls and women flocked to join the AUCE; the numbers rose from 500 in 1908 to six thousand in 1914. It has been estimated that by then over 12,000 women working for co-operative organisations benefited from the minimum wage.

Margaret's report of an AUCE meeting in October 1911 hints at the entrenched attitudes of some, though not all, AUCE activists. As Miss Kidd, the Guild's formidable clerk and an experienced trade unionist, pointed out, its annual report made no mention whatsoever of the women's minimum wage campaign, then in full flow. When a male supporter suggested that the AUCE should have a woman organiser, the Chair suggested, to laughter, that 'the gentlemen had been paying more attention to the ladies than to their own sex'.[402]

Harriet Kidd, one of only three women at the meeting, was not having any of this. She protested, took a prominent part in the discussion, and, at the end, successfully challenged the Chair's reading of the vote. Revealing the progressive views of many of the men attending, a formal count then showed a substantial majority in favour of appointing a woman organiser.

The following year Miss Kidd herself became the AUCE's first female elected official, but it was not until 1915, with the impetus of wartime change, that the union finally appointed its first paid women's organiser. She was the young Ellen Wilkinson, subsequently dubbed 'Red Ellen', who later had a long career as a Labour MP and government minister.

This was the campaign which first showed the Guild as a major force to be reckoned with in the co-operative world. Despite the difficulties, Margaret had put into practice her mantra that trade unionism and co-operation were 'two halves of the same circle'. Moreover, it was the first time – though not the last – that the combination of her tactical and networking skills at the centre and the determined, nationally organised, local lobbying, came fully into play. Above all, this was a campaign which confirmed grass-roots Guildswomen's commitment to women workers.

Wages for housework?

Although she was committed to supporting trade union struggles, Margaret herself was increasingly concerned about the position of those married women who, like most in the Guild, depended on their husbands' wages.

Like many other feminists, Margaret opposed to the principle of the family wage, which was sacrosanct in many parts of the union movement. This was based on the idea that a man's wages should be high enough to support his whole family, so that wives and mothers were not forced by poverty to go out to work. Critics argued that this encouraged employers to use women as cheap labour, and underpinned male dominance within the home. Furthermore, as Margaret and others pointed out, it was a myth that only men had dependants; many women financially supported their mothers, children or other relatives. And the family wage principle assumed that, as most women would be unable to gain a living wage, single women and widows should depend on fathers or brothers.

Married women's lack of rights came under the spotlight in August 1907, quite out of the blue. A judge in Middlesbrough ruled that a husband had the legal right to any savings which his wife had put aside from the housekeeping money which she had provided. The Guild was advised that the ruling would apply to the co-operative dividend. As this was paid out on the basis of the amount spent at the co-operative store, it had previously been seen as the wife's property. Now, a husband could legally claim it – even if his wife were a co-operative member in her own right.

Some in the movement simply assumed that there was no problem – of course co-operative men behaved well and dealt fairly with their wives! But it was worrying for local co-operative managers, who would have to decide whether to release the dividend, and to whom.

This could be a minefield. Moreover, it was potentially a body blow for Guildswomen. They were responsible for making ends meet, in bad times as well as good. If they were able to save through the dividend, it was entirely thanks to their careful management, and they relied on it to cover big one-off expenses, or to tide them over when the family fell on hard times.

Margaret organised Guild discussions to publicise the problem and made a point of speaking at several. All but one of the meetings agreed that the Guild should seek advice on getting the law changed, and it is likely that she had a hand in persuading the Co-operative Parliamentary Committee to consider the need for legal changes to give married women rights to maintenance. But she does not seem to have taken this demand any further, and there is no evidence that Guildswomen were pressing for further action.

It seems that, in the event, the judgement may have been a damp squib. At the request of the Guild, the movement obtained legal advice that a husband would need a court order before he could insist on receiving the dividend against his wife's will.[403] This would make it difficult, if not impossible, to take advantage of the Middlesbrough ruling.

However, the Middlesbrough judgement did stimulate debate within the Guild. Margaret had arranged for Mrs Gasson, a veteran leader and the wife of a Bermondsey plumber, to write the introductory paper for the 1907 discussions.[404] She not only explained the judgement but went on to argue that, because of her domestic work, a wife 'earns a certain amount of the family income. Services lovingly rendered by her have a monetary value, for without her they would have to be paid for.'

Most Guildswomen would agree that being a housewife was a job, and a demanding one at that, but this was going much further. Mrs Gasson also suggested that the marriage service should prescribe for a wife to have the same amount of money for her personal use as her husband, and that the Married Women's Property Act should entitle her to a proportion of family income, 'in recognition of her moral claim in contributing to the household expenses'. This was strong stuff – although, as we have seen in chapter 3, similar ideas had been suggested in *Woman's Corner* as early as 1885.

With women's rights to the fore in public debate, Margaret herself hoped that the Middlesbrough judgement would encourage Guildswomen to support the struggle for the vote. With typical enthusiasm, she wrote to Bertrand Russell:

> It looks as if we were at the beginning of what might be a real sort of revolution of our married women ... the Middlesbrough Court decision ... is going to do more for us than anything else ... Married women ... may now be made to see that they must have the vote ...[405]

Evidently, attitudes within the Guild were shifting. In 1910, a local branch put a resolution to the Guild's Congress demanding that, as the wife 'contributes by her work in the home to the maintenance of the family equally with the husband', she should be recognised as joint head of the household and be legally entitled to 'an equal form of economic independence'. After the branch agreed to soften the wording to 'some' form rather than an equal form – no doubt Margaret had an eye to Co-operative politics – delegates passed the resolution unanimously.[406]

Meanwhile, partly stimulated by the disagreements about minimum wages, Margaret was discussing with Lilian the broader aspects of married women's financial dependence and how it could be countered. The issue was being widely discussed at this time, and feminist and socialist women had varying ideas. Some backed the family wage, believing it would enable mothers to devote themselves to home and children if that was what they wanted. Among those who, like Margaret, wanted to promote women's financial independence from their husbands, many supported a state allowance for mothers: often referred to as an endowment for motherhood and a forerunner of Eleanor Rathbone's proposals for a family allowance (the origin of our current child benefit). They saw this as providing an independent income for mothers, but others disagreed; either distrusting state involvement in the matter, or fearing it would have the effect of tying women to the home.

More radical ideas were also floated. For example, socialist and trade unionist Ada Neild Chew opposed both the family wage and endowment for motherhood, suggesting instead that the state should provide day nurseries, and that domestic work should be a paid job.[407]

While Margaret supported state endowment of motherhood, she felt it was only part of the solution. For a start, it would leave many married women stranded once their children were grown. No longer qualifying for state support and having been out of the world of work for many years, they would be unable to command a living wage.

She was also tussling with the issues surrounding equal pay. Although theoretically in favour, she still believed it was unrealistic to campaign for this as an immediate demand and felt there must be other broader changes before equality could be achieved. While she saw the family wage principle as a major obstacle, she also pointed to embedded social and cultural factors, including women's generally lower standard of living than men, and the fact that their labour was seen as having a lower value. As she wrote angrily in *A Co-operative Standard*:

> A girl is given less to eat, is supposed to require less exercise, less education, and less training. A woman has a cup of tea for her dinner, while she prepares her husband a beefsteak; a woman does not claim money to spend on herself as her husband does; she can rarely take a holiday – she will stay indoors for weeks together; she consents to a dependence which is humiliating.

Writing to Bertrand Russell, she linked an increase in women's wages with 'gaining a larger share of wealth for the whole working class', and argued that eventual equal pay would be 'the ideal, based on the right of the worker to the whole produce of his labour. But this could only be achieved by 'economic reforms, payment of wives, improved custom and destruction of women's [feeling of] inferiority'.

Wrestling with the inequality within and outside the workplace which still besets us, Margaret was momentarily and uncharacteristically pessimistic: 'The more independent women grow, the more they claim from life, the more impossible their problems become. Men must become angels before there's much of a life for [women].'[408]

CHAPTER 12

Gender Politics in the Home, 1909-1914

Margaret and the Royal Commission

On a November afternoon in 1910, Margaret went to tea with her old friend Dolly Ponsonby. She was full of the dramatic testimony from individual Guildswomen which she had presented to the Royal Commission on divorce law reform the previous week. Dolly confided to her diary that Margaret's, 'eyes burnt with indignation as she told me stories of the terrible injustices inflicted on poor women by the present laws'.[409]

Up till now, campaigning on questions like votes for women had been seen as controversial by some co-operators. This would surely be even more so. Venturing into the private world of husband and wife, publicly recounting Guildswomen's intimate experiences? How could this possibly have happened?

Because of its high cost, divorce was out of reach for most working people, and anyway they had to travel to London to get their case heard. Worse, there were different rules for women and men. While a husband could obtain a divorce on grounds of adultery alone, a wife also had to prove another offence such as desertion, incest, cruelty or bigamy. Many women disapproved of divorce in principle, on religious grounds, although opinion varied widely, and some feminists and freethinkers even argued that current laws and customs made marriage akin to prostitution.

The need for reform had come to the fore when Sir John Gorell Barnes, the most senior divorce court judge, publicly stated that the current law was riddled with 'inconsistencies, anomalies, and inequalities almost amounting to absurdities'.[410] With a reforming Liberal government in power, pressure mounted. Late in 1909, Prime Minister Asquith set up a Royal Commission, headed by that same judge, to investigate and recommend changes.

As might be expected, Margaret was all for reform. Despite her other commitments, she seized the opportunity when invited to give evidence to the Commission on behalf of the Guild. But she first had to get agreement from the Central Committee at its meeting in May 1910. The current Guild President, Miss Gration (whom Margaret described as 'Tory' but 'such a nice creature') was personally opposed to divorce, and reading between the lines of the minutes, this was a long and difficult discussion. Nevertheless, the Committee eventually agreed to support a change in the law although, unusually, Miss Gration's dissent was formally recorded. The Committee authorised Margaret to consult Guild members to see what they thought on this controversial question and she promptly circulated all 521 Guild branches, asking them – not, perhaps, in the most neutral terms,

1) Do you think the grounds for divorce should be equal for men and women?
2) Do you think divorce proceedings should be cheapened, so that the law may be within reach of the poor?[411]

The response to both questions was a resounding 'Yes' and the Guild's July Congress passed a motion on the same lines, again with a massive majority. Margaret now had an unquestionable mandate to argue for these two reforms at the Royal Commission.

However, she wanted to go further, much further.

Margaret already had advanced ideas about divorce, and suggested a number of additional reforms, including, most controversially, that a couple should be able to divorce solely on grounds of 'mutual consent' or 'serious incompatibility'. This would mean that a marriage could be dissolved 'on the sense of the sufferer himself or herself that the marriage was unendurable'. Although there might be conditions such as a period of separation before divorce, and judges would still decide on custody and maintenance of children, marriage itself would be based on consent.

Margaret was keen to obtain Guild backing for this and other additional proposals before she gave evidence to the Commission in November. Her opportunity came in September, at the first meeting of a newly elected Central Committee, which thanks to the rule that members could only serve for three years consecutively no longer included Miss Gration. Even so, Margaret only persuaded the Committee to agree to another consultation after a long discussion.

She immediately wrote to 124 selected branch officials, asking for their opinion on her additional proposals. When the replies came back, most of them supported divorce on grounds of cruelty, insanity or persistent refusal to maintain. A smaller number, though still definitely a majority, was in favour of her other suggested changes, including divorce on grounds of mutual consent.[412] Many women wrote in at length, voicing their opinions and giving detailed examples of their own and other women's experiences.

It was clear from Margaret's two surveys that most Guildswomen were in favour of increasing access to divorce and that even though there was disagreement about her more radical proposals, these also achieved significant support. So, many of the Guild's respectable wives and mothers had ideas about marriage and divorce which were astonishingly ahead of their time. Not surprisingly, this would lead to trouble.

Margaret finally appeared before the Royal Commission on a chilly November morning, in Winchester House, an imposing but gloomy edifice in London's exclusive St James's Square. She found herself facing ten Commissioners: eight men, including a number of senior lawyers and Churchmen, and just two women. These were the gentle though determined May Tennant, long active in improving women's working conditions, and the imposing, energetic Lady Frances Balfour, a prominent suffragist, daughter of the Duke of Argyll and sister-in-law to ex-prime minister Arthur Balfour. Thanks to her wide range of contacts, Margaret already knew them both.

Margaret presented herself to the Commission not as an expert but primarily as speaking for Guildswomen. She organised her arguments around quotations from the responses which Guild officials had sent in, also summarising in writing each of the 131 individual case examples which they had provided.

While acknowledging that a minority of Guildswomen was opposed to divorce, mainly on religious grounds, she stressed that many more believed that easier divorce would promote a truly moral family life. She quoted one Guildswoman who spoke for many:

> It is said that marriages are made in heaven, but in my opinion the only real marriage is when men and women are real comrades. When they are not, then in the sight of God it is not marriage. Never, never will I believe that submission to a man who has killed every scrap of affection and respect by his unfaithfulness and neglect is accepted in the eyes of a loving and just God.[413]

After advocating cheaper divorce, and equal laws for men and women, Margaret went on to put forward the more controversial proposals which had been approved by the selected branch officials. These included divorce on grounds of mutual consent.

Citing their letters, Margaret made some more general points. She described the plight of both women and men who were currently unable to remarry even where they had been deserted or were living apart by agreement. More controversially, she attacked the accepted view, enshrined both in law and in custom, that a wife was her husband's property and that he possessed conjugal rights over her body. One Guildswoman put this in a nutshell. 'We want to get rid of the idea that a man owns his wife just as he does a piece of furniture.'[414]

The Guild officials had reported cases not only of adultery, mental cruelty, neglect, and failure to provide financial support but also of domestic abuse. Margaret read out some shocking reports to the assembled Commissioners, of which these two are presented as examples:

I know of women who always try to bring on abortion when first they are pregnant ... because the husband will grumble and make things unpleasant because there will be another mouth to fill and he may have to deprive himself of something. In one case the man always thrashes his wife and puts her life in danger in his anger on discovering her condition.[415]

The tenth day after the [first] baby was born he [husband] came home drunk and compelled me to submit to him ... I felt so degraded. I had not the same privilege as the beasts of the field. No one can possibly imagine what it is unless you go through it, to feel you are simply a convenience to a man ... I believe that it is immoral in God's sight for a man and woman to live together as husband and wife when there is no possibility of them living together happily.

For Margaret, the role of witness at a quasi-judicial enquiry, held in public and reported in the press, was new and difficult. To start with the Chairman (now Lord Gorell) took her through her evidence. He was mild-mannered and studiedly courteous, but nevertheless pressed her closely on some points. When he asked if she had any religious affiliation, Margaret had to reveal that she did not; an embarrassing public admission as her father was a well-known Anglican clergyman.

It was another Commissioner, Sir Lewis Dibdin, a barrister and Church of England official, whose cross-examination proved particularly challenging. Dibdin tied Margaret in knots on why and how she had selected the individual branch officials whose backing she used to justify her more controversial demands.

> Have you any reason to think that their views would be shared by the branches themselves?
> – Yes. On the whole ... they were typical of the other members in the branches. The branch opinion on the whole might not be so advanced, but from the evidence we have had ... I may say it would very closely represent the branch view.
> – Do those 124 individuals represent all the ... officials or a selected number?
> – ... They were women who were selected from those whom we know to be specially intelligent – on no other ground at all.

Pushed further, Margaret snapped back, 'They do not represent the official class; they do not represent anything.'

Dibdin moved on to a more specific point, her proposal for divorce on grounds of mutual consent or incompatibility:

> Was there any reason why this very important question as to incompatibility should not have been submitted to the branches themselves?
> – We only submitted the two questions to the branches, the equality and the cheapening ...
> – Why did you not go further?
> – We did not go into any of the [other] questions with the branches; we did not think they had yet had sufficient study of the subject.
> – ... you think they would agree with the view you yourself and the majority of the 124 [officials] formed?
> – I should think the majority of the branches would, though all might not be so advanced. But these women are drawn from the same class as the branch members, and would to a very large extent be representative of the branches.'[416]

Margaret was struggling.

Wisely, however, she had arranged for a working-class Guildswoman to present additional evidence. At this time, Eleanor Barton was the secretary of one of the Guild's Sheffield branches, although she later rose to become General Secretary. A tailoress when young, Mrs Barton originally hailed from Manchester and had interesting political connections. Her brother was a leading local anarchist, and she was arrested at least once when the police fought to break up one of their open-air meetings – a regular occurrence. After she married Alfred Barton, another Manchester anarchist, they moved to Sheffield and became more 'respectable'. Alfred Barton became an official of the local ILP, involved in the Trades Council, while his wife joined the Guild. When she gave her evidence to the Royal Commission she was in her late thirties, with two children.[417]

Eleanor Barton appears in photographs as delicately pretty. But she was a tough character, and her background of militant protest helps to explain her un-deferential approach to the members of the Royal Commission. Spirited and articulate, she described the thirty-six members of her Guild branch as wives of 'the better class of artisan', and, 'thinking women, and women who mix with others, and take an intelligent interest in their neighbours'. She told the Commission that during branch discussions, all but one member had agreed with making divorce cheaper and ensuring equal laws for men and women, while most also supported extending the grounds. Like Margaret, Mrs Barton attacked the current view of married women as their husbands' property and emphasised their need for financial independence. As she explained:

> ... a married working woman in the home has no money of her own at all and that makes it very hard for women to escape from any amount of cruelty. I do not mean physical cruelty; there are different causes and different cases of cruelty; but to understand the position of working women one has to live among them. There is a great deal of suffering which never sees daylight ...

Here and elsewhere, Mrs Barton was effectively alluding to rape within marriage. She pointed out that 'working women ... are not able to get away the same as people in a better class of life', and openly referred to the suffering caused by 'a lustful husband, by bearing children unwillingly. They [wives] feel they are married and because they are married they must submit ...'[418]

The two women's dramatic evidence inevitably attracted press attention. *The Times* reported Commissioner Lady Frances Balfour's reaction, delivered in the course of a speech at a suffragist reception:

> ... she did not think she had ever listened to anything that was a stronger and more convincing argument as to the need for representative power for women. She would that such things as she had heard that day could

go forth with all their burning force and power to give the lie to the statement that women had nothing to complain of. [419]

But to others, and to conservative opinion generally, the challenge this presented to accepted notions of Christian morality was deeply shocking.

Margaret under attack

It took time for the Commission to finish its work, and although Margaret continued to organise information-giving and discussion within the Guild about her proposals, with other campaigns needing urgent action divorce temporarily faded into the background. But in the spring of 1912 a short, explosive item in *Woman's Corner* signalled trouble ahead. It reported that members of the Guild's Darwen branch in Lancashire, 'firmly convinced that any broadening of the ground for divorce ... would prove disastrous', formally dissociated themselves from any action the Guild might take in favour of liberalising the law. [420]

The largest branch in the Guild, Darwen was headed by Mrs Bury, who had already clashed with Margaret over the Guild's suffrage policy. Never before had an individual branch repudiated national policy in this way. If not a declaration of war, this was at least a shot across the bows.

The Darwen rebellion did not have any immediate repercussions, and the next significant event was the publication of the Royal Commission's report late in 1912. Perhaps unsurprisingly, it had been unable to arrive at a consensus. The *Majority Report* recommended a number of reforms which the Guild and other organisations had supported, including regional divorce courts for low income applicants; equal rules for wives and husbands, so that either could sue for divorce on grounds of adultery alone; and some additional grounds for divorce which included desertion, cruelty (with a wider definition than previously), habitual drunkenness and incurable insanity.

Three powerful Commissioners objected: the Archbishop of York, and two lawyers with ecclesiastical links, Sir William Anson and Sir Lewis Dibdin, who had already crossed swords with Margaret. While accepting equal laws for men and women, their *Minority Report* opposed any extension whatsoever of the grounds for divorce. In a sign of their influential position, *The Times* published it in full. Amongst other things, the *Minority Report* singled out Margaret and Mrs Barton for virulent attack, claiming that they had advocated 'a facility of divorce hitherto unheard of in any civilised country'. Picking up on Dibdin's earlier criticism, it described Margaret's evidence as wholly biased, based on, 'the extreme opinions of a comparatively few individuals selected by a witness who shares those opinions'.[421]

This public and personalised denunciation really stung. Margaret immediately sat down to pen an angry rebuttal, published in *The Times* and elsewhere, in which she categorically denied that she had pre-selected officials who agreed with her for the consultation. She also challenged the authors' unfavourable comparison between the Guild's evidence and that of the Anglican Mothers' Union, the only women's organisation to give evidence against reform, which had submitted a large petition backing it up.

Margaret stressed that she and Mrs Barton had been elected by members and were putting forward Guildswomen's opinions. The Mother's Union, she argued, was 'a working-class body managed by another class', while the Guild was a 'self-governing organisation of workers'. Whereas the Mother's Union quoted people who worked *among* the poor, she insisted that Guild officials 'belong to the workers themselves, and it is to such as they that intimate tragedies are confided by other women of their own class ... The views of independent, intelligent women cannot be stifled and ought to be listened to.'[422]

For the time being, the dispute ended there. Although furiously upset by the publicity given to the *Minority Report*, Margaret was undeterred.

Dissent in the Guild

Margaret saw the *Majority Report* as a great opportunity and was keen to start a national campaign based on its proposals, plus several additional demands including divorce on grounds of mutual consent. Typically upbeat, she suggested to Leonard Woolf that he could help her organise, 'a deputation to [Prime Minister] Asquith on Divorce – Guild with as many good people backing as possible'.[423]

Meanwhile she continued to organise discussions within the Guild, and in 1911 arranged to publish the text of the Guild evidence to the Commission, which as we have seen included a large number of case examples.[424] However, to make the ongoing campaign official she needed the approval of the Guild's next Annual Congress, due in June 1913. Having speedily won the unanimous backing of the Central Committee, she clearly thought that Congress was bound to agree.

However, dissent was already surfacing. A couple of months before the Congress, Margaret Bondfield spoke for the leadership at a Lancashire Guildswomen's conference on divorce. Although several women supported her, one complained that her branch would not discuss the subject because members were 'afraid of becoming "the new woman"' (caricatured in the Press as ludicrous, unfeminine creatures). When Mrs Bury spoke powerfully against divorce on grounds of mutual consent, she was backed up by laughter and applause.⁴²⁵

Margaret felt impelled to respond personally in *Women's Corner* (the new name for Woman's Corner from 1913), and over the next couple of months arguments on both sides were aired in its correspondence columns. Mrs Bury was a major player, writing that it would be a 'national peril' to implement the leadership's proposals and that she had support from, 'thousands of our members'.⁴²⁶ The stakes were high.

After years of apparent harmony, Mrs Bury had recently found herself thoroughly out of tune with Margaret and other Guild leaders. Now, she was once again in open opposition. She was not against all divorce but opposed making it any easier than at present, claiming widespread grass-roots support in the Guild. A pugnacious opponent, prepared to brush aside the consensual traditions of the Guild, Mrs Bury was clearly acting in accordance with her nonconformist conscience. Nevertheless, there was perhaps also a tinge of unconscious personal and class antagonism towards Margaret.

As the June Congress approached, several branches, including Mrs Bury's, formally put forward amendments opposing the leadership's divorce policy. Margaret had to recognise that she might not win the day. She put a brave face on it when writing to Bertrand Russell, welcoming the fact there would be 'clear votes' to decide the issue once and for all. But she admitted that she was anxious about the outcome: '… other influences have been at work + the women have it instilled into them that the home is to be broken up + they are fearful for children.' [she was probably referring to religious bodies]. She was still furious with Anglican attacks on reform, adding, 'Did you see the Bp of London to his Diocesan Conference *and* the Archbaggar [sic] of York to the Mothers' Union? *Atrocious!* (I shd like to hear your denunciations!).'⁴²⁷ [original emphasis and abbreviations]

Mrs Bury had vowed to lead the opposition to reform at the Congress. But three weeks before it was due to start, the news came that she had suddenly died. This was a shocking, tragic development and she was much mourned in the Guild. But Margaret would have been a saint not to register that this death might well work to her advantage.

The crucial debate took place on Tuesday 9 June, the first day of the 1913 Congress. Over 600 delegates, plus numerous visitors, packed into a co-operative hall in Newcastle. It was only at the end of the afternoon that Anna Blair from Lancashire, well known to delegates as a recent President, finally rose to propose the leadership's resolution on divorce.

Mrs Blair asked Congress to approve the Royal Commission's *Majority Report* recommendations with some additions: primarily, mutual consent after two years' separation as grounds for divorce.[428] It is indicative of the confusion in many Guildswomen's minds that she felt the need to stress that this did not mean divorce would be compulsory after two years' separation, and to reassure members that women would usually be given custody of children after divorce. At the end of her short speech, Mrs Blair expressed the hope that delegates would support the proposal on mutual consent, 'so that they might help to sanctify and make marriage purer and more holy'.

Mrs Booth from Derby, seconding the resolution, regretted that many Guildswomen did not want to discuss divorce. She added that '… it was an injustice to bring up children in homes where love did not exist'.

Now it was the opposition's turn. Immediately, Mrs Gibson from the Cambridge branch put forward an amendment opposing any extension of grounds for divorce. This was put to the vote, apparently without discussion, but was overwhelmingly rejected.

The crucial amendment, however, came next, proposed by Mrs Eccles for the Darwen and Bristol branches. While approving the Majority Report proposals, she asked delegates specifically to oppose divorce on grounds of mutual consent. Only a few short speeches were reported in *Women's Corner*. On one side, Mrs Bye from Gloucester drew attention to people forced to live together 'in immorality' because one or the other, previously married, could not get a divorce. On the other Miss Gration, while against all divorce, particularly opposed extending the grounds to mutual consent: 'Any irresponsible couple could get married, and when tired of each other would be able to get a divorce.'

Delegates now had to vote on Mrs Eccles's amendment opposing divorce on grounds of mutual consent. The result was unnervingly close. 182 supported her, while 199 disagreed. Margaret's adversaries had lost – but only just. After this, came the vote on the Central Committee resolution which backed the *Majority Report's* proposals with crucial additions including mutual consent. This got through comfortably.

So the Guild had not spoken with one voice. There was undoubtedly substantial support for some degree of reform, and even for divorce on grounds of mutual consent. But more than a third of the six hundred plus delegates had simply not voted either way on Mrs Eccles's amendment to rule it out. As we have seen before this was not uncommon at Guild Congresses, where abstentions were often not recorded and there was a strong impetus towards consensus and loyalty to the leadership. It is reasonable to suppose that a large number of delegates were either still unsure about mutual consent, or definitely against but not prepared to oppose the leadership.

Margaret seems not to have been perturbed by this near defeat and continued trying to work up support for a national campaign, both in and outside the Guild. Later in 1913, having won over Yorkshire meetings of the Guild and of the Women's Liberal Federation, she recounted with gusto, 'how we are stirring things up re: Divorce, + how nicely impressionable even sheepish Liberal ladies are'.[429]

Nevertheless, the young journalist Rebecca West's assessment that the Commission had produced 'A Report that will not become law'[430] turned out to be all too accurate. *The Times* had already shown its colours by reproducing the *Minority Report* in full for free, while *The Spectator* thundered that if the grounds for divorce were extended, 'the inevitable result would be the undermining of family life, by the maintenance of which the nation stands or falls'.[431] The Archbishop of York told Anglicans that it was their Christian duty to 'resist any further extension of the grounds for divorce'.[432] Predictably, given the trouble it faced on so many fronts at this time, the Government failed to take action on the *Majority Report*'s recommendations.

For Margaret, other campaigns took precedence. In any case, without substantial public support, proposals for divorce law reform sank into obscurity with the advent of the First World War. While the double standard for men and women was abolished in 1923, it was not until 1969 that the law caught up and finally allowed divorce where a marriage had irretrievably broken down.

The Guild in jeopardy

Meanwhile, however, more trouble erupted. It started in a deceptively small way in mid-1913, when the general secretary of the Salford Diocese Catholic Federation wrote to the Guild demanding that it give up the divorce campaign. The Federation – founded by the Bishop of Salford to defend Catholic interests locally – claimed that the campaign was 'illegitimate', and that Catholic co-operators were being 'mulcted of a portion of their dividends in order that your Guild may propagate divorce'.[433] After delaying for several months, the Central Committee sent a curt refusal. Divorce law reform, it insisted, was 'one of the most crucial moral and social reforms which affect co-operative women'.[434]

Because of the large number of Catholic co-operators in the north-west, the Salford Federation potentially carried considerable clout. It was not going to let the matter drop. It went on to write formally to the United Board, which acted as the executive committee of the whole co-operative movement and held the purse strings for a large annual grant to the Guild. The letter threatened that Catholic co-operators might exit in large numbers unless the divorce campaign was abandoned.

Faced with this intervention, the United Board caved in and requested the Guild give up the campaign in order to avoid 'disruption in the movement'. This received a speedy and determined refusal. In mid-April 1914, a long letter signed by Margaret and Mrs Essery, the Guild president, challenged the right of the Catholic Federation to interfere, stressing the majority support for the campaign within the Guild. Crucially, they also claimed that the Guild had the right to act independently, and to campaign on social issues without seeking permission. They proudly defended such campaigns as wholly appropriate for co-operative women, arguing that 'the best definitely Co-operative work is done by those Branches and individuals who are the keenest supporters of social reform.'[435]

This was very serious. The Catholics' intervention gave conservative co-operative leaders an unexpected but welcome opportunity. Although by now the Guild had won widespread respect and recognition for its work, this only went so far. Many influential men still felt the Guild should stick to spreading co-operation, rather than campaigning on controversial issues like divorce and women's suffrage. Given the Guild's reliance on the United Board's substantial grant, this was an opportunity to whip it into line.

The Co-operative Congress took place at the end of May 1914, a few weeks before the Guild's own gathering. The venue was Dublin, where the issue of divorce would be particularly contentious. In a pre-meeting, co-operative leaders decided to take a hard line. Whatever their personal views on divorce, almost all the speakers were critical of the Guild campaign, fearing that it might raise religious division within the movement. And there was more. One man said 'if the board had to pay the piper, they should be able to call the tune', another that it would be 'a mistake to allow the women to go on agitating, not only on that question but on other questions'.

The meeting decided that the Guild's annual £400 grant would only continue on condition that it stopped the divorce law campaign, and in future only took up work approved by the United Board.[436]

This major escalation had frightening implications for the Guild and its work. When the Guild's Congress took place a few weeks later in Birmingham, an emergency resolution from the Central Committee proposed outright rejection of the conditions.

Delegates were furious. Mrs Beattie from Birkenhead moved the resolution:

Where would the members of the United Board be, she would like to know, if women decided to withhold their support from the movement? They wanted to work with the men side by side, not as subordinates with restrictions, for they possessed the powers and abilities of adult women (Hear hear and applause). They were not prepared to be dominated (Loud and prolonged applause). They were open to criticism; but they did not take any action without having first carefully considered a question. (Hear hear) ... in taking the action they had done on this question of divorce, they were not interfering with the private opinions of those people who did not want the divorce laws reformed.

She went on, to loud applause, to attack the further condition that the Guild must not take up work to which the United Board objected: 'I for one prefer to work without this grant if it means the foregoing of our freedom.'

Mrs Holderness from Derby, who seconded, argued that if they accepted the United Board's conditions, they would lose their independence – to which Guildswomen in the audience interjected, 'We're not going to accept it'. She went on, 'It was repeatedly said that the women were the backbone of the movement; was it not time they showed the strength of that backbone?' (Applause.) There was 'loud and prolonged' cheering when the resolution was declared carried, with only a few abstentions.[437]

So, with the Guild's right to independent action at stake, members were fully prepared to sacrifice the annual grant rather than give in. And somehow, in the course of all this, the heated opposition to Margaret's proposals for divorce reform had dissipated. It was clear from the discussion that that even if Guildswomen did not agree on all the specific proposals for reform, they backed the campaign as a whole. A resolution essentially repeating that of the previous year went through with relative ease. Thanks to the United Board, the details of divorce law reform were no longer the issue.

Elated, Margaret told Leonard Woolf that the debate was primarily about women's autonomy, and showed that members would 'work out their own salvation and not be driven, + just take on men's view'.[438] She applauded the Central Committee's handling of a deputation from the United Board which tried belatedly to engineer a fudged compromise: 'The way each in turn of our Central Committee women went for the Board men – each with different points – was magnificent.' Margaret was overwhelmed by the Guildswomen's strength and unity. 'Someone said the Guild had found its soul, it has certainly found its feet. I feel the women have now "arrived" – and they will never go back ...'[439]

Coda

From the beginning, Margaret's approach to this campaign had been controversial. As we have seen she had been thinking for some years about the various economic and cultural factors which held women back. She seized on the opportunity of the Royal Commission to move on from the public world to the apparently private – and show how they were linked.

The letters from Guildswomen, exposing the hidden reality of what women endured, had a powerful effect on Margaret, fuelling her passionate commitment to this campaign. She had never lost her capacity for outrage at others' suffering, writing at one point: 'How people can settle into complacency in old age I don't know. *Bombs* is more likely I feel.'[440] [original emphasis]

Perhaps Sir Lewis Dibdin had a point when he attacked Margaret's use of a selective survey as her main mandate. But, personally committed to radical change, she knew that the Royal Commission represented a unique opportunity, and also that there was not enough time for the full-scale in-depth discussion with the membership needed on such a sensitive issue. So she organised the smaller, selective survey of officials which laid her open to criticism. Her decision was not wholly unreasonable.

Whatever the pros and cons, Margaret showed that, significantly, there was overwhelming backing among active Guildswomen at least for extending access to divorce, and considerable support even for her most advanced proposals. The Guild was at the forefront of progressive opinion, presenting 'arguably ... the most radical call for reform presented to the [Royal] Commission'.[441] Members' reaction, based on their own experience and on that of helping others, dramatically challenged stereotypes of respectable, middle-aged working-class wives.

The divisions exposed by the campaign also highlight the range of opinion and experience which the Guild contained as times changed and it matured. Mrs Bury and Mrs Barton illustrate two contrasting currents – partly reflecting differences in the movement as a whole – but there was more diversity still. Neither were differences straightforward. It is interesting that some deeply religious Guildswomen actually justified support for radical divorce reform on the basis of their moral principles.

Above all, Guildswomen on different sides were united in their extraordinarily self-confident rejection of the United Board's attempt to exert control, which surprised and delighted even Margaret. As Gillian Scott has perceptively commented, this not only demonstrates how they and the Guild had changed over the years; it can also be linked to the context of industrial unrest and suffrage agitation at this time, which encouraged independent action and refusal to give in to unreasoning authority.[442] It would be four long years for the dispute with the United Board to be resolved.

As for Margaret, her long-lasting achievement in this campaign was her presentation of members' letters and stories directly to the Royal Commission, and her decision to publish them subsequently. In this she was truly ahead of her time. This was a first step towards working-class women having a voice in debates about public policies which affected them, rather than them being presented as passive victims.[443] In the next chapter, we shall see how the same approach was used later, to even more powerful effect.

CHAPTER 13

Mothers First![444] 1911 onward

At the beginning of 1911 the campaigns on suffrage, divorce and the minimum wage were relatively quiet. Margaret might have been forgiven for taking a breather. But characteristically, when a major new opportunity came up she jumped at it.

Part one: Money for Mothers

A new maternity grant

Lloyd George was preparing his ground-breaking national insurance bill at this point. His scheme meant that, for the first time, workers would qualify for some free medical treatment and for cash while off sick, and there would also be a very limited unemployment benefit for certain trades. In return, each worker would contribute four pence a week, to which the state added tuppence and the employer threepence. As the saying went, the worker would get 'ninepence for fourpence'.

Margaret leapt into action early on. Working closely with both Lilian and Rosalind, she hoped to influence the bill even before it was finalised – a measure both of her self-confidence and of her ambitions for the Guild. However, it was soon clear that Lloyd George's national insurance would do little or nothing for working-class women. Their wage rates were low, on average much lower than men's, so most would not be able to afford the fourpence a week insurance contribution. The scheme also excluded the huge numbers of women who did not work regularly for pay, thus ignoring both their unpaid work in the home and their widespread occasional or casual work.

Nevertheless, Margaret believed that the bill was a step in the right direction, and that it was worthwhile agitating for improvements. Already interested in including some sort of maternity grant, Lloyd George arranged a private meeting between the Guild and his close ally, Sir Rufus Isaacs, the Attorney General. Margaret organised a deputation armed with feedback from a rapid Guild enquiry which concluded that most families could only cover maternity expenses, 'at the cost of the woman'; and also with a fully costed proposal for a grant.[445] But when Mrs Layton told Rufus Isaacs that a mother needed a minimum of £5 to cover maternity costs, he insisted that it was impossible to pay a grant of more than thirty shillings (£1.50).[446]

With the national insurance bill due to be published soon, Margaret rearranged the Guild's regular spring conferences at the last minute to include a discussion about it. Unusually, she took the trouble to introduce the topic herself at several, and all the meetings passed model resolutions to go to Lloyd George demanding both a maternity grant and inclusion of non-wage-earning married women in the insurance scheme. Not long after, the Guild Congress sent a similar message; demanding that the state contribution be extended to married women, and for women who were not employed to be entitled, if they wished and were able, to pay voluntary contributions.

Despite overall support for national insurance, there were some interesting objections. While some Guildswomen pointed out that women workers would not be able to afford the fourpenny contribution, others were generally sceptical about state welfare provision; whether insisting that it was unnecessary because 'There was already plenty of help to be had', or, from the opposite perspective, arguing that it would come 'out of the pockets of the workers'. Indeed, some Guildswomen saw the proposed insurance scheme as a con, forcing the poor to fund their own protection. And as in earlier discussions of state-regulated minimum wages, there was a view that assistance from a capitalist state would only further capitalist interests.[447]

Meanwhile, Margaret was building alliances. In June she and several other Guildswomen took part in a high-profile delegation to Lloyd George, along with representatives of the Women's Labour League, the Women's Trade Union League, the Women's Industrial Council, the National Federation of Women Workers and others. As the bill now included provision for a lump sum maternity grant, the delegation concentrated on attacking the effective exclusion of women from the insurance scheme. It also demanded that those women who *were* included – that is, who were earning enough to pay full national insurance contributions – should be guaranteed at least four weeks' sickness benefit around childbirth.

Lloyd George was combative about increasing potential claims on the insurance fund, complaining that the women wanted to 'get more out of a pint pot than it is capable of containing'. When Margaret joined with Margaret Macdonald of the Women's Labour League to press the claims of home-based married women, he refused on grounds of cost. They suggested voluntary contributions as a possible fall back, although they also pointed out that most married women would not be able to afford them.

Margaret then came up with another compromise. The state could credit wives of insured men with twopence per week, the same amount which it contributed to their husbands' insurance. Twopence would finance at least some limited benefits and a sympathetic Lloyd George promised to consider it.

In another statement, Margaret welcomed the maternity grant, even though it had now been confirmed that it would only be thirty shillings rather than £5. But, while the bill provided that national insurance payments would be administered by 'approved societies'– insurance companies, friendly societies or trade unions – she insisted that the maternity grant was different. Instead, she wanted it to be administered by the county health committees, an early indication of her belief that all maternity provision should be controlled by local authorities. She also stressed that any balance left over from the grant after medical fees were paid should be treated as the mother's property, payable to her in cash.

Margaret's pragmatic approach to negotiation was evident, but this did not stop her from pressing home her points of principle elsewhere. She wrote to *The Times* to publicise the Guild Congress's 'forcible protest' against the exclusion of six million married women from the bill, using the same arguments as in earlier debates about wives' rights to family savings:

> The fourpenny contribution from the family income of the worker gives the wife an equal right with her husband to a grant from the state. By her work as mother and housewife, the woman contributes equally with the man to the upkeep of the home, and the family income in reality is as much hers as the man's. Therefore the woman is entitled to claim the State's contribution of twopence without any further contribution from herself.[448]

While the bill proceeded through parliament Margaret continued writing to the press and MPs, working closely with her allies. She ensured that the Guild joined with other organisations to support the inclusion of domestic servants in the insurance scheme, in the face of an orchestrated backlash from their employers, and over a third of the Guild branches answered the call to write to their local MPs about the bill. Significantly, Margaret also persuaded the co-operative movement's Parliamentary Committee to issue a statement endorsing her proposal for a state contribution of twopence for benefits for the wives of insured men.

Lloyd George also came across Margaret with her People's Suffrage Federation hat on around this time, and he later singled her out among the women who came to the lobbying meeting on the insurance scheme for her useful suggestions. Nevertheless, it soon became clear that while he would agree to voluntary contributions from married non-wage-earning women, her proposal for the state to contribute twopence towards their benefits was not going to succeed.

By October Margaret had reluctantly accepted this, and suggested that the campaign should now be for the voluntary contributions to be as low as possible. She urged branches to continue their good work and write to their MPs demanding that their voluntary contribution should be, at most, twopence per week.

In the end, though, it was fixed at threepence, effectively excluding most working-class women. And although there would be a state contribution, this was fixed at a penny rather than the twopence Margaret had suggested. Her skilful campaigning, and that of her allies, had achieved very limited victories. But the story did not end there.

Once the bill had been passed, Margaret made national insurance a major focus for the Guild. Up to 500 Guildswomen attended classes about it, and within months over sixty had joined the new local insurance committees that oversaw the Act's administration. These were clearly set up with the great and good in mind rather than working women, and Guildswomen reported having to miss meetings or walk long distances because they could not afford the fare. Mrs Wimhurst, the Guild Vice-President, raised this with the central Insurance Commissioners, and 'entertained them greatly with the account of the grand lady on her insurance committee who drove up in a motor car [at this time unaffordable for most people] + told Mrs W it was immoral to ask for expenses'.[449]

In 1912 Margaret's temporary collapse following her father's illness led to the arrival of Margaret Bondfield, specifically to work on Guild campaigns. This might have freed Margaret up to look after Llewelyn, and indeed herself. Instead, it would seem, this new and able help enabled her to take the maternity campaign to a whole new level.

Margaret knew Margaret Bondfield from the People's Suffrage Federation, and despite their very different backgrounds they made an excellent team. Twelve years younger, one of eleven children of a foreman lace-maker and his home-based wife, Margaret Bondfield had started work at thirteen as a pupil teacher. A year later she became a shop worker, and as a young woman worked undercover for the Women's Industrial Council, exposing how West End shops treated their workers. By the time she came to the Guild, she was a highly experienced trade unionist, active in the TUC, the ILP and the Women's Labour League. A lifelong, committed Congregationalist, she had a brisk manner, and was a powerful public speaker.[450]

Margaret Bondfield took enthusiastically to the Guild, remembering much later the 'outstanding' women Margaret had gathered around her, like Lilian and Rosalind. But while she was an impressive and effective campaigner, she did not share Margaret's easy rapport with Guildswomen. When she led a 1914 discussion about maternity care, the Guild audience laughed at her bald statement that women should notify public health authorities as soon as they knew they were pregnant. With no insight into what might lie behind their response, an angry Margaret Bondfield went straight into lecturing mode: '[she] could not understand the amusement ... it seemed as if the women here were ashamed of themselves ... Motherhood was a sacred and beautiful thing.'[451] Nevertheless, she made an impressive contribution to the Guild's campaigns.

A grant – but who to?

In the early summer of 1913, government plans for a tidying up amendment bill on national insurance presented a fresh opportunity. Early lobbying indicated that Ministers would concede on two demands: to abolish a prescribed fee for doctors' maternity care, and, as previously demanded, to provide four weeks' sick pay to insured women around the birth of a child. Margaret had thought that they might also agree to make a maternity grant paid on the basis of her husband's insurance contributions the property of his wife. But when the new amendment bill was published on 24 June, these hopes were dashed. Coming hard on the heels of a worrying dispute about divorce at that year's Guild Congress, this must have been a blow.

Undaunted, Margaret and Margaret Bondfield found a sympathetic MP to take forward their demand for the maternity grant to be paid to the wife. They had a mountain to climb, as the amendment was due to be discussed in a House of Commons committee in only a few weeks' time. The situation was all the more difficult because, in the event, none of the other women's organisations which had campaigned for the maternity grant agreed with Margaret's proposal that the grant should be the wife's property. The Guild was on its own.

Margaret's tactical skills came to the fore during the lightning campaign which followed. 337 Guild branches answered the call, while she and Margaret Bondfield lobbied carefully selected MPs, backing their arguments with real life examples gathered from the Guild and elsewhere. They publicised the Guild's proposals widely in the press, from *The Times* to *Reynolds News*, and even managed to gain support from a number of the approved societies which administered insurance benefits.

The Guild's arguments, deemed 'persuasive and convincing' by the *Manchester Guardian*, were carefully framed. They agreed that the vast majority of men would pass the maternity grant to their wives, but suggested that explicit legal provision was needed to prevent the possibility of abuse. They also reiterated Margaret's argument that because of the wife's unpaid work in the home, in reality she and her husband had contributed equally to the insurance scheme.

The parliamentary committee debate took place on 26 July, and Margaret pulled out all the stops. Margaret Bondfield arranged for Central Committee members to attend the proceedings, while Margaret and Lilian are said to have come accompanied by a barrister; presumably to help them feed suitable arguments to supportive MPs.

It soon became clear that the Guild had lost friends. Liberal minister Charles Masterman, who had earlier been sympathetic to including a maternity grant in the insurance scheme, spoke against the proposal that it should be paid to the mother or to someone nominated by her.[452] He argued that abuse by husbands was rare, and that the amendment, if passed, would cause, 'great resentment among the working classes'. It must have been hard for Margaret to hear the (male) Labour members on the Committee vehemently agreeing with him.

Trade unionist George Roberts led the Labour attack, arguing that the Guild-backed amendment constituted 'unnecessary interference by the state between a man and his wife'. He proposed a compromise: that either husband or wife could receive the payment, but the husband would be legally bound to pay it to the wife, or to use it to maintain her and the child. Labour Party chair Ramsay Macdonald dealt a major blow when he announced that the Women's Labour League, which was affiliated to the party, did not feel strongly on the question; more, that Labour did not see the benefit as belonging to the mother alone.

After a heated debate in which the Guild had to rely on a Conservative to propose its amendment, the Committee decided that the benefit was the woman's and should be paid to her 'in some fashion'. This was only the beginning, however. The final decision would be made a couple of weeks later, at the bill's 'report stage' in the full House of Commons.

To her chagrin, Margaret now had to rely not on her natural Labour allies, but on Conservatives. She wrote to Leonard Woolf, 'We are now up to our ears preparing for Report stage ... when the [Insurance) Commissioners and the Labour Party are going to try to defeat us ....' Furious at what she termed Macdonald's 'incredibly bad behaviour', she went on, 'What with the negotiation and all the doings , + our supporters + failing friends it's all a nightmare when one gets a little outside it'.[453]

In the days before the report stage, Margaret and Margaret Bondfield again lobbied sympathetic MPs. At breakneck speed, they gathered 681 signatures on a petition in favour of payment to the mother from officials and professional in the field: 'councillors, midwives, nurses, members of insurance committees, sanitary inspectors and health visitors, poor law guardians ... doctors ...' and more.[454] They sent this to all MPs and publicised it widely. The *Daily News*, the *Manchester Guardian* and the *New Statesman* all came out in support.

When the report stage debate took place on 6 August, there was a vigorous fight. Once more, George Roberts moved his proposal for either husband or wife to be entitled. He was backed by Masterman, and by all the Labour MPs except Philip Snowden. After a tumultuous debate, a slightly amended version of Roberts's proposal passed with a majority of nine. Apparently, the campaign was lost.

But proceedings rapidly descended into farce. As is still the procedure, MPs registered votes for and against by filing through different lobbies. Because this was a free vote, they had not been guided by the party whips as usual, and so some MPs who supported the Guild realised they had gone the wrong way. The confusion was perhaps understandable, as 'Members before both lobbies were shouting "This way for protecting the women!"'[455]

Lord Robert Cecil, a Conservative backbencher primed by the Guild, saved the day. He swiftly moved an 'amendment to the amendment', providing that the husband could only claim the payment if specifically authorised by his wife. After a little more debate, this passed with a majority of 21. Parliament had finally confirmed that the maternity grant was the mother's property. This was rightly seen as the Guild's achievement, the *New Statesman* declaring 'We take our hats off to Miss Llewelyn Davies and Miss Bondfield in recognition of a singularly successful campaign on behalf of married women'.[456] And it had a wider significance. As Margaret herself later emphasised, this was 'the first public recognition of the woman's place in the home, and a new step towards some economic independence for wives'.[457]

Although Margaret normally loved campaigning, all this had taken its toll. Later on, she was able to present the whole thing light-heartedly. But at the time, she was worn out. On top of her continuing anxiety about her father's health, and the frantic pressure of work during those crucial weeks, she was profoundly disturbed by the isolation from her natural allies. Labour MPs' attitude seems to have come as a shock to Margaret, although with hindsight it was perhaps predictable that they would think that her proposal undermined the husband's status as head of the family; and also, by reducing the need for a family wage, weakened trade unionists' bargaining power.[458]

Margaret had worked consistently over the years with labour women's organisations, including recently on the original national insurance bill, and Margaret Bondfield was closely associated with them. Their lack of support on this issue must have been galling. However, just as on other occasions, external events – in this case the timetable of the amendment bill – meant that Margaret did not feel she had time to discuss with potential allies and bring them on side. While some key labour women were committed to the family wage and would have opposed her proposal, those who supported state-provided endowment of motherhood might have been expected to have backed it. They may have resented Margaret going it alone without consultation, and in any case may well not have seen this as a priority.[459]

In the event, Margaret's ability to react quickly paid off; even if it meant going out on a limb. By grasping the opportunity to put into practice, though in a small way, theoretical arguments about wives' rights to their own independent income, she actually achieved something remarkable. The principle of payment to the wife, included when family allowances, were introduced decades later, was now an accepted part of the system. Margaret's feminist perspective on the seemingly private world of the family had produced a significant result.

Part 2: Money is Not Enough

Fortunately, Margaret regained her equilibrium within a short time of this battle, and with it her customary energy and dynamism.

What did mothers and babies need?

Margaret had never seen the maternity grant as a cure-all. It was too low, many women were too poor to benefit, and in any case, mothers and babies needed much more than a cash grant. Years before, she had suggested 'a great National Health Crusade' for free maternity care. Now, she and Margaret Bondfield kick-started a new and ambitious project.

Since the 1890s, a falling birth rate and high infant mortality among the poor had led to increasing public anxiety about the future of the 'British race'. A new and influential movement to improve infant welfare came into being. Organised by a mix of charities and local authorities, increasing numbers of health visitors checked on mothers and babies at home, while infant welfare centres, often called 'schools for mothers', sprang up, offering advice about feeding and baby care. Many centre workers were volunteers, usually middle class, and the main focus was on educating and instructing poor mothers, often perceived as ignorant and/or feckless. Little emphasis was put on alleviating the poverty, insanitary housing and lack of medical care which played a major part in causing infant deaths.

Although the result could be intrusive and patronising, it did not have to be so. Margaret would have concurred with Sylvia Pankhurst's criticism of the 'purse-proud patronage and snobbery' permeating much charitable infant welfare work, but would also have shared her view that, for all their limitations, infant welfare centres could provide poor mothers with welcome support.[460] Some years earlier, in the course of suggesting that the Guild might take up other countries' examples of co-operative-run welfare services, she herself had floated the idea that branches might organise 'schools for mothers'. Indeed, Sarah Reddish and her local Guild, working with other groups, had set one up in Bolton which ran very successfully for years. The Women's Labour League, too, had its own mother and baby centre in North Kensington.

More recently, Margaret had dropped the idea of Guild-run health and welfare services, and now saw state funding as the solution. Just as in the campaign about co-operation and the poor, she started with research. Beginning in October 1913, working with Margaret Bondfield, she contacted government departments and local officials, from midwives and doctors to public health officials and sanitary inspectors; travelling to Bradford, Sheffield and Birmingham to find out about promising infant welfare work going on locally.

At least as important as this background research was Margaret's decision, drawing on the experience of the divorce campaign, to find out from mothers themselves about their experiences and what they wanted. At this time, long before the advent of the NHS and modern social security benefits, if women could not afford to pay for maternity care themselves they had to fall back on whatever charitably-run medical services they could find, or do without.

Late in 1913 Margaret wrote to around 600 current or past Guild officials, asking them to reply to her 'privately', describing their experience of maternity. In an echo of the investigative approach she had become familiar with in Sunderland, she also asked them to enumerate their pregnancies, miscarriages and infant deaths, and for details of their husbands' occupations and wages. The 386 replies that she received revealed shocking poverty and suffering. They fundamentally affected how she saw the problem.

Margaret later wrote that these letters provided some of the most valuable material she collected during her research. In line with the age profile of Guildswomen, many of the writers were now middle aged. Some covered page after page, reliving what they had gone through years earlier. As active Guildswomen they were used to helping and campaigning for others, rather than thinking of themselves as in need. They had not been the poorest mothers whose deficiencies so preoccupied infant welfare workers. Yet Margaret confessed that she found their letters too harrowing to read straight through one after the other. How much worse would the experience of maternity have been for less well-off women?

Nearly one in four of the women who replied had lost at least one child before its first birthday, and there were high rates of miscarriage and stillbirth. While some recounted positive maternity experiences, the majority told a very different story. Writer after writer graphically described the ill-health and exhaustion caused by frequent pregnancies and lack of medical care:

> For fifteen years I was in a very poor state of health owing to continual pregnancy. As soon as I was over one trouble, it was all started over again. In one instance, I was unable to go further than the top of the street the whole time owing to bladder trouble, constant flow of water. With one, my leg was so terribly bad I had constantly to sit down in the road when out, and stand with my leg on a chair to do my washing. I have had four children and *ten* miscarriages ...[461] [original emphasis]

Women became seriously ill as a result of inadequate or non-existent medical treatment, and/or lack of proper care from a nurse or midwife – if indeed they could afford one at all. Although they often wished they had known more about how to look after themselves when pregnant, many did not have the money, or the extra help with heavy housework and childcare, to follow medical advice to rest and eat well.

If there was not enough money to feed a family, the mother came last. As one woman explained:

I nearly lost my life through want of nourishment, and did after nine months of suffering lose my child. No-one but mothers who have gone through the ordeal of pregnancy half starved, to finally bring a child into the world to live a living death for nine months, can understand what it means ...[462]

Many made a point of saying they wished they had known more about procreation before they got married. Desperately wanting to limit their pregnancies, some simply relied on abstinence, and a number wished they had known about contraception and abortion: the former frowned on, the other illegal. A mother of three who had previously unsuccessfully attempted an abortion, described how

Many a time I have sat ... a baby two and a half years old at my back, one sixteen months and one one month on my knees, and cried for very weariness and hopelessness. I fed them all as long as I could, but I was too harassed, domestic duties too heavy, and the income too limited to furnish me with a rich nourishing milk ... [463]

Even though most Guildswomen had husbands on relatively good wages, there was frequently not enough money to provide for a large family. And crucially there was no safety net against hard times. If a woman became pregnant while her husband was off sick, on short time or laid off work, as was common, she frequently had to take on casual work even when unwell – if only to scrape together a little money for the birth, in order to pay for an unskilled midwife or a doctor's visit.

And while some women described loving, considerate husbands, not all were so fortunate. As Guildswomen's responses during the divorce campaign had exposed, belief in a husband's 'conjugal rights' was still strong.

... within a few days of the birth ... she [a woman] is tortured again. If the woman does not feel well she must not say so, as a man has such a lot of ways of punishing a woman if she does not give in to him.[464]

It is remarkable that Guildswomen volunteered their intimate stories to Margaret, and specifically in order to help the maternity campaign. This is startling testimony not only of their personal courage but also of the trust and sense of community within the Guild, and which Margaret herself also inspired. Many letters included expressions of hope for a better future for women, support for 'our' maternity campaign, or ideas about the proposed maternity scheme. A few wrote as if to Margaret personally, for example, 'While I am writing I almost fancy I am talking to you. I hope I have not tired you with this letter.'[465]

Perhaps even more than in the divorce campaign, Margaret was now confronted by suffering normally hidden behind what she later called the 'thick curtain that falls on ... married life'.[466] This affected her deeply, and fuelled her commitment to changing conditions for mothers.

Although Margaret herself was childless, the maternity letters may have struck a personal chord. One of the closest relationships of her life was with her mother, who had had seven children in ten years. Margaret, the only girl, was the second eldest and her early years were punctuated by the births of five brothers. Hers was a comfortably-off family which could afford servants, and we know from the 1871 census that when the three youngest were all under five, there was at least one nurse living in, as well as a cook and a maid.[467] So, unlike Guildswomen, Margaret's mother had plenty of help. From what we know about Margaret, on some level she would have made, and felt, the comparison.

The plan for the 'National Care of Maternity'

Drawing both on Guildswomen's letters and on their other research, Margaret drew up a Guild maternity scheme, together with Margaret Bondfield, in spring and early summer 1914. This built on current thinking about improving babies' welfare, but turned it around to include their mothers' welfare, which it put centre stage. The scheme linked baby care advice with medical, financial and practical help, gave decision-making control to local authorities rather than charities or private insurance bodies, and above all insisted that women, and working women to boot, should play a leading part in running the scheme.

It proposed radical change to Lloyd George's maternity grant. Local authorities would now administer new, increased maternity benefits which would no longer require insurance contributions. Authorities would also have to ensure that there was a wide range of local services, based around what the plan, significantly, termed '*maternity and* infant welfare centres'. These would serve not only babies, but pregnant women, new mothers and children from birth to starting school. They would offer advice about baby care, but also minor medical treatment, and would be linked with well trained, well paid health visitors and midwives (i.e. not volunteers). In an attempt to address some of the problems recounted in Guildswomen's letters, there would be home helps, maternity homes and designated maternity beds in hospitals. Similarly, where medically recommended, mothers would receive free dinners and, in some cases, free milk. The scheme also urged the creation of municipal milk depots, already provided in some places because the milk generally on sale was expensive and often polluted.

All this, it was proposed, would be funded by central government but controlled by new local maternity sub-committees which would be attached to local authorities' public health committees. These sub-committees, the scheme emphasised, should be largely composed of working women. The plan also called for compulsory notification of births, to enable contact to be made with new mothers, and suggested that a Ministry of Health should be created, with a maternity department at least partly staffed by women.[468]

When a paper by Margaret Bondfield outlining an early version of the plan went to Guild conferences in early spring 1914, they overwhelmingly endorsed it, as did the Guild Congress a few months later. As one speaker declared, for her 'the scheme was coming fifty years too late; but what a grand and glorious privilege it was to be able to work for others'.[469] As with maternity benefit, there were some Guildswomen who distrusted state welfare on principle, and the conferences raised several other queries: concern about having to tell the authorities about births, suggestions that mothers might be wary of municipally-run centres, and ambivalence about more health visitors coming uninvited into the home. But overall the response was hugely positive.

Campaigning for the plan

In tandem with Margaret Bondfield, Margaret now steamed into action. Supported by allies such as the Women's Labour League and the Fabian Women's Group, they took every opportunity to publicise their scheme, lobbying doctors and public health officials, meeting ministers, and publishing letters and articles in *The Times*, the *Manchester Guardian* and other newspapers. With their combined contacts, skills and experience the two women operated a more sophisticated lobbying campaign than Margaret alone had previously achieved. It appears that Margaret Bondfield did more of the public speaking, and Margaret more of the press work. They made a formidable team.

The campaign came at a good time, when it was able to tap into changing thinking about infant welfare. Margaret's writings and speeches show her skilfully helping to shift the terms of the debate. For example, she contributed two unsigned articles to *The Times*, headed in conventional, imperial terms '*Mothers of the Race*'. These nevertheless outlined the Guild's scheme, drawing on the maternity letters to highlight the impact of mothers' poverty.[470] Commenting in the *Manchester Guardian* a few months later on a recent conference about infant mortality, Margaret felt less need to pull her punches:

> In seeking how to save infant life, the first thing of all to consider is the daily life of working women. It has to be remembered that the whole of the housework and the care of children and husband falls on the mother who, too, is often obliged to add wage-earning to her unpaid work in the home. Carrying her unborn child, she stands for hours at her washtub, reaches to hang up clothes, carries heavy weights, nurses husband and child when ill, baths and carries her other children, goes out to char or wash or sits at home sewing to provide for midwife or doctor, goes without food she ought to have, and all the time is worn with anxiety as to how to make ends meet.

We can see the impact of Guildswomen's letters here. And Margaret went on to a bolder challenge to accepted wisdom, attacking terms like 'schools for mothers' on the grounds that they obscured what a mother really needed: 'adequate money of her own, through increased maternity and pregnancy sickness benefits, and individual medical advice and treatment'.[471]

These were progressive ideas for the time, but there was more. As in a speech to London Medical Officers of Health, Margaret insisted that mothers wanted state provision, not charity and philanthropy. And explaining her vision of 'partnership of the individual woman with the State and science', she argued that 'while the remarkable public spirit of working women will lead them voluntarily to do what is for the good of others', they would 'resent any legal encroachment on their freedom of action'.[472]

The scheme's emphasis on local authority rather than charitable services fitted in with Beatrice Webb's ideas about reforming welfare provision, and the Webbs and the Fabian Society backed it. But Margaret and Beatrice Webb were light years apart. For a start, Beatrice kept aloof from the feminist movement. For her part, Margaret rejected the Fabian policy of achieving socialism from above, through permeation of existing institutions; instead sharing the humanistic socialism of the ILP. Margaret confided in Dolly Ponsonby that she 'really couldn't stomach' Beatrice Webb, criticising her lack of 'real burning love for humanity' and her mechanistic approach to social welfare: 'Mrs Webb thinks it would be so nice for the poor to be inspected regularly, their children put to bed by officials.'[473] So, although Margaret had to value their influential support, she firmly rejected the Webbs' characteristic social invitations.[474] Reading between the lines of her letters, we can almost hear her gritting her teeth: 'You'll be surprised to hear we've had to join hands with the Sidney Webbs + the [New] Statesman – which now backs us for all it is worth every week.' She went on to declare, with heavy irony, 'Mrs W is becoming quite an extreme feminist'.

> The Webbs' support is very amusing + also valuable just now. They are wirepullers. They instruct Samuel [Herbert Samuel, President of the Local Government Board], + even got Ll G [Lloyd George] to dine the other night ... Their patronage of the Guild every week in the Statesman is entertaining.[475] [original abbreviations]

The government would still not countenance changes to the national insurance maternity grant, but in a tribute to the campaign, Herbert Samuel did come on board about the rest of the scheme (perhaps due to all those instructions from the Webbs?) In July 1914 he issued a path-breaking circular to local authorities urging them to take up many of the Guild's maternity proposals – with the carrot that central government would meet 50 per cent of any costs. This was indeed a result. An overjoyed Margaret declared that this 'opened a new era for the mothers of the country'.[476]

Then, on 4 August, the First World War broke out.

Part Three: Mothers and Babies in Wartime

Shifting opinion

The war gave a powerful impetus to the maternity campaign. Stimulated by fears for Britain's capacity to produce healthy fighting men, infant welfare work was now seen as a form of war work. Both media and policymakers increasingly glorified motherhood, and maternity care came onto the public agenda in a new way.

Margaret recognised the potential opportunity. Within weeks of war breaking out, she wrote to *The Times* urging the local relief committees which were coming into being to give special care to mothers and babies. In October she helped to organise a broad-based deputation to a sympathetic Herbert Samuel, still the relevant government minister. Margaret later remembered, gleefully, how this included not only 'experts' but also ordinary women. 'It was a new thing one day when a lot of mothers and babies invaded Whitehall to tell Mr H. Samuel what they wanted.'[477]

Margaret presented the popular maternity scheme to members as 'the Guild's great contribution to the problems of the war'.[478] Over the next couple of years, official reaction provided at least a degree of satisfaction. Among other things, an act was passed confirming local authorities' legal power to provide maternal and infant welfare services, the government once again recommended local maternity sub-committees, and depots were set up selling baby milk at cost price.

Meanwhile Margaret took every opportunity to publicise the Guild's demands and decided to find a wider audience for Guildswomen's letters. Leonard and Virginia Woolf, to whom she had passed them on, both pushed her to do so. Leonard offered to draft an introduction, while Virginia tried unsuccessfully to interest her half-brother Gerald Duckworth in publishing them. Undeterred, Margaret found another publisher, and *Maternity: Letters from Working Women* came out in September 1915.[479] Edited by her, it contained 160 of the letters she had received. And it is worth noting that when asked for permission to publish their letters, only six women refused.

The book included a brief but glowing foreword from Herbert Samuel, along with details of the Guild's maternity proposals and Samuel's 1914 circular. Margaret herself wrote a lengthy, hard-hitting introduction highlighting the impact of poverty and lack of skilled treatment and advice, but also, more controversially, 'the personal relation of husband and wife'. She challenged the glorification of womanly self-sacrifice, suggesting that mothers' current predicament was leading to, 'a kind of strike against large families'. Finally, she reiterated that maternity care should be provided by the state, not by charities. Mothers should feel, 'as free to use a Municipal Maternity Centre as they are to use a Council School or a Public Library'.[480]

Maternity proved a runaway success; two editions quickly sold out, to glowing reviews. The *British Medical Journal* recommended it to doctors, particularly obstetricians, *The Times* praised its 'notable interest and singular distinction', while the ILP's *Labour Leader* called it 'the authentic voice of our working women mothers, imparting to the world a knowledge which the most rigid scientist cannot affect to disbelieve, a knowledge of their suffering'.[481] The climate was receptive. Two months later, an eminent doctor urged a prestigious meeting on the care of mothers and babies, 'See that every mother has proper and sufficient food, and rest and relief from heavy work, and you will have gone a long way to solving the problems before us.'[482] So influential opinion was shifting, and *Maternity* played its part.

Progress and challenge

At the beginning of 1917, Lord Rhondda, now the relevant minister, urged the creation of a Ministry of Health which would take over the health responsibilities of the poor law and national insurance, and even, it was suggested, provide some free services for women and children. Needless to say, Margaret wasted no time in securing a meeting. She presented Lord Rhondda with a copy of *Maternity*, and a lengthy Memorandum which outlined again the demands in the Guild's original maternity scheme. Again, she stressed that working-class women must be involved in the local maternity sub-committees. Otherwise, she suggested, the care might be too institutional, and also 'there might be differentiation between married and unmarried mothers, inquiries into family circumstances might be made, while doctors might insist on notification of pregnancy'.[483]

Margaret followed this up with what she later described as one of the Guild's most impressive delegations. Some Guildswomen who came had first hand experience of sitting on local maternity committees, and pulled no punches. They described the impact of appalling housing conditions; for example, mothers in Durham mining villages often had to give birth in front of their children, because one of their only two rooms was reached by a ladder, and open to the roof. Mrs Taylor and Mrs Lawton bluntly criticised charity workers, declaring that they often came with 'inquisitorial methods that to the honest working woman are well, abominable'. Mrs Lawton also recounted how mothers would rather do without help than be subjected to humiliating personal enquiries. Rather than encountering abuse of the free dinner service, 'We found, on the contrary, that the difficulty is, even among the poorest mothers, to get them to come'.

Margaret used the occasion to good effect, turning the Memorandum and speeches into a pamphlet which she circulated widely to an enthusiastic audience, ranging from civil servants and local public health officials to trades councils and other labour organisations.

And influential opinion had continued to change. Later in the year, Lord Rhondda, now the Government's Food Controller, spoke at the inaugural meeting of a high profile 'Baby Week' listing a series of priorities that could have come straight from the Guild. As well as pure milk, he argued, there must be, 'cleaner and healthier homes, proper food and care for expectant and nursing mothers, more maternity centres, more health visitors, and more skilled attention for mother and children'. The meeting unanimously adopted a resolution moved by the Duchess of Marlborough which demanded 'improved housing and sanitation, together with adequate provision for the care of maternity and infancy in their own district'.[484] While Margaret's more radical demands were still not generally accepted, times were definitely changing.

The problem remained that local authorities were not legally obliged to set up maternity services. Many refused. Some pleaded lack of money while others were just not interested.[485] As with the minimum wage campaign the battle had to be won in each area, and hard-headed local decision-makers had other pressures to contend with.

Margaret had gone into action about this early on, pressing Guild branches to make maternity care a campaigning priority, setting up a special fund, and deploying her extensive networks into play. As well as the Women's Labour League and the Railway Women's Guild, who were already involved, she brought in other labour, trade union and women's organisations and the National Union of Women's Suffrage Societies even provided an office and temporary organiser.[486] Clearly, this relatively uncontroversial campaign could attract broad support.

Margaret enthusiastically recorded local progress in her annual reports and *Women's Corner*, often employing popular rhetoric such as 'saving the nation's babies' to galvanise Guildswomen. By 1915, 71 branches had already started lobbying alongside other local organisations, but progress was slow.[487] Two years later, only fifty local authorities had taken the first step and established maternity sub-committees. And even when the 1918 Maternity and Child Welfare Act made such maternity committees compulsory, it did not compel them to organise any actual services. It clearly had an effect, though, as by spring 1919, Margaret was able to record a total of 122 new committees, in addition to others established before the Act came into force.

Overall, Margaret considered the maternity campaign one of the most important she ever undertook. It certainly demonstrated her strengths and those of the Guild as a whole Although it would be a long time before her vision of comprehensive, state run maternity services was achieved, the campaign's detailed proposals helped to shape ideas about future maternity services, and provided a focus for a broad based campaign in alliance with other organisations. Led by Margaret, with its co-ordination and support for local action across the country, the Guild was able to influence both national and local policy. Most importantly, the campaign put mothers' own experience and needs on the map, and kept them there. Margaret's personal vision played a central part in this.

The experience of the maternity campaign definitely affected Margaret's developing ideas about the position of women in the home. She summarised her current thinking in 1918 when she contributed, as an individual, not on behalf of the Guild, to a Labour Party book aimed at women who were now entitled to vote for the first time. Significantly, this was the first time that she had identified herself publicly with the Party.

In a chapter on 'the claims of mothers and children', Margaret explained the Guild's maternity scheme and acknowledged the urgent need to tackle poverty. She went on to make more challenging points, alluding to the 'thick curtain' behind which, until recently, a married woman's life and domestic labour had been undertaken 'in isolation + obscurity'. She praised women's demand for autonomy and vehemently criticised 'customs which impose a disastrous silence and ignorance on all questions connected with sex'. The current condition of marriage and motherhood was, she claimed, 'entirely out of keeping with democratic ideals of freedom, justice and equality, and fatal to the well-being of the nation'.[488] And once again, Margaret took the opportunity to attack married women's economic dependence. She went on to argue for the endowment of motherhood, for reform of the divorce laws, for equal treatment of married and unmarried mothers, and for the removal of the stigma attached to illegitimacy.

All in all, a challenging agenda for the Labour Party.

CHAPTER 14

In Time of War, 1914-1918

Part 1: Margaret's Home Front

In midsummer 1914, things were looking up for Margaret. The government had backed the maternity scheme; and, to her relief and delight, the Guild had refused to give in to the co-operative leadership's bullying over the divorce campaign. Happily absorbed in work, she would have agreed with Margaret Bondfield that talk of war was 'mere sabre-rattling'.

At the end of July, though, everything changed. Suddenly, war was imminent. The Guild pulled out all the stops to help arrange a last-minute women's peace rally, but it was all too late. On the very day the rally took place, Britain declared war on Germany.

This was a devastating blow. We can infer Margaret's feelings from those of like-minded friends. Helena Swanwick recalled an overwhelming 'rending pity, a horror of black darkness', while Bertrand Russell wrote to Margaret in anguish, 'I had never believed anything so frightful could happen ... I feel it *utter madness* for us to join this war. I try to fix my thoughts on the future – the present is too unbearable.' [original emphasis][489]

For Margaret, the general horror was compounded by personal grief. Her father's health was now failing, and he was not expected to survive for long. Then in March 1915 the family, like so many others, suffered an early, dreadful loss. George – Arthur and Sylvia's oldest son – was killed in action at the age of 21. When Margaret steeled herself to break the news to her father, he suffered such a frightening relapse that for a while she was unable to leave him.

Except for Margaret's two years at Girton, she and her father had always shared a home; initially with the rest of the family but, since her mother's death twenty years earlier, mostly on their own. In spring 1916, when 90-year-old Llewelyn was fading fast, she wrote that 'he is taking very little nourishment now ... He realizes the change – + in a strange natural + unnatural way talks of his end.'[490] That end finally came on 18 May.

Fortunately, Margaret did not have to face her grief alone; she had her brothers and her close women friends. Leonard Woolf immediately offered to help, recalling how Margaret had supported him during Virginia Woolf's breakdown the previous year. Uncharacteristically tentative, Margaret responded: 'If you could take a turn on the [Hampstead] Heath morning afternoon or evening, + would have a little rest here, it would be comforting to see you ...'[491]

Her father's great age and lengthy illness evidently made the loss easier to bear. Only two months later, Margaret wrote, 'However painful ... it has seemed so natural, and right in the midst of all the horrors of loss of young life.' And, in another letter, 'you cannot bear to let them go ... but there is a wonderful calm afterwards when the peace beyond understanding comes at the close of a fine life with its precious memories.'[492]

John Llewelyn Davies was still remembered, both in the Church and more widely. His funeral, conducted by the Bishop of Chester, was attended not only by a number of his eminent friends but also by the Master of Trinity, his old Cambridge college, and even by a representative of King George – presumably because of his previous post as honorary chaplain to Queen Victoria.[493] Margaret, who openly opposed the war, would have found this gathering of the great and good somewhat alien, though she would have appreciated the recognition, for her father's sake.

She would surely have been pleased, too, that her father's name also meant something in those other circles which meant more to her. The Working Men's College and the Guild both sent representatives to the funeral, and lengthy appreciations appeared not only in *The Times*, but also in *Co-operative News*. A remarkable personal tribute came from atheist Bertrand Russell, who wrote to Margaret:

> It is a wonderful thing to have lived consistently and nobly through such a long life – to have remained free in mind and spirit ... I had a very profound admiration for your father – his stoicism + courage + disinterestedness + real liberality of outlook were a perpetual encouragement.[494]

Her father had completely accepted Margaret's commitment to the Guild, and made no difficulties about its gradual encroachment into their home. Margaret was proud of him and made a point of publicly praising his achievements. Although herself without religious belief, she was strongly influenced by his Christian Socialist ideals. Nevertheless, over the years she had become much more radical. One does wonder what Llewelyn felt about Margaret's campaign for divorce law reform, in which she clashed directly with Anglican worthies, spoke publicly about sex and abortion and was pushed into publicly declaring her lack of religion. Later, too, father and daughter almost certainly disagreed about the war.[495]

After meeting John Llewelyn Davies at a lunch party, not long before his stroke, Dolly Ponsonby confided to her diary,

> Dear old Mr Davies was so charming & modest + retiring + yet so full of quiet humour. He talked about Margaret being so keen on so many things + he said – "Do you feel as strongly as she does on divorce?" I said yes. "Oh, said he with a charming smile, I rather hoped you'd say *you did not.*"[496] [original emphasis]

This was perhaps as far as he would go in implicitly criticizing his formidable daughter.

Once the initial impact of her loss had softened, Margaret was able to look around her and, perhaps, appreciate her new found freedom. For the first time in her life, she had only herself to consider. She already had some income of her own thanks to family bequests, but now, in her mid 50s, she was comfortably off. After various legacies, her father had divided his remaining estate between Margaret and her brother Harry. She inherited around £8,500.

Margaret did not take long to carve out a new home life. In February 1917, she moved a short distance from the imposing house in Hampstead Square to a smaller, though relatively spacious, mansion flat in Church Row, Hampstead. So she stayed very close both to the Guild office and to the Parish Church where her father had worshipped and was buried. The flat was in Margaret's name, but the 1918 electoral register, which included women for the very first time, shows that Lilian was now living there, too.

Part 2: Margaret and the Guild

War work and more

Margaret's first job was to ensure that the Guild kept going in wartime; by no means an easy task.

Money was very tight. From 1914 onwards, the withdrawal of the Co-operative Union's grant forced the Guild to manage on half of its normal funding. Despite fundraising, extra subscriptions from branches, and even a £100 loan from her own pocket, Margaret could not bridge the gap. This made difficulties for campaigning as well as administration – the latter hampered also by long term staff sickness. Margaret Bondfield, who had other irons in the fire anyway, resigned at the beginning of 1915, a few months before the special 'citizenship' fund which had financed her post ran out.

As we've seen, the maternity campaign provided a unifying focus for Guildswomen. But there was much more for them to do. The beginning of the war produced a temporarily chaotic situation, as men enlisted in their thousands and women and children were left penniless. Margaret immediately urged Guildswomen to join the local committees for the relief of distress which sprang up, and stressed the need, as with local maternity committees, for working-class women to have a voice. By the spring of 1915, nearly 500 Guildswomen had answered the call. Like other women's organisations, the Guild continued throughout the war to raise relief funds, and to provide what practical help it could.

It became increasingly obvious, though, that this was not enough. Although the initial chaos soon subsided, life on the home front was increasingly tough. Women flooded into jobs on trams and railways, in factories, offices, shops and especially in the hugely expanded munitions industry; and the Guild worked with other groups pressing for equal pay, for union rights, and for better working conditions. It protested loudly at rising food prices, and demanded an increase in the inadequate separation allowances paid by the government to servicemen's wives. Among other things, the Guild joined a successful feminist campaign against police surveillance of women receiving the allowances, and against stigmatising treatment of the unwed mothers of 'war babies'.

Needless to say, Margaret steered the Guild in all this, speaking on its behalf at national level. Later in the war she sat on various national committees including the Government's Food Commission, and the labour movement's Standing Joint Committee of Industrial Women's Organisations (SJCIWO). Sylvia Pankhurst vividly remembered her at one meeting, 'tender in her broad humanity', arguing against the 'cruelly' long working hours in munitions factories.'[497]

Conflict within the co-operative movement

The decision to withdraw the Guild's grant, taken shortly before war broke out, had shocked some male co-operators. An editorial in *Co-operative News* had insisted that whatever the immediate rights and wrongs, 'The triumphs standing to [the Guild's] credit, and its record of work well done are too precious for its hands to be shackled in the manner proposed'.[498]

Margaret's most urgent task was to try to regain this vital source of income. This proved more than difficult. In spring 1915, when hopes were raised informally, Margaret and Eleanor Barton (now Guild President) offered a compromise. But at the Co-operative Congress shortly after, the mood was hostile. Mrs Wimhurst, present as a delegate from her local Co-operative society, felt impelled to rise and object to 'sneering' about the Guild, and to a speaker who 'referred to wild cats'.[499] It came as no surprise that the Guild lost the vote by a substantial margin.

A couple of weeks later, the Guild's own Congress was still defiant. As one speaker put it, 'Much as we deplore the loss of the money – the freedom to control our own actions is much dearer to us.'[500]

The following year, while struggling with her father's final decline and death, Margaret found herself dealing with yet more conflict. Over the years she had consistently argued that education and campaigning were integrally linked, and insisted on the Guild's right to organise its own education classes for its members. However, this could be seen as a challenge to the movement's Central Education Committee (CEC) and its control over co-operative education. A dispute arose, in the course of which Margaret and Lilian wrote a paper for the Guild's 1916 spring conferences which argued for greater democracy.

The response to the paper was painful for Margaret. Some Guildswomen supported her, complaining that, 'when they wanted to study questions of national importance, they were told [by the CEC] the present was not an opportune time'. But she also faced considerable criticism. Some praised the CEC's classes, or argued that she was 'stirring up mud'. Then, on top of all this, an anonymous CEC member used the letters column of *Co-operative News* to mount a vituperative attack on Margaret and Lilian's paper. He went so far as to make personal accusations not only aimed at Margaret, but also at Leonard Woolf, who had written in to support her, referring to Woolf's 'almost Teutonic obliquity of vision'.[501] Although the editor closed the correspondence at the end of June, the dispute rumbled on.

Around the same time, an unusual drop in Guild membership led to other complaints. *Co-operative News*, resurrecting previous criticism, demanded: 'Has the power of the Guild as a progressive agent in the State detracted from its strength as a Co-operative body?' Margaret responded vigorously, pointing to inevitable wartime organisational problems. In the event, membership rallied again from 1917-18 onward,. but at the time it must have been worrying. At the Guild's 1916 Congress, just a couple of months after her father's death, Margaret uncharacteristically acknowledged the 'considerable stress and trial' she had suffered over the last year. This was surely an understatement.

Somehow, though, the Guild remained generally in good health. Despite reduced funds and the difficulties of wartime travel, the 1916 Congress managed to bring 750 delegates from around the country to London, to discuss everything from votes for women to conscription, peace and day nurseries for working mothers. Leonard Woolf penned an enthusiastic report, but then he was a friend and keen supporter. An interesting accolade came from a visitor from Ireland, who paid tribute to

> ... what I might term "the wonder of the rank and file" ... There were genuine flashes of humour; there were inimitable home thrusts, indicating that the working woman of today is keenly alive to what is going on in the sphere of public and political activity; there was the "human touch"... There was also in evidence that diversity of opinion indicative of life and health. The rank-and-file are thinking for themselves – the most hopeful sign in any organisation.[502]

Amid all the difficulties, this must have been music to Margaret's ears.

Resolution

Just when the outlook for regaining the movement's grant to the Guild seemed at its bleakest, the tide was about to turn. This was thanks to two apparently unrelated external changes.

In 1916 over three and a half million people were members of British co-operative societies, and with their families depended on the food they bought at co-operative shops. Yet the government completely denied the co-operative movement the same influence on wartime food and consumer policies which private business enjoyed. When it decided that a new tax on 'excessive profits' should be applied to co-operative societies' surpluses – which they used to finance dividends to members – that was the last straw. Outraged, co-operators set up a Co-operative Representation Committee in 1917, to organise their own candidates for the House of Commons. Margaret enthusiastically backed this new development.

Meanwhile, another major crucial change was also in the offing: this time, for women.

The outbreak of war had stopped the suffrage movement in its tracks. The Pankhursts immediately called a suffragette truce, and from then on enthusiastically backed the war. Millicent Fawcett's National Union of

Women's Suffrage Societies (NUWSS) also suspended campaigning, and concentrated on developing relief work. But as the war dragged on, the government was under pressure to do something about electoral reform – if only to respond to public pressure for all soldiers to be entitled to vote. In spring 1916, with rumours spreading about the possibility of introducing votes for women, the suffrage movement emerged into new life.

There was still disagreement about whether to demand adult suffrage, votes for all women as well as men. This now provoked particular hostility both within and outside parliament, because of fears that women, now outnumbering men by two million or more, would form a majority of the electorate. The issue came to the fore when the Government set up an all-party Speaker's Conference, meeting for the first time in October 1916, to design proposals on electoral reform. With the People's Suffrage Federation defunct, Margaret now joined the executive of a new National Council for Adult Suffrage, and the Guild also affiliated, taking part in a major London demonstration organised by the NCAS the following February.

The Speaker's Conference's eventual decision to introduce a much higher age threshold for women voters than for men was opposed by many in the suffrage movement. But in the end, while Margaret and other adult suffragists were particularly dissatisfied, all the suffrage leaders except Sylvia Pankhurst eventually bowed to what seemed to be the inevitable.

The act which finally passed in February 1918 was truly historic. While it finally granted the vote to all adult men over the age of 21, for the first time it also enfranchised women, over eight million of them. But to be included, a woman had to be over the age of thirty, and in addition either she or her husband had to qualify to vote under local government election rules – that is, they had to own or rent accommodation in their own right. Although Margaret put a positive spin on this partial victory, arguing that the Act gave the vote to 'practically all Co-operative women', it is worth noting that the new law excluded many of the women workers whose 'loyal war work', especially in munitions factories, it was said to recognise. As young, unmarried women living with their parents, they would not qualify. It would be another ten years before all adult women gained the vote.

Margaret did everything she could to encourage Guildswomen who qualified to take up their new rights. In February 1918 *Women's Corner* announced 'The vote is ours. The first thing to do – get registered!'[503] Other articles followed, explaining how women could take advantage of their new rights. Margaret also urged readers, where possible, to vote for co-operative candidates (in fact only ten stood nationwide in the 1918 election, and just one was successful). Penning a pamphlet for the Co-operative

Union entitled, '*The Vote At Last! More power to Co-operation*', she used the opportunity to stress women's 'basket power' as consumers, and the links between co-operators and trade unionists: 'If our Co-operative Party were to throw its great weight on the workers' side, we might ... secure a Parliament and a Government which would place the lives of the people before the interests of wealth and class.'[504]

As election day approached, the *Corner* pressed Guildswomen to help wherever there was a local co-operative candidate. Days before the election, which was fixed for 14 December, an article headed 'Women, Arise!' exhorted members, 'Your responsibility next Saturday is great! March to the poll! Vote for Justice and for Right!'[505]

The Guild's work to harness women's support for the Co-operative Party does a great deal to explain a mellowing in the co-operative leadership's approach to the Guild towards the end of the war. This was also against the background of a generally leftward shift in labour movement opinion around this time. Despite some festering disputes, there was a new will to resolve the deadlock over the Guild's £400 grant.

Inevitably, there were a couple of false starts. But when fresh negotiations began in June 1918, after several months during which the Guild had loyally promoted the Co-operative Party, both sides were ready to compromise. An initial agreement was reached by September. The Guild would receive its grant each year on the basis of the previous year's annual report to the Co-operative Congress. If at any time the grant were withheld, the Board would have to give reasons. Significantly, it was also agreed that the Board and the Guild would meet at least once a year, 'to discuss the possibility of co-operating in work in which both organisations are interested'. The extent of the change was signalled when, for the first time in its history, the Guild was formally invited to send its own delegate to the Co-operative Congress, to give an address.[506] After four long years, the Guild had won.

Part 3: War and Peace

Sadly, though, for Margaret the war years had also brought even more painful conflicts; this time with fellow Guildswomen.

Against the tide

When the war began, Margaret and her anti-war friends had found themselves in a tiny minority. The TUC had agreed an industrial truce, and the Labour Party had abandoned its earlier opposition, leaving only the Independent Labour Party (ILP) to stand firm against the war. While men and boys trooped off in their thousands to enlist, voices for peace were swamped by war fever.

As trench warfare set in, Margaret lost much of her usual optimism. In a low moment, she wrote to Leonard Woolf:

> The only refuge to be found from the appallingness of things is in the thought of the possibility of a new civilisation without armaments and war being built up on the ruin now coming ... But my horrible fear is that we shall just sink back again.[507]

It is difficult to appreciate the courage that it took to stand up and publicly call for peace at this time. As Ramsay Macdonald put it, you were treated as if you were 'tainted with leprosy'.[508] Nevertheless, there were signs of opposition from early on – and women were at the forefront. As we've seen, women's suffrage would not return to the top of the political agenda for several years. For Margaret, as for many other feminists, ending the war was now the burning issue.

A women's anti-war movement began to take shape at the end of 1914, by which time over 90,000 British soldiers had already lost their lives. The first step was a heartfelt *'Open Christmas Letter'* to the women of Germany and Austria, published in an international suffrage paper on New Year's Day 1915. Declaring that 'our very anguish unites us', the letter urged women to unite across the battle lines to strive for peace; ending, 'We are yours in this sisterhood of sorrow'.[509]

Margaret and Lilian were among the hundred prominent British women who signed, many of whom Margaret already knew through the suffrage and labour movements. A response came through a few months later, signed by 155 German and Austrian women.

A split was emerging within the National Union of Women's Suffrage Societies, which as we have seen had suspended campaigning once the war started. When Dutch women went on to propose an International Women's Peace Congress, to take place in The Hague in April 1915, the NUWSS's refusal to send official representatives was the last straw for some leading activists who emphatically opposed Millicent Fawcett's line that talk of peace could be seen as treasonable. At this point, they resigned from its executive and began to organise a British delegation to The Hague.

Margaret gave her name to a General Committee of supporters and spread the word, using her position and contacts among co-operative women, while Lilian became a prominent figure in the Executive Committee which did much of the organising. With Eleanor Barton, a committed pacifist, now

Guild President, the Guild Central Committee agreed to back the Congress and to send her as official delegate. Other Guildswomen, too, were keen to go.

Against a background of press ridicule deriding them as a 'shipload of hysterical women' and, 'folly in petticoats', and government determination to thwart them, 180 British women tried to get to The Hague. Only three succeeded. This dramatic story, and that of the extraordinarily impressive Congress, has been told elsewhere.[510] Up to 1,200 women from twelve countries made it through to the Hague, and the Congress later sent envoys to travel across war-torn Europe, visiting political leaders to demand neutral mediation. But while there were some positive reactions, no single country agreed to be the first to commit.

When an international women's peace committee was set up in the wake of the Hague Congress, the NUWSS finally split irrevocably. A number of its leading lights became central to a British branch: the Women's International League (WIL, later the Women's International League for Peace and Freedom). The Guild joined WIL, and Eleanor Barton, now Guild President, represented it on the WIL executive. The organisation went on to campaign bravely for peace throughout the war.

We might have expected Margaret, a convinced pacifist and internationalist, to have been more involved with the Congress and with WIL than she was. But from early on, she had been faced with an agonising dilemma. Although she was committed to opposing the war, her dying father had to be her major priority, along with her responsibility to the Guild. In the latter, she had to be cautious. While there was a strong anti-war current, especially among its socialist members, others felt very differently. Many had soldier husbands or, more commonly, soldier sons. Like Sylvia Pankhurst, Margaret would have felt acutely the difficulty of 'having to tell the relatives of soldiers that the war was in vain'.[511]

Margaret's solution was two-fold. She supported peace organisation as an individual, rather than a Guild representative, and she avoided taking on much active responsibility. And while she promoted debates about war and peace within the Guild, initially she trod very carefully.

Early on she joined the Union of Democratic Control (UDC), which had been set up at the outbreak of war and was fiercely critical of the secret diplomacy which had preceded it. Demanding democratic control over foreign policy, the UDC promoted the principle of durable peace terms which would not involve annexation of territory or humiliate the loser. It became more outspoken from 1915, and increasingly campaigned directly for peace by negotiation. Moderate though it was, the UDC was seen as an important anti-war organisation and subject to press-fomented hostility; Arthur Ponsonby was beaten up on one occasion, Bertrand Russell was sacked from his university post, and members were subject to police raids. Prominent activists included not only Arthur Ponsonby and Bertrand Russell, but also Charles Trevelyan and Helena Swanwick, so this would have felt like a natural home to Margaret. She publicly backed the UDC and was elected to its General Council.

Margaret drew heavily on the UDC approach in her work within the Guild. Perhaps remembering the rows back in 1909, when she had wrongly assumed that the Guild would support the People's Suffrage Federation, she started cautiously. She organised discussions in spring 1915 about, 'how nations should live together' in future and made sure that *Women's Corner* included several articles about the Hague Congress. However, at the Guild's own Congress in June, the resolution she drafted was about ways of avoiding future wars rather than stopping this one. It linked permanent peace with democratic control of foreign policy, economic reforms including extension of co-operation and, of course, votes for women.

This went through without difficulty, but a few months later there was the first hint of trouble to come. Mrs Moxon, a long-standing branch secretary, resigned from the Guild; declaring in *Women's Corner* that she 'would not sign a petition for peace if it was not a peace which embodied those principles of justice and liberty for which so much precious blood has been spilt'.[512]

The Guild divided

As the relentless slaughter in the trenches dragged on, patriotic euphoria was gradually replaced by grim endurance. 1916 was a particularly terrible year. 21,000 British soldiers were killed in the first day of the battle of the Somme alone, most within a single hour.

Margaret continued to support peace movements, though still in a personal capacity. She remained on the committee of the Union of Democratic Control, and in April 1916 publicly demonstrated her support for the much vilified No Conscription Fellowship, which supported conscientious objectors, by appearing alongside other prominent sympathisers on the platform of its National Convention. Later in the year, she was to join the committee of the National Council Against Conscription, a spin-off from the NCF.

As the war situation worsened so, perhaps inevitably, did splits within the Guild. The Central Committee had sent a protest when plans for conscription were first announced, but when it asked branches to discuss the issue early in 1916, the lack of consensus was clear. Of the 254 branches that responded, only 112 were opposed to conscription, while 85 were in favour and 43 divided. It is not surprising that the Committee reluctantly turned down a request to join a committee for a negotiated peace, explaining that this did not have sufficient backing among Guildswomen.

Margaret's resolution for the 1916 Congress in June tested the waters, combining a protest against conscription with a demand for negotiations for a 'just and lasting peace'. Eleanor Barton, the mover, begged delegates to 'do the right thing at this time of crisis'. The resolution was indeed passed with a large majority, but only after a debate which revealed heartfelt disagreements.

However, by 1917 the public mood was beginning to shift. In February, the first Russian revolution, with its promise of ending the war, gave radical and peace movements a huge fillip. With no end in sight to the agony of trench warfare, life on the home front was more and more grim. There was increasing anger at rising rents, soaring food prices, and even food shortages. This was all intensified by the impact of conscription, curtailment of workers' rights and punitive restrictions on civil liberties. Anti-war feeling began to grow. Social unrest spread, with strikes and demonstrations nationwide.

Margaret welcomed the Russian revolution as 'transcendent'. The Central Committee, though, seems not to have been quite so enthusiastic. When the Guild was invited to a Workers' and Soldiers' Convention in Leeds, organised to bring together trade unionists, co-operators and socialists to celebrate the revolution, the Committee decided that if Margaret and Lilian attended, it should be at their own expense. Needless to say, they went ahead and did so.

The Russian revolution also gave a powerful boost to a radical new peace movement, spearheaded by working-class women. The Women's Peace Crusade linked opposition to the war with support for women's suffrage and protests against high prices, food shortages and repression of dissent. Its grass-roots protests and demonstrations erupted in industrial towns across Britain from 1917 onward.

Although many Guildswomen played a part in the Crusade, especially in the north-west, Margaret was careful not to suggest involving the Guild officially. But its spontaneous militancy, along with the increasingly radical mood of the times, helped to convince her to take a stronger anti-war line than before. The resolution she drafted for the Guild's 1917 Congress applauded the 'new hope' brought by the Russian Revolution and looked forward to a Russian co-operative state, 'which will lay the foundations for the International Co-operation essential to world-wide peace'. It went on to praise the Russian appeal for negotiations for a peace without conquest.[513]

If Margaret hoped that linking peace with international co-operation would gain broad support within the Guild, she was wrong. The debate on this resolution was unprecedently bitter. In a charged atmosphere, reflecting divisions in the country at large, opinions were noticeably more polarised than before. What is more, Guildswomen seemed to have lost the tolerance which had so impressed the observer from Ireland the year before. In an episode which would hitherto have been unimaginable, when Mrs Allen suggested that Guildswomen should consider 'for the sake of argument' what would happen if Britain were defeated, she was howled down and prevented from speaking.

Margaret's resolution was passed by 207 votes to 73. While she must have been relieved that a substantial majority of Guildswomen were in favour of a negotiated peace, a damaging split was clearly in the making. As 1917 wore on, this also came out in the correspondence, often acrimonious, in *Women's Corner*.

In March 1918 Germany broke through the Western Front and Britain and her allies were suddenly on the defensive. Bertrand Russell, facing a prison sentence for publishing an anti-war article, wrote to Margaret the following month: 'things are very despairing just now, it hardly seems to matter whether one is in prison or out.'[514]

By this time grass-roots anti-war movements had been gaining ground, and the Labour Party had begun to discuss possibilities for a negotiated peace. At the Guild's traditional evening meeting at the 1918 Co-operative Congress, one speaker was cheered when he declared himself a 'peace man'. Mr Maxwell, a leading co-operator, got a similar reaction when he called for the war to end, and for a League of Nations.

When it came to the Guild's Congress, though, the mood was very different. Buoyed up by the second, Bolshevik revolution in Russia the previous October, Margaret had drafted a long and wide-ranging resolution, which not only called for immediate peace by negotiation, without annexation of territory, but also for universal disarmament. It went on to demand international action to ensure that 'all Peoples ... substitute Co-operation for Capitalism and ... place a People's Government in power, thereby removing the chief causes of war, and creating those world wide economic and ethical foundations on which alone Peace and Freedom can rest'.[515]

This openly socialist plea will have been music to the ears of some Guildswomen, like those active in the Women's Peace Crusade. But, given the divisions in the Guild, it was probably a tactical mistake.

Moving the resolution, Eleanor Barton argued that any annexation of territory would only lead to more wars, while peace by negotiation would ensure that militarism was defeated. She ended, 'peace must not be left in the hands of the diplomats; it must be "A People's peace"'. But among other speakers, Miss Gration argued, 'How could they consider peace negotiations with "brutes" who bombed hospitals and torpedoed ships?' while on the other side, Mrs Close appealed for 'humanity and sanity'. The vote was close, and unusually, delegates insisted on a ballot rather than a show of hands. In a shattering result for Margaret, this showed that the resolution had been defeated by a decisive 399 to 336.[516]

The Guild's powerful socialist current had been consistently anti-war, and other Guildswomen too supported a negotiated peace. However, especially with the increased threat of a German victory, many members had been convinced by the press and government that to support peace moves would be to 'betray their nation by making them tools of Germany', and that the Allies were only fighting for, 'justice, righteousness and to crush Prussian oppression'.[517] While both sides opposed what they saw as militarism, they could not agree on causes or solutions.

In an article arguing for a negotiated peace, Lilian wrote presciently that a crushing defeat was likely to 'arouse that intense spirit of nationalism which never submits until it has, in its turn, overthrown its conquerors'. But others passionately concurred with the member who wrote that 'we can safely talk about peace negotiations when our brave fellows have kept the German menace from our shores'.[518]

Margaret was devastated by the Congress defeat and the deep divergences among Guildswomen that it exposed. However, the debate came at an inauspicious time. With Britain and the Allies temporarily embattled a German victory seemed all too possible. More broadly, she had clearly misjudged the mood of delegates. We have to ask whether she might have been more successful if she had gone for a straightforward demand that maximised the common ground, rather than a long and complex resolution linking peace with socialism.

When the armistice was finally announced in November, Margaret's message in *Women's Corner* once again linked peace with co-operation:

> The horrors of war are over. Let hatred and revenge die too, overcome by reconciliation ... May the workers of the world unite to remove all barriers, and create the Co-operative commonwealth in which alone peace can endure. [519]

Margaret penned this with special feeling. Her nephew Roland, Maurice's son, had been reported killed in action only weeks earlier. Rushing to be with his family, she wrote in her grief, 'The pain has been very great ... Oh to think that the war is almost over – But for us, it has come just too late'.[520]

CHAPTER 15

Entr'acte 2: Lilian

Margaret and Lilian Harris lived together for over 25 years, from 1918 until Margaret's death.

They had first met as far back as 1889, not long after Margaret moved to Kirkby Lonsdale. 24-year-old Lilian, trapped in a highly conventional middle-class home nearby, was desperate to do something with her life. She soon began helping Margaret with the Guild, and within a couple of years was roped in to accompany Mary Spooner, a more experienced volunteer, on a recruiting trip. The two young women travelled alone across the southwest and Wales, drumming up support for new Guild branches. At times, this must have been a baptism of fire for Lilian; in Newport, for example, five hundred men and women turned up to hear the two visitors. Despite its mock complaints, a rare surviving letter conveys Lilian's exhilaration at being let off the leash:

> Our meeting last night was the climax of our experiences. The chairman's address was a prayer, in which we were mentioned by name! He "thanked the Lord for the ladies who had come from a distance"!! Have you ever had a like experience?
>
> The next time you send your disciples out two and two it would be as well to enquire how far their tastes agree. We have not actually come to blows yet, but there is no knowing what another week of dirty Temp. [Temperance] inns and fleas may do! [521] [original abbreviations]

However, like many other young women from her background, Lilian still had to struggle for autonomy. Her parents had already been uneasy about the recruiting trip to the southwest. A few months later, when she fell ill while in London with Margaret, working on the trade union campaign, they exploded. In a reminder of the Llewelyn Davieses' relatively advanced views, Mary Davies recounted a fierce argument with the Harrises who, she complained, spoke of Lilian as if she were 'a naughty girl who has shown herself entirely incompetent to take care of herself'. Her father did not wish her to continue with the Guild, and in the Harrises' view, 'nothing can prosper that is done against a parent's wish'.[522]

Lilian somehow managed to bring her parents round; although there seem to have been no more campaigning trips. And in the end, she achieved her independence. When her family moved away in the late 1890s, she stayed on in Kirkby Lonsdale, sharing lodgings with another Guild volunteer for ten years or so before moving down to Hampstead not long after Margaret. She was now her own woman and, like Margaret, devoted to the Guild.

Margaret recognised Lilian's potential from early on. After stints as secretary of the Guild's north-western section and then as national cashier, Lilian was formally designated Assistant Secretary from 1901 and quickly made herself indispensable. In particular, she became central to the smooth running of the Guild's huge Congresses and to the production of the facts and figures about branches and membership which appeared in each Annual Report. She was a well-liked and trusted figure for Guildswomen, especially at Congress; always there to provide practical help and advice.

However, Lilian was much more than just a gifted administrator. Her contribution became essential to Margaret's success, both within and outside the Guild. Margaret Bondfield, who knew first-hand what it was to work on Guild campaigns, remembered that 'Margaret was our inspiration and driving force. Lilian was the practical mind which kept us on the rails of the possible.'[523] Tellingly, ex-Central Committee member Mrs Dewsbury concurred, writing that Margaret always took the long view but 'left Miss Harris and us to work out the details'.[524] Margaret herself acknowledged how much she came to rely on her friend's judgement.

Lilian was an able researcher and writer. While especially good with figures, she produced occasional pamphlets for the Guild, and indeed, in the 1920s, one for the Fabian Society. By nature more retiring than Margaret, she nevertheless stepped in to replace her at Congress in an emergency. As Margaret's campaigning became ever more ambitious, the two worked closely together, developing ideas on tactics and policy, for example on maternity benefits and suffrage. As the years went by, they worked more and more in tandem and were increasingly recognised as providing an ideal combination. It was not at all unexpected that the Guild paid joint tribute to the two women when they retired.

Photographs of the younger Lilian show her sporting either pince-nez or rather dashing spectacles. Her style was definitely that of the New Woman of the 1890s. She rejected the constrictions of contemporary fashion in favour of a neat shirt, sometimes with a tie, and as we have seen, intrigued the girls at the Sunderland settlement by wearing bloomers. She also sometimes rode a bicycle, a symbol of independence for young women at this time. Even in later years, as fashions changed, she still stuck to a plain style of dress.

Virginia Woolf first got to know Lilian properly in September 1916, on a joint holiday with Margaret and Leonard in Cornwall. Initially, she did not take Lilian very seriously, reporting in a light-hearted letter (probably embellishing to make a better story): '[Lilian] smokes about 8 pipes a day, and is very fond of good wine and cigars … her other taste is for statistics.'[525] But Virginia's liking and respect soon grew. Less than two years later, she mused on how Lilian was

> always to the point, + surprisingly ready with her views, considering her air of modesty … in clothing, manner, appearance, she is of the most ordinary type possible: + thus her talk, and her pipe, come with force.

On another occasion, Virginia recounted Lilian's characteristic 'serene quiet' response, calming her down after a distressing row with Margaret who had, somewhat tactlessly, criticised her just-published novel *Night and Day*.[526]

Although outwardly a much less powerful personality than Margaret, Lilian, too, attracted love and admiration. When she was old and frail, Dolly Ponsonby's husband Arthur summed her up as 'the incarnation of one of my beliefs, the wonderful influence of a completely obscure person … handicapped by stone deafness and partial blindness yet cheerful, wise, thoughtful and really helpful'.[527]

It has been suggested that Lilian and Margaret were a lesbian couple. This could be reinforced by the contrast between Margaret's flowing garments and Lilian's severe clothes and pipe (although in their generation, women often used these to signify independence rather than sexual preference). And there seems to be further confirmation in Virginia Woolf's claim that on the shared holiday with the Woolfs, the two women occasionally called one another 'John' and 'Jim'.[528]

As with other parts of Margaret's personal life, there is a lack of concrete evidence. While there seems to have been a romantic element to Margaret's youthful friendship with Rosalind Nash, there are no hints of this in her early relationship with Lilian. Instead, this seems to have focused much more on their shared work. As late as 1904, in her history of the Guild, Margaret mainly stressed Lilian's administrative prowess, calling her an 'assistant in everything'. This contrasts with a much stronger, more personal tribute to Rosalind later in the book.

As time went by, though, the relationship moved to a different level and Lilian became vital to Margaret both in and outside work. They did not live together until after Margaret's father died, when they were both in their mid-fifties, and it is tempting to speculate, though impossible to know, whether they would have done so much earlier if Margaret had not had him to consider. From now on, in many ways they operated, and were seen, as a couple; although each had her own bedroom and sitting room, and they often socialised and went on holiday separately.

Margaret's niece Theodora, who knew both her and Lilian well at the end of their lives, felt that if there was what she termed an element of lesbianism in their relationship, they were totally unaware of it.[529] Both born in the 1860s, Lilian and Margaret came from a generation with very different ideas about sexuality from those of today. They certainly would not have recognised the labels we use. Many middle-class women of their time, who like them chose a life of public service rather than marriage, relied on close female friendships. It was only later that such relationships came under the microscope in terms of sexual orientation. It's possible that, like Eleanor Rathbone – of a similar generation, and also relying on a close partnership with a woman – they too would have been distressed at being seen in this way.

Margaret and Lilian undoubtedly had a productive working partnership, and from middle life onwards became devoted companions. They went on to sustain one another, finally, through illness until death. More than this we cannot know.

WHY BUY SWEATED GOODS AND SUPPORT SWEATING FIRMS?

All TRADE UNIONISTS and their Wives should lay out their money at the

CO-OPERATIVE UNIONIST STORES,

436, COMMERCIAL ROAD,
227, BOW ROAD,
70, BRUNSWICK ROAD, POPLAR.

WHY?

1. Because the articles are good, and **made under fair conditions.** Let women boycott bad employers by refusing to buy their goods.

2. Because women can thus raise their husbands' wages. The Stores are managed by working people, who all share in the profits. **For every £1 spent there, each Member gets 1s. as his or her share in the profits.**

3. Because at the Stores you have a Free Library, Free Classes, Free Entertainments, etc.

Women's help is wanted in the Labour Movement.

Women must rally together and help on the good time coming by joining the Women's Co-operative Guild.

Women are the purchasers. They must be Co-operators.

Women also want help themselves. They need less work, more change, more to spend, more to read, more interests.

Come and give a hand, and see how the Guild can help you, at any or all of the following Meetings:

THURSDAY, FEB 18th, at 8 o'clock, in the CO-OPERATIVE HALL, Johnson Street, Commercial Road, **Joint Social Evening** for Tower Hamlets, Bow, and Poplar Branches. Music and Singing. ADDRESS by Miss LLEWELYN DAVIES (General Secretary, Women's Co-operative Guild). DIALOGUE between Mrs. STORE and Mrs. SHOPPER.

TOWER HAMLETS MEETINGS, at Toynbee Hall, Commercial Street, at 8 p.m.

MONDAY, MAR. 7 —DIALOGUE between Mrs. STORE and Mrs SHOPPER.
MONDAY, MAR 21.—ARGUMENT: "Must Women always be Household Drudges"?

BOW MEETINGS, at the Stores, 227, Bow Road, at 8 p.m

WEDNESDAY, FEB. 24.—DIALOGUE: "Must Women always be Household Drudges"?
WEDNESDAY, MAR. 9.—ADDRESS by Miss TOURNIER (Vice-President of the Women's Co-operative Guild), on "How Women can help in the Labour Movement"?
WEDNESDAY, MAR. 23 —DISCUSSION: "Is it worth while to join the Women's Guild"?

POPLAR MEETINGS, at the Stores, 70, Brunswick Road, Poplar, at 2 30

MONDAY, FEB. 22.—DISCUSSION: "For and Against the Women s Guild."
MONDAY, MAR 7 —ADDRESS by Mrs. JONES (President of the Women's Co-operative Guild).
MONDAY, MAR 21.—DIALOGUE "Must Women always be Household Drudges"?

Margaret's early attempt to link co-operators and trade unionists, 1891-1892.
(M. Ll. Davies, 1904. Archives and Special Collections, Bishopsgate Institute)

Group of Guild members, taken around the time Margaret became General Secretary. (Catherine Webb, 1927)

Leading Guildswomen: Central Committee, 1892-93, annotated by Margaret. (Jane Wynne Willson)

Leading Guildswomen: Central Committee, 1903-1904. Note this includes Mrs Bury, prominent in opposition to Margaret over suffrage and divorce.
(M. Ll. Davies, 1904. Archives and Special Collections, Bishopsgate Institute)

Sarah Reddish, prominent Guild activist; leading radical suffragist, also at various times paid trade union and suffrage organiser.
(Catherine Webb, 1927)

of whole heart cometh hope.

This is to Certify that Mrs Cox is enrolled a Member of the Women's Co-operative Guild: a self-governing organization of 25,500 Women, who work through Co-operation for the welfare of the people, seeking Freedom for their own progress, and the Equal Fellowship of men and women in the Home, the Store, the Workshop and the State.

Date. January 18th 1909   General Secretary.
Died October 1914

Guild membership card, 1900s. The image is well known, but not the text, which is rarely reproduced. (Archives and Special Collections, Bishopsgate Institute)

'Radical suffragists': Lancashire and Cheshire delegates on a suffrage deputation to the Prime Minister, 1906. Guildswomen were heavily involved in these groups, note Sarah Reddish: centre second row, without hat.
(Lancashire Record Office, with thanks to Jill Liddington)

Radical suffragist banner. (Working Class Movement Library, Salford)

Section Four

WINDING DOWN

CHAPTER 16

Leaving, 1918-1922

In October 1921 Margaret dropped a bombshell. A brief letter to *Our Women's Pages* (the new name for *Women's Corner*) explained that she was resigning as the Guild's General Secretary. Lilian Harris, too, would be leaving.

This came as a complete shock to most Guildswomen, but in reality it had been a long time coming.

Why Margaret resigned

The lack of lead-up immediately led to speculation as to the reasons behind Margaret's announcement. In fact she and Lilian had been thinking about retirement for several years, and had been actively planning it for at least two. Both were in their late fifties, and in poor health. Although Margaret always pushed herself to go on working, it was now becoming a real struggle. And Lilian, who had so often rescued Margaret when she had taken on too much, was herself troubled with increasingly poor sight. She worried about possible blindness, and on at least two occasions had spent time in a nursing home.

Margaret's health was particularly bad during the final years of the war. Although she never formally took sick leave, she had to go away for extended periods of rest. She put this down to heart trouble and in August 1917 explained to Dolly Ponsonby that she had gone away for several months with Crompton and his family, 'to try to get my heart right, + generally set up'. She had been told to rest for two hours a day but found this hard: 'One has to cut off so much when one is more of a crock.'[530]

Between August and early October 1918, Margaret's health broke down again, and she had to go to a sanatorium for several months. She put a brave face on it: writing chatty letters, receiving visitors and, as we shall see, occasionally dealing with work. But such a long period suggests that her illness was more than temporary.

Margaret appears to have often felt unwell in this period. Whatever the nature of her heart trouble, its impact had clearly been exacerbated by the stresses and strains of the later war years. Ever since her father fell ill, she had been under particular pressure. As well as the horror of the war, there was the anxiety of caring for him, and the grief and loss of his final decline. 1916 had seen not only his death, but a few months later that of Harriet Kidd, the Guild clerk, after a prolonged illness. Margaret had become very attached to her, and made time to help look after her at the end. On top of all this, as we have seen, there were some painful disputes within the Guild and the movement.

In the past, when Margaret had been exhausted, it had not been hard to see that she herself was at least partly responsible. Like so many campaigners, she found it impossible to say 'No' to demands, or to refuse new possibilities. Now, it was different.

If managing the Guild had been fraught with difficulties during the war, once peace returned she found herself coping with all the problems of success. The Guild grew by leaps and bounds: after an influx of five thousand new members in 1918-19, women still flocked to join. By April 1921, a few months before Margaret retired, the total number of Guildswomen had gone up to fifty thousand. This dramatic expansion partly reflected a growth in co-operative membership at the time. But also, women who had tasted greater freedom and independence during the war were now perhaps looking for a new outlet.

Whatever the cause, there was a mountain of extra administrative work. The Central Office, with only two paid clerical staff, just could not keep up with it. Although Lilian was key on the organisational side, even Margaret, with her overall leadership responsibility, sometimes found herself perforce dealing with much detail. The problem was not only one of practical administration. It was also a challenge to incorporate the mass of new members smoothly into the Guild. Many had joined hundreds of new branches which had sprung up from 1917 onwards, where they did not have the support of already knowledgeable and experienced Guildswomen. They had to be trained up, and at speed. They needed to understand the Guild's aims and its approach to campaigns, to learn about co-operation and how the movement worked, and more. The workload was daunting.

By 1918, Margaret and the Guild had come a long way. After more than thirty years, this may have seemed the right time for her to execute a graceful withdrawal.

Later campaigns

Understandably, it took several years to organise leaving the Guild. During this time Margaret continued to campaign, though in a different way. She seems to have coped with her ill-health by doing more writing and less travelling and organising, producing a small flurry of pamphlets between 1919 and 1921. Significantly, she had help; she co-authored several pamphlets with Lilian and/or Honora Enfield, an Oxbridge graduate who had been informally acting as her assistant since 1916. Some of these were designed to help with the Guild's internal work, but others focused on broader issues.

The war had irrevocably changed Margaret priorities, and Lilian's, too. Both now increasingly focused on the big picture for co-operation as a whole, and on how to ensure international peace.

For years, Margaret had been to the left of many in the co-operative movement. But even before the war, co-operative opinion had begun to move in a more radical direction. Since it ended, this had accelerated. After the wartime food shortages and price rises, the immediate post-war years saw yet more speculation and profiteering in the retail sector. Business interests, influential in government circles, were joining together and consolidating. As consumer co-operation expanded, it had always been opposed by powerful competitors. Now, many members believed, 'entrenched private enterprise' would use its position to try to weaken the movement – or even destroy it.

There were other influences as well. Old certainties had been challenged by the bitter experience of the war, and now the mass return of demobilized soldiers, all too often jobless, fuelled social dislocation. Along with inflation, there were major strikes in the mines and railways. The Russian revolution had opened up new possibilities for a fairer society. In this climate, many more co-operators accepted the idea of joining forces with trade unions, and even with the Labour Party, now a major national political force.

Early in 1919, the movement launched a campaign to defend and expand co-operation against the threat of what it now termed the 'capitalist menace'. In the lead-up, Margaret was busy pulling strings. Confined to a sanatorium for some of the time, she typically managed to correspond with leading co-operators, persuaded Leonard Woolf to write some publicity material, and organised Lilian to 'coach up' the sympathetic chair of the ruling United Board.

One aspect of this campaign was to promote an alliance between co-operation and trade unionism, something which had always been dear to

Margaret's heart. Despite her fragile health, she spoke at several public meetings. In January 1919, a conference of co-operators and trade unionists enthusiastically applauded her when she declared that both movements supported a Co-operative Commonwealth. *Co-operative News* reported her claim that

> ... they could no longer tolerate a system in which the trade, industries, factories and workshops were autocratically controlled; they could no longer tolerate a system in which the many were toiling to make a profit for the few.[531]

Margaret also looked outward, to international contacts. Increasing trade with co-operatives in other countries was much discussed in the British movement at this time, and was backed by influential voices, including the CWS. There was particular interest in relationships with the co-operative movement in the new Russia. Thanks to Margaret, the Guild – which consistently supported her approach – was the British co-operative movement's 'most active advocate' for international trade at this time.[532]

Co-operation versus Capitalism, a pamphlet which she co-authored with Honora Enfield, was widely disseminated in the movement. The pamphlet stressed that if British co-operation were to become independent of capitalist suppliers, it needed to find new sources both of raw materials and of finished goods, and immediately. This could be achieved, it argued, through international co-operative trade – especially with Russia. Margaret and Honora made other ambitious proposals too: to change CWS rules so it could greatly extend its production and trading, to create a co-operative shipping and transport business, and to raise the capital urgently needed for such expansion through trade union funds, insurance and even a loan.[533]

For Margaret, international co-operative trade would not only help the British movement, it would also promote international peace. More, it could be the basis of an incremental, peaceful, transformation to a worldwide Co-operative Commonwealth. She was not alone in suggesting this. Other co-operators took a similar view, though unlike Margaret, most probably saw it more as a long-term vision rather than as an immediate, concrete aim.

With the wartime split a thing of the past, the Guild backed Margaret on broader questions of peace and internationalism. Guild Congresses registered opposition to continuing post-war conscription, supported disarmament, and backed a critique of current proposals for the League of Nations: demanding instead that the workers of the world unite to create a 'true' League of all Nations 'with direct representation of the peoples, and the total rejection of all military alliances with individual powers'.[534] The Guild also protested against British repression in Ireland, and opposed British intervention against the Bolsheviks in the Russian civil war.

There is one disturbing footnote to this story of Guild internationalism. Sandwiched in the middle of the 1919-20 Annual Report's discussion of 'Foreign and Irish Affairs' is a brief report that the Central Committee had agreed to write to the prime minister expressing its 'horror and indignation' that French African troops were stationed in occupied Rhineland.[535]

This came out of a campaign which had recently gathered considerable support among left-wing and women's groups. Publicised with headlines like 'Black Scourge in Europe', it alleged that because of their 'barely restrainable bestiality', the African troops were regularly raping German women. The Guild not only protested to the prime minister, but also publicised a meeting called by the Women's International League which was promoted under the heading 'Barbarisation of Europe: Mass meeting against importation into Europe of troops belonging to primitive peoples'.[536]

It is a salutary reminder of the blatant racism prevalent at the time that even Margaret, with her ardent belief in human equality, was prepared to countenance, even support, such a venture.

One of Margaret's main post-war aims was to develop links between co-operative women in different countries. She had always promoted international contacts for the Guild, and had invited the first foreign visitor to its annual meeting as early as 1894. At the onset of the First World War she found a new ally in Frau Emmy Freundlich, a remarkable social democrat and co-operative activist from Vienna. It was partly thanks to Frau Freundlich that, early in 1915, Margaret wrote to co-operative women in various countries urging them to take part in the Hague Congress.

Immediately after the war, internationalist slogans took on a new, grim reality. The situation in Germany and Austria was desperate. Post-war upheavals and the allied blockade, which continued until July 1919, had led to acute starvation. German and Austrian children were dying in their thousands. When British women decided to organise relief and set up the Fight the Famine Council (shortly to become the Save the Children Fund) Guild branches donated, keen to help.

Then, in April 1920, Frau Freundlich visited Britain with a terrible but all too realistic message: 'Vienna is dying'.[537] Margaret promptly organised a Guild collection which generated a lorry load of supplies for Austria, and also pointed up the link with co-operation. When two Guildswomen visited Austria, she wrote in *Our Women's Pages* that she hoped this would 'lay the foundations of an International Women's Guild' and promote international co-operative trade. After they had produced a pamphlet describing the appalling suffering they had witnessed, *Our Women's Pages* stressed that Austrian women needed 'the loving sympathy of English co-operators and the helping hand of co-operative trading to restore them to take their part in the development of the great International Co-operative Commonwealth'.[538]

Then came a not-to-be-missed opportunity. The International Co-operative Alliance, founded in 1895 but in abeyance since the onset of war, was resurrected in 1919. Its first post-war Congress was scheduled to take place at Basle in August 1921. Why not use this as a base for linking up co-operative women? During 1920 and 1921, Margaret was increasingly preoccupied with achieving something along these lines before she retired. She and Frau Freundlich jointly decided to invite women from thirty Co-operative organisations in different countries to a women's meeting at the Basle Congress.

Perhaps stimulated by Margaret and Frau Freundlich's intervention, over a third of the delegates to the International Co-operative Alliance's main Congress were female. Forty women from England, Holland, Switzerland, Austria, Czechoslovakia, Russia and the US came together in a 'thrilling' meeting to set up an International Co-operative Women's Committee. As one male congress delegate put it (himself not permitted to attend), the women were 'making history'.[539]

Needless to say, the Guild had supported this venture. In addition to Eleanor Barton and Mrs Gasson, the two official delegates to the meeting, nine other Guildswomen chose to go to Basle at their own expense. Lilian was one of them.

Margaret herself did not go, almost certainly because of her health. However, her background work for the women's meeting was crucial, especially a paper of 'suggestions from the English Guild' which she produced, setting out the practicalities of creating an international committee. Although it was read on the day by Honora Enfield, the paper had an authentic Margaret ring, ending with a rousing call for the meeting to create an international union in which 'the combined power of the basket and the vote shall be utilised in the interests of Industrial Democracy and World-wide Peace'.[540] Later, when Margaret retired, Frau Freundlich paid a warm tribute: 'When we in Basle founded our international women's organisation, we had the feeling that you are always with us, and that you will be our good spirit ....'[541]

The Basle meeting elected Frau Freundlich as President of the new

International Committee and Honora Enfield as Secretary, while the English Guild offered its office as administrative base. With the groundwork for the international organisation now in place, Margaret could retire with an easier mind.

Preparing to leave

Back in 1919, the Central Committee had recorded a decision to review payments for Guild work, 'which would necessarily include payment for the Gen Sec, on the retirement of the present G. S.'[542] [original abbreviations] This was the first official hint that Margaret was considering retirement.

Traditionally, the Guild had relied on voluntary effort. Margaret, joining in the 1880s from a background of middle-class philanthropy, had always worked for it unpaid, as had Lilian. But times had changed. This high-profile post required what were increasingly seen as professional skills. In any case, an unwaged post would exclude less well-off women.

However, there was a problem with deciding to pay future General Secretaries. Other officials also did a great deal of work, and although the Guild had a strong voluntary tradition, informal 'honoraria' had been introduced in some places, to compensate those who could not afford to work for free. The Central Committee recommended that these should now be abolished, and that the only paid posts should be the General and Assistant Secretaries (along with the Central Office clerical staff, who were already paid). As might be expected, this led to something of a row. Margaret, who made a point of taking part in the discussions, expected that it would all be settled at the next Congress, in 1920, leaving her and Lilian free to retire.

As decision time approached, Margaret had cold feet about leaving for good. The Guild had been the centre of her life for over thirty years. However, her dithering appears to have been fleeting. She was evidently convinced by Leonard Woolf's sensible advice that even if she did take a break rather than resign for good, '... you'll find things overwhelm you again as soon as you come back'.[543] It is worth adding that, despite this, he was clearly unable to envisage Margaret abandoning public life. Leonard even suggested that she organise a Labour Party 'women's wing', apparently unaware of the party's recently created women's department and its chief officer.

The 1920 Congress did indeed agree to the Central Committee's proposal about payment, but then another dispute reared its head. While the Committee wanted the power to select a future General Secretary, Congress delegates suggested instead that the power should go to the branches.

Margaret and Lilian had to put their plans on hold for a year while the disagreement was sorted out.

It was a difficult period for Margaret. She was ill enough to go back to the sanatorium towards the end of 1920 and the beginning of 1921, and there were also several family anxieties and tragedies around this time.

Since the end of the war, Crompton's wife Moya had been living in Ireland with their children Richard and Katherine. During the battle for Irish independence which followed the war, Moya, closely involved with the nationalist struggle, had been providing a safe house. In March 1921 the news came through that she had been arrested by the Black and Tans and imprisoned. This left the children, aged nine and six, stranded. Crompton was liable to be arrested if he went to Dublin and it is said that Margaret, nearly sixty and in poor health, was unwilling to go. It was Maurice's 25-year-old daughter Mary, then a medical student, who saved the day, travelling to Dublin and bringing the children back to England and safety.

Then, in May 1921, came the shocking news that Arthur's twenty-year-old son, Michael, had drowned, possibly in a suicide pact. Margaret, who had kept in touch with him and the other 'lost boys', was deeply upset.

Finally, Emily Davies died in July. She had moved to Hampstead around the same time as Llewelyn and Margaret, and Margaret is said to have seen her 'constantly' at the end of her life.[544] Although they do not seem to have been especially close, her death marked the end of a significant and distinguished link with previous generations of the family.

Parting from the Guild

All finally went according to plan at the Guild Congress in the summer of 1921. A compromise was agreed, giving the Central Committee power to shortlist for General Secretary and make recommendations, with the branches then making the final decision. Margaret, who had still not said anything formally about retiring, insisted that it should not be mentioned at the Congress. She wanted to get through the summer first, with the foundation of the International Guild, and to 'do the horrid deed' after that.[545]

As the months wore on, Margaret and Lilian had to plan carefully to make sure they left things in good order. Margaret was finding the process hard, confiding in Leonard Woolf that the formal announcement of the resignations would be 'rather an ordeal'.[546]

In September, at the first meeting of the newly elected Central Committee, the moment finally came. Margaret gave a short speech on behalf of both herself and Lilian which nevertheless encapsulated her feelings about the

Guild and its members after over thirty years:

> ... it had been the greatest privilege to have helped to build up an organisation of those who had previously been without organised power, and to have seen it grow into a vital force in the Co-operative Movement and in the Nation. She expressed her affection for her fellow guildswomen, and her admiration for their unselfish devotion and courage. Guild work had been a wonderful experience with such fellow workers for such ideals as the Guild stood for.[547]

As we know, this was not news to the Committee. Margaret recorded in the minutes that they formally accepted the resignations with 'utmost regret and deepest gratitude'– and went straight on to plan recruiting and selecting replacements.[548]

However, when the decision appeared publicly in *Our Women's Page* ten days later, the floodgates opened. Shocked letters began to pour in. Such were the rumours flying around, both of internal splits and of Margaret's outside ambitions, that she felt obliged to write to the *Pages* insisting that she was retiring for 'purely natural and personal [reasons] ... health and old age'. She added, 'To clear up matters further ... I have no hidden intention of being called to the Bar, and ... the House of Commons is the last place in which I should wish to find myself!'[549]

Emotions ran high. On receiving the news, Annie Bamford Tomlinson, a long-time close colleague, editor from 1904 of *Woman's Corner* and then of *Our Women's Pages*, confessed that she 'just put my head in my hands + ... wept'. Others reacted with similar consternation. Even though the rule changes made it clear that the leadership would change at some point, few would have thought this would come so soon, and so abruptly. Whilst it may not have meant much to the large number of members who had recently joined, many long-standing Guildswomen simply could not imagine how the organisation would cope, or even manage to continue at all, without Margaret's leadership.

Most unusually for her, Margaret preserved nearly eighty letters sent to her when she announced her resignation, mostly from rank and file members. She may well, of course, have discarded any that were difficult or sensitive. The prevailing tone of the letters that survived was very personal. Some described Margaret as a 'friend', a 'big sister', or a 'guiding spirit'. Mrs Wakeham, writing for Guildswomen in Cardiff, summed up their feelings:

... for the time our beacon light is dimmed .... Words cannot say and would be wasted if we tried to say how much we feel we owe you for all you have done for working women when you could have had a selfish life.

Other letters illustrated Margaret's remarkable personal rapport with many activists. Mrs Hood, who rose to be Guild President, wrote about her first speech at a public meeting:

I was almost frightened to death, but when I stood up to speak, I saw your face in the audience ... when you smiled and clapped I went on with a fresh heart ... I am not the only one who has to thank you for showing them what they are capable of doing, over and over again. [550]

Praise indeed.

Events now moved swiftly on. The elections took place in November, and went smoothly. The candidates recommended by the Central Committee were successful: Honora Enfield as General Secretary, and Eleanor Barton as Assistant Secretary.[551]

November also saw an emotional leave-taking, when Margaret was asked to unveil the Guild Southern Section's new banner, patterned with marguerites as a tribute to her. As she said in her thank-you speech, this was her 'own' section, including as it did London, where she had first joined the Guild, and where she and Lilian had both lived for the last dozen years. She called for the banner to be a symbol of courage to welcome new and unpopular ideas, and of comradeship, calling on 'each one of us [to] do our part in promoting the spirit of internationalism by destroying the spirit which breeds hate and war'.[552]

In mid-December 1921, Margaret attended her last Central Committee meeting and produced her very last minutes. She and Lilian went on to pen a farewell letter to Guildswomen, which appeared in *Our Women's Pages* at the end of the month.

After thirty-two years, it was all over.

Coda

Except that it wasn't quite.

Less than a month after her resignation took effect, Margaret received a remarkable invitation. At the end of January 1922, Mr Whitehead wrote on behalf of the United Board to ask her to preside over the next annual Co-operative Congress, the first woman ever to have done so. After praising her achievements for the Guild and for the whole movement, Mr Whitehead affirmed that if she accepted she would be 'performing a symbolic act, demonstrating to the whole world that women have at [last] won the right to fill equally with men the highest office in the British Co-operative movement'.

Given Margaret's battles over the years with the co-operative establishment, this was astonishing, but it illustrates how much the movement and, indeed, society as a whole, had moved on. No doubt Margaret's recent work alongside the mainstream movement promoting international co-operative trade and the campaign against the 'capitalist menace' had also helped.

Mr Whitehead offered to ensure that a senior Co-operator would be on hand to assist Margaret if, in the event, she was not strong enough to chair the full Congress. This was not a patronising suggestion; Margaret explained in her reply that she had hesitated because of her state of health, and gratefully accepted the promise of help if needed. She clearly felt that she must accept the invitation, stressing that it represented recognition of the contribution made by co-operative women and adding her gratification 'that our British co-operative movement should be the first of all co-operative and labour movements to give so striking an example of the equality and comradeship of men and women'.[553] *Our Women's Pages* promptly published both letters under a huge heading: 'Woman President for Brighton Congress'.

Margaret's presidency evoked a great deal of interest. In the run-up to the Co-operative Congress, *Co-operative News* carried a whole-page article about her. The *Manchester Guardian* also had an article, and *The Observer* a 'special interview'. Both pointed out that there was also other evidence of progress for women in the movement. Around this time, Guild activist Mrs Cottrell had become the first woman director of the CWS, and Eleanor Barton a prospective parliamentary candidate for the Co-operative Party.

In its report of the Congress proceedings, *Co-operative News* reported Margaret's opening address in full, under the banner headline, 'Welcome to First Woman President'.[554] Finally, after all these years, Margaret could feel that women were being recognised as a real, positive presence in the movement.

Understandably, Margaret approached the task of chairing the Congress with some trepidation. The proceedings, due to take place in Brighton in early June 1922, would last for three days and bring together getting on for two thousand delegates, mostly male.

Months before, she had already drafted her introductory address and given it to Leonard Woolf for comments. Interestingly, he suggested she should, 'leave out words like "I venture to think" – you are too modest all through'.[555] Although Margaret tried hard to dissuade Virginia Woolf from accompanying Leonard to witness her performance, luckily for us, she was unsuccessful and we have the great writer's acute, if partial, observations of the occasion, which appear in the introduction to this book.

As we saw in the Introduction, Margaret made no attempt to play down her criticisms of the movement in her address. After she had finished, the Co-operative Central Board formally presented her with an elaborately bound and illuminated address.[556] Carefully preserved by Margaret, this took a very different approach, thus neatly illustrating the range of interweaving ideas and traditions present in the movement.

Concentrating on Margaret's Christian Socialist heritage and her humanitarian ideals, the address did not repeat her claim that co-operation's main aim was not social reform, but social revolution. Instead, it emphasised that

> you have always taught that ... although [co-operation] promotes the material welfare of each and all, it seeks higher ends than any change in social organisation or industrial relationships, inasmuch as it seeks to make men and women conscious of their true relation as members of the great Human Family.

Nevertheless, the address also praised Margaret's campaigns within the movement and her role, as a 'fearless champion of married working-women', in encouraging the Guild to fight for social and 'domestic' reforms.

It was a generous tribute, and another signal that times had changed.

To Virginia Woolf's approval, Margaret responded, once again, that she was not accepting the honour for herself personally but on behalf of all co-operative women. Then, briskly and no doubt with relief, she started the Congress business. Despite her anxiety, Margaret dealt with the rest of the Congress with aplomb. The only sign that it had cost her dearly came at the very end. *Co-operative News* reported that when she responded to the gifts presented to her, she was, 'almost breaking down under stress of emotion'.[557]

The Congress marked a major milestone for the Guild and, indeed, for the whole movement.

Soon after, on 15 June, there was a very different public occasion, this time much less arduous, and much more pleasant. It had been decided to offer Margaret and Lilian the Freedom of the Guild, along with a testimonial of £700 raised from Guildswomen. With Lilian temporarily in a nursing home, Margaret alone received the presentation, which took place at the end of the Guild's own Annual Congress. She delivered a relaxed speech of gratitude, recalling campaigns of the past and looking to those of the future. She ended:

> We are glad to make room for others, but we feel we are still united with you, and can never, never be grateful enough to you all for the life and love you have given us.[558]

That was the moment when Margaret really took her leave of the Guild.

CHAPTER 17

After the Guild, 1922-1933

'How awful it would be to "retire" at 60: to sit down & look at poplar trees?'[559]

Twenty years younger than Margaret and Lilian, Virginia Woolf was convinced that they had made a great mistake in leaving the Guild when they did. As the years went by, increasingly influenced by her own feelings about ageing, she sometimes portrayed the two women as both depressing and depressed. After one encounter in 1930, she wrote that Margaret 'deserved better than this dishevelled and undistinguished end'.[560]

Certainly, the abrupt break with the all-consuming demands of the Guild must inevitably have created a sense of loss. And for both Margaret and Lilian, health worries persisted. Lilian's eyesight worsened, and Margaret was still forced sometimes to abandon her plans when her heart played up; at which time her doctors, presumably following the accepted treatment of the time, encouraged her to do as little as possible. She found this terribly frustrating, feeling like 'such a slacker in all things except rest'.[561] Significantly, her old friend Dolly Ponsonby connected the crises with emotional strain: 'Her enthusiasm reacts on her health. Her heart is bad and she gets over excited.'[562]

For Margaret and Lilian, then, the backdrop to these post-retirement years was one of ageing and poor health. But it was not by any means the whole story,

Still campaigning

Predictably, various pieces of work presented themselves once Margaret had retired. First of all, the Central Committee suggested that she write a history of the Guild, updating her previous work from 1904. Although this would have been an obvious retirement project, Margaret refused, referring them instead to veteran Guildswoman Catherine Webb, an experienced and accomplished writer well known in the movement, who did indeed publish her history five years later. Perhaps Margaret did not want to commit herself so soon to such a major piece of work, but it may also have felt too sensitive to research and write about what had, after all, been her life's work.

A few months later, another request came up. Following her successful chairing of the 1922 Co-operative Congress, Margaret was invited back to do much the same in 1923 – another accolade. However, she explained to Leonard Woolf that she did not feel well enough to take this on: 'I can't get my heart right.'[563]

Margaret was now, evidently, seen as a respected and respectable public woman. Trying to find her another niche – it would seem not particularly at her request – Leonard Woolf suggested her as possible Principal for Newnham College, Cambridge. This clearly did not attract Margaret, and no more is heard about it. Instead, she concentrated on campaigning; above all for co-operation, peace and internationalism.

Having already ensured that the International Co-operative Women's Guild got successfully off the ground, Margaret wisely resisted any temptation to get personally involved with organising it after that. However, she did go with Lilian to the next full ICWG conference in 1924. It took place in Ghent, perhaps recalling memories of 1906 when she had had to miss a trip there at the last minute because of Arthur. When Margaret was about to give a paper, Frau Freundlich introduced her as, 'the mother of the whole Guild'. To a woman, the audience promptly rose to its feet and sang 'For he's a jolly good fellow [sic]'.[564]

Margaret's pacifism also led her to support several British peace campaigns which had grown up in reaction to the horrors of the First World War. In the early 1920s she backed the No More War movement and War Resisters International. A few years later, when Dolly Ponsonby's husband Arthur initiated a 'peace letter' campaign which gathered over 100,000 signatures, Margaret enthusiastically spread the word to her contacts in the co-operative and labour movements.

'Life as We Have Known it'

Inevitably, the Guild remained very close to Margaret's heart even after her retirement. Although she carefully kept away from interfering in internal matters, she retained a lifelong affection and respect for the organisation, and for Guildswomen. This came out very clearly in four commonplace books (scrapbooks) which she started towards the end of her time in the Guild but continued into old age. They include a handwritten copy of the excerpt from D.H. Lawrence's *Sons and Lovers* that appears in Chapter 7; one of many hints of her enduring pride in the guild.

Margaret carefully folded into one of the commonplace books some notes she had made of conversations on a train journey, almost certainly dating from the time when she was travelling round as general secretary. One quotes a woman who had borne nineteen children, of whom fourteen survived into adulthood. 'For 15 years never went out except on a Saty to do marketing. Never joined anything but Guild – 'I should have been dead but for Guild'[565][original abbreviation].

A few years after she retired, stories such as this led Margaret to think about pulling together a book of Guildswomen's reminiscences. She floated the idea with the Woolfs, who were running the Hogarth Press, and they agreed to publish it.

The project was slow getting off the ground, probably because of Margaret's ill-health, and at times she was despondent about it. She offloaded her feelings onto Dolly Ponsonby: 'I am not very pleased or happy about it. I doubt if it will be felt at all interesting – + people really don't care about women's lives.' Nevertheless, she was determined that guildswomen should be recognised: 'I should like people to see what they have gone through, and how they have built up a new life for themselves, and how much the "bringing of them out" has meant in their lives.'[566]

When the Woolfs brought out *Life as We have Known It* in 1931, Guildswomen's contributions certainly lived up to Margaret's hopes.[567] The writers had been born in the mid to late Victorian years, most into poverty. Yet they had come through to hold positions in the Guild and the co-operative movement, and some even in wider public life. Their reminiscences movingly evoke their hard lives from childhood onward, and their determination to overcome the barriers they faced. They all pay tribute to the Guild – which, as one put it, discovered her 'latent sparks' and made them 'burn brightly'.[568]

Margaret herself contributed an affectionate chapter on the life and achievements of Harriet Kidd, the Guild's clerk, who had died in 1917. This vividly brings home the potential vulnerability of young working-class women like her and would have been shocking to many readers. When she was seventeen and working in a silk mill, Miss Kidd had been raped by her rich, respected employer. As a result, she became a single mother bringing up a much-loved son on her own. Despite all the odds, Miss Kidd went on to be the much-respected mainstay of the Guild office, as well as a leading activist for women in the Amalgamated Union of Co-operative Employees.

Although a sympathetic review in the *Manchester Guardian* praised 'the amazing energy and grit' of the contributors, the book did not have the same impact as its predecessor, *Maternity*. Also, the process of bringing it out brought up a particular, rather personal, difficulty. Margaret had decided to ask Virginia Woolf to provide an introduction, and although initially insisting that she was 'too much of a picturesque amateur',[569] in the end the writer produced an *Introductory Letter*, purportedly addressed to Margaret, which has since become extremely well known. This started with a fictionalised account of her 'contradictory and complex feelings' when she went to the Guild Congress way back in 1913. It only later discussed the memoirs themselves, and then in terms which were not always flattering. Virginia Woolf stressed the gulf between herself, the upper middle-class observer, and working-class Guildswomen; suggesting at times that this could never be bridged, and criticising what she presented as their limited capability to understand art and literature.

Margaret was not happy with the draft, apparently objecting in particular to unflattering descriptions of Guildswomen, not to mention the depiction of Lilian smoking her pipe. Irritated and upset, Virginia reluctantly agreed to some, but by no means all, of the alterations she suggested, and after a few difficult exchanges they came to a compromise for the final published version.

Thankfully, there seems to have been no lasting bad feeling, at least on Margaret's side. Indeed, a couple of years later she was able to tell Dolly Ponsonby that she felt Virginia had changed for the better since the early days. She no longer felt that Virginia was 'just looking at the Guild as a spectator'.[570]

Whether or not one reads the *Introductory Letter* as written to reflect Virginia Woolf's own attitudes – some commentators argue that it was not[571] – she was certainly interested in the material that Margaret sent her, and wanted it to see the light of day. Much later, she wrote to Margaret on the spur of the moment, 'I wish we could bring out another volume,' and added '… I'm always on the look-out for a real Co-op autobiography.'[572] It is likely that this off the cuff remark was not intended be taken too seriously. Yet, despite finding it irritating and difficult, Virginia Woolf gamely chaired a local Guild branch for several years, and even hosted it in her house. And, as we have seen, she insisted on being present to see Margaret preside over the Co-operative Congress. Whatever her ambivalence, her friendship with Margaret and her involvement with the Guild were significant for Virginia Woolf, giving substance to her vision of the contribution of women 'outsiders' to the world.[573] She was more than the uneasy observer portrayed in the *Introductory Letter*.

Margaret and the Russians

For years before the revolution, Margaret had shared with others on the left a romantic admiration for Russian culture, and an indignant sympathy with political exiles from the Czarist regime. She was enthusiastic when, in October 1917, the Bolsheviks seized power. In subsequent years, as we have seen, she saw the new Soviet Russia as a potential future linchpin of international co-operative trade, and the creation of a socialist USSR as the possible first step towards the transformation of the whole world into an international co-operative commonwealth.

At the end of 1923, moves to set up a Society for Cultural Relations with the USSR fitted perfectly with Margaret's socialism, her internationalism, and her love of the arts. In January 1924 she wrote to Dolly Ponsonby that she had become the temporary chair of a provisional committee which aimed to recruit 'the learned + distinguished in every dept of life' to a society, 'for fostering intellectual relations between the peoples of the *USSR* and the *British Commonwealth*!'[574] [original emphasis and abbreviations]

A few months later, Margaret invited Dolly and Arthur Ponsonby to a party organised by the Soviet ambassador. She seems to have been thrilled by the whole occasion. Somewhat amused, Dolly was more sceptical:

> Margaret trembling with enthusiasm said had I seen the group of real Russians at the further end of the room with beards smoking pipes & most characteristic. I did not feel inclined to move from my seat – but the said Russians proved to be English Communists who smoked & spat on the floors all the evening so that Claridges the next day informed Radovsky [Rakovsky, the Russian ambassador] they would not let their rooms to Bolshevists again.[575]

Margaret was ever the networker, and the task of chair of the committee suited her down to the ground. When the Society was formally launched in July 1924, it rapidly drew in a range of outstanding British intellectuals. The philosopher and journalist Leonard Hobhouse, an old friend of the Llewelyn Davies family, was the first president, and the mixed Anglo-Russian executive committee included Leonard Woolf and the leading co-operator Henry May. Bloomsbury connections figured prominently. Virginia Woolf, E.M. Forster and J.M. Keynes were all among the initial supporters, along with other notables such as Bertrand Russell, Bernard Shaw, and H.G. Wells.

The Society brought together a range of influential figures from the worlds of politics, social activism and the arts. There was particular interest in co-operation, reflecting the British movement's early interest in co-operative developments in the new Russia, and also Margaret and Henry May's involvement. Margaret's organising experience and her connections both in the labour and co-operative movements and among the liberal intelligentsia made her a valuable chair.[576]

Margaret filled pages of her letters to Dolly Ponsonby with her work in the society. She evidently took to it with gusto, much as she had enjoyed setting up the People's Suffrage Federation some fifteen years earlier. When J.M. Keynes gave a public lecture for the society in November 1925, she was full of comment on the content, but also of pride at the turnout:

> Little Lopokova [Keynes' wife, a renowned ballerina] was there, looking so sweet and simple. Also Bertie R[ussell] *and Mrs* – + H.G. Wells, + Hawtrey, + E.M. Forster, + Francis Burrell + Mary Murray + Emily Hobhouse …' [577][original emphasis]

The list went on.

Although the Society's British members were generally pro-Soviet, they were not, for the most part, communists, and it always claimed to be interested solely in fostering cultural relations in a non-political way. According to Dolly Ponsonby, this initially frustrated Margaret: '[as] Margaret cares for political action more than anything – + upholds on the whole the regime in Russia, it is rather too difficult for her.'[578] Margaret certainly remained sympathetic to the Bolshevik government during its early years and when it forcibly took over the Russian Co-operative movement in 1920, she and Lilian published a long article in *Co-operative News* in defence.

Despite her support for the new Russia, the evidence is that Margaret never actually joined the Communist Party; indeed, her commitment to pacifism would have ruled this out. As chair of the Society for Cultural Relations, she firmly held the line that it must remain genuinely independent of the Soviet regime. In 1925 she wrote bluntly to Varvara Polovtseva, a Russian-born executive committee member living in Britain whom she had known and admired for some years:

> … from the beginning I have said that we must choose between being a Communist cultural Society and a Society which, while being on friendly terms with the Soviet Government, must not be in any way dominated by it.

She added, 'I would not remain Chairman if the Society became an official Communist one'.[579]

Margaret soon had to draw on her Guild experience of handling sensitive negotiations. In the summer of 1927, alleging espionage, the British government severed all diplomatic relations and trade agreements with the Soviet Union, and deported many Russians. Almost all the society's Russian members – who had previously numbered a quarter of the total – were eventually forced to leave Britain. There was alarm and despondency as Margaret led a series of executive committee discussions about whether or not the society could continue at all in its current form. Margaret eventually managed to persuade enough people to support her positive approach, and eventually the committee unanimously agreed that the society should continue, albeit on a reduced scale.

Sadly, Margaret had to resign within a year of this success. Her continuing ill-health had regularly forced her to miss executive committee meetings, and now it was getting worse. In February 1928 she had to go away for three months, 'on doctor's orders', but a short break was not enough. In June, she had to submit her resignation.

This must have been a bitter pill. It was the last time that Margaret, now 67, took on any organising responsibility.

Life goes on

In early 1925 Margaret and Lilian had moved from their mansion flat to 26 Well Walk, still in Hampstead, where they were to stay for the next ten years. This was a good-sized terraced house and more roomy than their previous flat. It also possessed a garden, something which became more and more important to both women.

As Margaret gradually relinquished her role on the public stage, other interests, though always combined with politics, came to the fore. She loved holidays and visited various parts of England, perhaps making up for the long years when she had been tied to home because of her father. She wrote enthusiastic letters about the countryside she saw, and also about the people she came across – an unending source of interest to her.

Music continued to be Margaret's great love. In her late sixties she turned to the gramophone, writing excitedly that she had, 'nearly decided to get His Master's Voice ... I shd so love to have all the possibilities, as I can hardly ever manage concerts nowadays'.[580]

Margaret read voraciously and eclectically, and when she needed relaxation was to be found devouring Dickens, Laurence Sterne's *Tristram Shandy*, or Daisy Ashford's *The Young Visiters*. Surprisingly, she approved to some extent of D.H. Lawrence. Although she found his ideas about the position of women 'totally unacceptable', she nevertheless felt he was 'sincere + courageous' and that 'a good deal of what seems right is to be found in his extraordinary kind of harmony'.[581]

Much of our scanty picture of Margaret's personal life in the 1920s and '30s comes from her letters to Dolly and Arthur Ponsonby and from the diaries which they both kept. As the years went by, a shared commitment to the peace movement strengthened this old friendship. Margaret was a regular visitor to Shulbrede Priory, the Ponsonbys' Sussex home. She wrote long, gossipy letters to Dolly about friends, family, books, health problems, gardens, holidays, the countryside – and, still central for Margaret, political ideas, particularly peace and disarmament. Both Dolly and Arthur admired her; Arthur enjoyed their political discussions, while Dolly confided to her diary that Margaret was

> without exception the most remarkable woman I know – absolutely uncompromising about what she thinks right + with a burning belief in things. Warm hearted to a degree, emotional + yet strong + with a tremendous love of beauty ... In this scrappy cynical present world she is an immense support.[582]

Despite their long-term friendship, though, Dolly, rather like Virginia Woolf, did find Margaret irritating at times. The old enthusiasms had definitely not dimmed, and if anything, her left-wing political allegiance had hardened. At times she was off-puttingly intense and inflexible, annoying Dolly, who saw the world rather differently. After one breakfast-table discussion Dolly's son Matthew, who was otherwise fond of Margaret, exploded. If she went on any longer, he protested, she would, 'turn him into a Tory!' Dolly herself let off steam to her diary when Margaret sent her a newspaper cutting to persuade her to change her views about birth control, 'I have told her quite definitely I am against State birth control – but she is a propagandist beyond everything'.[583]

There was a particularly painful disagreement at the end of 1929 when Arthur, now a Labour junior minister, accepted a peerage. Margaret, still a convinced republican, was horrified. But in a long letter which otherwise threatened to become an angry rant, she eventually put out a disarming olive branch: 'After all, it is only a Peerage we are discussing! Think what it would have been if you had become Roman Catholics, or I a bloody Communist!'[584]

Fortunately the friendship remained unscathed, and if anything was to grow still closer as the years passed.

Margaret's adventurous side did not diminish with age. As Dolly put it, although Margaret was now in her sixties and seventies, she was 'always ready for experiments of any sort'.[585] While she was not always good with children, she had a real talent for getting on with young people. When her nieces Mary and Theodora, Maurice's children, went to Girton, their friends apparently thought she was wonderful. She even went on holiday with a group of these young women, and kept in touch for a while with one who was to become extremely eminent, 'My clever young economist Barbara Wootton'.[586]

Instinctively a helper, Margaret would still drop everything, her own health permitting, if someone she knew was sick or in trouble. Thus when a friend with serious mental health problems turned up unannounced, she took it upon herself to find suitable care for her. And she tried to use her contacts to help Varvara Polovtseva, by 1930 an impoverished exile from the Soviet Union.

Margaret's inner life

Margaret had been drawn to co-operation in the first place because of its ideals of mutual aid. Influenced by her father's Christian Socialist traditions, and also by the Positivism on her mother's side of the family, she stressed the importance of putting values into practice in personal relationships, believing that altruism was 'the only finally satisfying course of conduct',[587] and that co-operation should aim to make people 'not only richer, but better'.[588] These beliefs had never left her during the intervening years, although she became preoccupied with campaigning and running the Guild, and grew much more radical politically.

In her later years Margaret had time to create the commonplace books, which comprised a huge jumble of hand-copied or pasted-in poems, aphorisms and other writings, jokes, children's sayings, press cuttings, cards, photographs and cartoons – all in no particular order. In this eclectic mix, some things stand out, and politics and the Guild figure particularly prominently. In a lighter vein, her inclusion of this piece of doggerel provides an interesting sidelight on her friendship with the Woolfs:[589]

> Confident that art + brains
> Reside with them (and Maynard Keynes)
> The School of Bloomsbury lies here
> Greeting the unknown with a sneer.

Above all, though, the books provide a moving record of Margaret's inner life, and especially a reflection of her over-arching preoccupation with peace and non-violence. In early entries, we see her struggling to come to terms with the violence perpetrated by the Bolsheviks and Irish nationalist movements, both of which she supported. Apropos of Irish nationalism, she copied poems about the 1916 Easter Rising, and explained to Leonard Woolf, 'I cannot, as an Englishwoman condemn acts which we have caused. Nor do I think that actions by oppressed + oppressors are on the same plane'.[590] Under the heading, 'Compare the Russian Revolution with the following' she copied out descriptions of the French Revolution, and an extract from Macaulay which ends 'There is only one cure for the evils which newly-acquired freedom produces, + that cure is freedom'. Although Margaret's own pacifism was absolute, she was not prepared to condemn others out of hand.

The books also contain a great deal about ethics and about spiritual ideas, drawing on eastern as well as western philosophy; and demonstrate Margaret's deep love of literature, art, poetry and music. She quotes from a wide range of British writers but also from Gogol, Nietzsche, Turgenev, Dostoevsky and more. She was evidently drawn to poems about the beauties of nature; and the Romantics, especially Keats, are well represented. Significantly, she wrote in one of the books, 'Where there is no beauty, there is no spiritual power'; reflecting her lifelong belief, following William Morris, in the cardinal importance of beauty in everyday life.[591]

CHAPTER 18

The Final Years, 1933-1944

On 20 June 1933 almost three thousand women converged on Central Hall Westminster from all over the country for a giant congress celebrating the Women's Co-operative Guild's 50th birthday. A special supplement in *Co-operative News* marking the occasion included an article by Margaret and Lilian, reminiscing about their time in the Guild. It was entitled, perhaps pointedly, *Peaceful* Campaigns.[592]

On the day, the hall rang to the rafters with a rapturous ovation when the two women appeared on the platform. Margaret made a speech presenting a new national banner for the Guild, which she and Lilian had commissioned. It showed a woman carrying a shopping basket, with her arm round a young girl. Seen in the background were a factory, a co-operative shop and a rainbow; the latter symbolising the guild's motto, 'Of whole heart cometh hope'. The accompanying text was 'Co-operative buying builds the new world'. The huge audience cheered Margaret again and again as she urged them not to rest on past triumphs, but to 'go forward with faith and trust in the irresistible advance that is bringing the new civilisation'.[593]

For both Margaret and Lilian, the proof that they were still appreciated in the Guild was obviously a tonic. A photograph shows them flanked by old friends and fellow campaigners Frau Freundlich (over from Austria), Margaret Bondfield and Eleanor Barton.[594] The two women had both dressed up for the occasion – Margaret even seems to be wearing make-up – and they look relaxed and happy. The image is a salutary contrast to the depressing picture which Virginia Woolf painted of Margaret in these later years.

From what we know, this was Margaret's last public speech. It was a high note to end on.

Pacifism and the threat of war

Despite her optimistic speech at the Congress, Margaret could not help feeling already that 'Public things ... get worse and worse – but I fear Lilian + I can do little to help now. The W.C.G is the only cheering thing – and the International Guild ...'[595] Her sense of powerlessness inevitably worsened as the 1930s wore on, with mass unemployment and continuing poverty at home, and ever stronger fascism and the threat of war abroad.

While Margaret maintained her interest in politics, her focus became narrower. The commonplace books include some items about current British developments, including Edward VIII's abdication, which seems to have interested her a good deal,[596] but they are virtually silent on the major developments in European politics which preoccupied others on the left, such as the rise of Stalin and Hitler, and the Spanish Civil War. A rare exception is a 1932 press cutting of 75-year-old Communist Clara Zetkin defying the Nazis in the Reichstag.[597]

Margaret was now almost exclusively preoccupied with the need to preserve peace. She rejoiced that, with Eleanor Barton at the helm, the Guild continued its anti-war campaigning and became a leading women's peace organisation. It is still remembered today for its introduction of the white 'peace' poppy, to be worn on Armistice Day instead of red, in memory of the dead of the First World War.[598]

In the mid-1930s Margaret was buoyed up by a temporary groundswell of support for British peace movements. This was largely due to the new and highly successful Peace Pledge Union, which appealed to individuals to pledge themselves to renounce war. Although she was initially critical of its religious connections and its lack of links with working-class organisations, Margaret supported the PPU, as did Lilian. Margaret met and talked to the Reverend Dick Sheppard, its founder, and soon both women felt they had now found an organisation for which they could 'do what (little) we can'. No longer able to be active in the old way, they nevertheless wrote an article for *Co-operative News*, and Margaret spread the word among people she knew; hopefully reporting that 'there seems to be considerable peace feeling about'.[599]

Towards the end of the 1930s, as the threat of war drew closer, divisions grew between 'absolute' pacifists and those who abandoned their pacifism because they believed Nazism to be an existential threat which could only be defeated by force of arms. Margaret took the absolute pacifism line. In 1938 she supported the Munich Agreement, which permitted Hitler to take over the Sudetenland in the mistaken belief that this would guarantee 'peace in our time'. She signed a manifesto sponsored by a wide range of peace and labour organisations which repudiated appeals to support a war which would 'maintain and extend Imperialist possessions and interests'.[600] Tucked into her very last commonplace book are press cuttings from August 1939 showing members of the Peace Pledge Union's National Council.

After nearly thirty years of campaigning for peace and international harmony, Margaret simply could not justify war and killing on any grounds. Like her friends the Ponsonbys and, most famously, Vera Brittain, Margaret proclaimed herself a stronger than ever pacifist after the outbreak of the Second World War. She would remain so until her death.

Dorking and Patterdale

Margaret and Lilian finally left Hampstead for good in 1935. A couple of years earlier her brother Maurice and his family had moved to Surrey, just outside Dorking, and the two women decided to join them there. Margaret found two small cottages immediately down the hill from Maurice's house and had them knocked together. Hillspur would be home for her and Lilian for the rest of her life, except for a period during the war. She chose a woman architect for the renovation; something of a statement at the time. Janet Potts, a distant relative, remembered her as a friendly, enthusiastic client, closely interested in all the decisions.[601]

The house provided Margaret and Lilian each with her own bedroom and sitting room. There was a garden which joined up with Maurice's, and a tree under which Margaret would sit and enjoy the beautiful views of the Surrey hills. Maurice's daughter Jane, who loved coming down the hill to visit her great-aunt, remembers Margaret's living room as beautifully furnished and decorated, in her favourite William Morris style, and smelling of fresh flowers or potpourri.[602]

Brothers Charley and Harry, had died in the 1920s, and in 1935 Crompton suddenly succumbed to heart failure. Maurice, 'the last of my much-loved Six', was in poor health for some years and would also die from heart failure in 1939.[603] So Margaret survived all her brothers.

Meanwhile, though, there were good times. She and Lilian had become very close to Mary and Theodora, Maurice's daughters, who lived virtually next door, and bonded with Mary and Jane, Theodora's little girls, as well as with other neighbouring children.

However, the move away from Hampstead proved to be a milestone. As her health deteriorated, Margaret's world gradually narrowed. So did that of Lilian, who eventually became completely blind. By the later 1930s, Margaret had become something of an invalid, and a worried Rosalind Nash felt that what she needed was 'some easy change of scene and thought'. Rosalind was not convinced that Margaret really needed to be quite as careful with her health as she was, pointing out that she had managed to get to Hampshire to visit Janet Case – probably during Janet's last illness in 1937 – without apparent problems.[604]

However, Margaret stuck to the restrictive medical advice she received about her heart trouble. As early as 1933, she complained that when she had one of her regular crises 'I have to ... refrain from so much – talks, walking, reading, music'. Yet she had not lost her old enthusiasm. The same letter continues 'there is so much I would like to do, + to get through'.[605]

Margaret and Lilian always enjoyed political discussions, and they and the Ponsonbys relished like-minded company. After tea with Margaret and Lilian in May 1940, Arthur wrote, 'In spite of illness and physical incapacities, both of them [were] full of wisdom and satisfactorily violent against the hypocrisies and imbecilities of the day'.[606] Months into the Second World War, and just weeks before the Battle of Britain, they must have all welcomed being able to share their unpopular pacifist beliefs.

Maurice's family owned Broad How, a house near Patterdale in the Lake District that they used for holidays. Anxious about air raids, Mary and Theodora took the children to live there after war broke out, and eventually Margaret, Lilian and their housekeeper, Mrs Redhouse, on whom Margaret relied a great deal, came to join them. What with the three of them each requiring their own room, Theodora's two daughters, a Hungarian child refugee whom the family had taken in, and, for a while, an evacuee, Broad How was bursting at the seams. Somehow, Mary and Theodora coped with running it all amid the rigours of wartime, 'do[ing] the necessary digging, not for victory but for peace'.[607]

Despite both the war and her worsening health, there were new compensations for Margaret. She loved being with the family, and especially enjoyed Theodora's children. By this time she only left the house to walk the few yards to the garden gate, but she still managed to indulge her lively interest in people by starting up conversations with unsuspecting passers-by, waylaying them from her deckchair.

The family remembers Margaret as otherwise spending most of the time on the sofa, unlike Lilian, who despite her blindness 'never used to behave as if she was ailing'.[608] Niece Mary, an experienced doctor, apparently thought Margaret did not need to rest as much as she did; although her anxiety was understandable, perhaps, as her mother and three of her brothers had all died of heart related conditions. Everyday life was becoming harder. As

Margaret wrote to Dolly Ponsonby, 'My eyesight and memory are failing + my dear Lilian is blind + deaf + neither of us can remember anything.'[609]

There were more losses. At the beginning of April 1941, a letter came from Leonard Woolf with the terrible news of Virginia Woolf's suicide. Recalling how much Margaret had helped during the earlier crises, he explained in anguish why he had not insisted on bringing in nurses. Margaret managed to reply the same day, comforting and supportive, '… how perfectly right you were. Don't ever think differently – and she would not have wished it …' The letter ends, 'No more poor words – but you know I love you both, and what that means'.[610]

Margaret hated everything about the war, and at times found it too depressing to read the papers at all. The last commonplace book, much of it created while she was at Patterdale, is dominated by her continuing commitment to peace and by her concern with 'living rightly'. Given the feeling of isolation that her pacifism must have meant at this time, she pasted in a telling quotation from the Quaker historian and theologian Rufus Jones:

> There are occasions when an individual can serve society best and most fittingly, not by yielding to its conventions, nor to its historic customs + estimates, nor to its requirements of what is necessary for its status quo, but by standing out under the compulsion of some vision of advance in the championship of an ideal which ought to prevail, but does not yet prevail.

And another from Goethe: 'Thinking is easy; action is difficult; to act in accordance with one's thoughts is the most difficult thing in the world.'

At this stage in her life, though still resolutely non-Christian, Margaret was pondering religious and spiritual ideas. There are a couple of entries in the Patterdale book about Buddhist ethical teachings, and a significant passage citing A.N. Whitehead's view that 'Metaphysical principles … are truths about the nature of God. [His] God, however, is not omnipotent, and cannot be identified with the God of the Christian religion.'[611]

Last days

Concerned to avoid the rigours of another wartime winter in the Lakes, Margaret and Lilian returned to Dorking after two years or so at Patterdale, followed soon after by Theodora, Mary and the children.

By now Margaret's sight was failing and she found it difficult to read or write. In April 1944 Rosalind wrote to Dolly that Margaret felt too weak to enjoy going out, or even being visited: 'Theodora says she does not care to be in the garden + they think it is because she can't see the flowers. It is strange to think of anyone of such vitality as Margaret being so cut off from everything.'[612]

Margaret died peacefully at home a few weeks later, on 28 May 1944 – just over a week before the D Day landings which would herald the end of the war in Europe. Mary, who had cared for her at the end, wrote to Dolly that the last short illness had been without pain. She added that recently Margaret had found it hard to endure old age.

As Margaret would have wanted, she was cremated privately. The cause of death was recorded as left ventricular failure and senile myocardial degeneration. Finally, her generous heart had given up.

Coda

Margaret left a little over £23,000. Her will, which runs to almost six pages, is a remarkable illustration of the rich variety of her life and interests.[613]

By far the largest of forty-nine legacies or annuities to individuals went to the two women who, apart from her mother, had been most significant to Margaret over her lifetime: Lilian and Rosalind. As might be expected other bequests went to surviving relatives, and several former colleagues in the Guild were remembered. But friends were always important. She left a number of legacies to a whole range of friends and neighbours; and also to some of their children, including Rosalind's and Dolly's sons. Reflecting her interest in the younger generation, she also left bequests to some of Mary and Theodora's friends and their children. Mrs Redhouse was remembered, as was Annie Tandy, the Llewelyn Davies family servant from many years before.

Inevitably, Margaret set aside substantial sums for the causes to which she had devoted her life. Given her central commitment to peace and internationalism in her final years, it is not surprising that the largest of these was to the International Co-operative Women's Guild, followed by others to the Peace Pledge Union and War Resisters International. Perhaps she felt the Guild was less in need of funds; she left it considerably less, and the same amount went to the International Co-operative Alliance.

Her interests had remained wide-ranging. Bequests went to the Elizabeth Garrett Anderson Hospital, with which her father had been closely associated in its early days, and smaller legacies to the path-breaking Pioneer Health Centre in Peckham; the Rachel Macmillan Training College; the Pedestrians' Association; the Commons, Open Spaces and Footpaths Preservation

Society; the National Council for the Abolition of the Death Penalty; the Howard League for Penal Reform; and local hospital and nursing charities.

Nieces Mary and Theodora, who had been so essential to Margaret and to Lilian during her final years, jointly inherited the rest of the estate. They decided to use some of their inheritance to ensure that Mrs Redhouse could continue looking after Lilian, and bought her a house near Hampton, close to Lilian's niece, on the understanding that Lilian would stay there with her for the rest of her life.[614]

Lilian lived on for another six years. Theodora remembered going to see her at Hampton, near Richmond, where she found her still interested in politics and wanting to discuss what was going on. 'By that time she was blind and very deaf, but far more intelligent than everybody else.'[615]

CONCLUSION

Margaret's Afterlife

Margaret's death at the end of May 1944 was announced in *Co-operative News* with a front page article and photograph under the banner headline, 'Women's Guild loses one of its greatest leaders'. Over the following weeks, *Our Women's Pages* printed tributes from Guildswomen old and new.

It was more than twenty years since Margaret had retired as General Secretary, and over ten since she had taken part in public life. Yet despite the short notice and the difficulties of wartime travel, over a hundred people found their way to the Guild's memorial meeting, which took place in London on 15 June. Margaret would have been gratified that four of the six speakers were women, and especially that one was her old Viennese friend Emmy Freundlich, now a refugee from fascism living in Britain. However, she would have been embarrassed at the praise which was heaped on her. And we can imagine her wry amusement when a director of the C.W.S., with which she had been locked in battle thirty years earlier, described her as a 'great and gracious lady ... a great democrat, noted for clear thinking and courage'.[616]

An obituary in the *Manchester Guardian* was accompanied by an anonymous 'Appreciation by an old friend' – almost certainly, Rosalind Nash. A personal tribute from Margaret Bondfield in *The Labour Woman* ended, 'Margaret Llewelyn Davies has joined the immortals, whose work lives on after them'.[617]

As time passed, Margaret and her achievements gradually faded into the background, although she was never entirely forgotten. Then, in the 1970s, the second wave of feminism brought with it an explosion of interest in women's history and Margaret once more came to the fore. In 1977, the British feminist publisher Virago began a hugely successful programme of reprinting forgotten books by and about women: producing cheap, attractively designed paperbacks which rapidly found their way on to thousands of bookshelves. *Life as We Have Known It* was among the first of these, and *Maternity: Letters from Working Women* soon followed.[618] Together, they opened readers' eyes to the hidden history of working-class women and helped to inspire a generation of women historians. As Margaret was the editor, her name was prominently displayed, and newly commissioned introductions discussed her life and work. Decades after her death, she was beginning to emerge from obscurity.

From the 1980s, Margaret and the Guild began to be the focus of detailed research. Jean Gaffin and David Thoms broke new ground in 1983 with their pioneering history of the Guild, which they produced for members to mark its centenary year. This laid the foundations of a new phase.[619] Research on the co-operative movement now began to include the Guild, and with the burgeoning of academic women's studies there came new interest from a different angle; stimulated by Gillian Scott's in-depth, authoritative study of the Guild which appeared in 1998.[620] This was followed by Barbara Blaszak's 2000 account, which, while offering some valuable insights, provided a highly negative assessment of Margaret and her leadership – in my view, unjustified. Despite its strengths in some areas, I agree with those who point to this study's over-reliance on argument by inference and its one-dimensional picture of working-class women; downplaying the diversity of their lives, opinions and social status.[621]

Meanwhile, Margaret and the Guild are now routinely referred to in general accounts of women's history of their time, and also in more focused studies, particularly on the suffrage movement, and in research on co-operative history. Nevertheless, although interesting work has illuminated her connections with Bertrand Russell and with Leonard and Virginia Woolf, Margaret has still received little detailed attention in her own right.[622]

What of Margaret's beliefs in today's world? Sadly, by the time it celebrated its centenary in 1983 the Guild, renamed the Co-operative Women's Guild in the 1960s, was already struggling. Overarching social changes, with the decline of manufacturing industries and the growth of supermarket trading, had led to a drastic decline in co-operative shops; with a knock-on impact on the Guild.[623] In 2016, it finally closed as a national organisation.

Nevertheless, co-operatives are still here, and indeed have had a new lease of life, though in a different form. While the old-style co-op shop and its 'divi' have gone, 'The Co-operative', owned and controlled by members, is now a major high street retailer. Co-operative production is very much alive and well – and growing. In 2019 there were over 7,000 British co-operatives, small and large, employing nearly 234,000 people, with a turnover of £37.7 billion and 13.7 million members.[624] And co-operation is international. At a time when the globalised capitalist economy is producing devastating poverty and inequality and frustrating attempts to tackle the climate emergency, it is widely recognised radical new solutions are essential. Many agree with Nobel prize-winning economist Joseph Stiglitz who wrote, in terms which would have resonated with Margaret, that if we learn from co-operatives, we can 'construct a world in which the economy works better for all'.[625]

Meanwhile, there are small signs that Margaret is beginning to receive the public attention which she deserves. On a windy day February day in 2017, a small but significant ceremony took place in Kirkby Lonsdale. Margaret's great-niece Jane, Maurice's granddaughter, unveiled a large information board about Margaret and her work in the Guild. Produced by the local Civic Society, it occupies a prominent place in the churchyard, close to the vicarage where she lived and worked for nearly twenty years.

More came later. Idly Googling Margaret's name one day, I was surprised and delighted to come across Margaret Llewelyn Davies Close, a street in Redditch. When I visited, I found something wholly remarkable. The Close, part of Breedon Housing Co-operative, is a small street of attractive timber framed houses, built using state of the art, environmentally friendly materials. The tenants pay genuinely affordable rents, and thanks to the latest methods of insulation their fuel bills are extremely low. There is a green space opposite, and as the Close is a dead end, children can play safely. Carl Taylor, the manager, explained that the housing co-operative had found out about Margaret when, having already named several streets after famous co-operative men, it was searching around for a co-operative woman to commemorate in this new development.

Carl stressed that the Close is not only about providing good housing, vital though that is. All the tenants are members of the co-operative, and through monthly meetings have a voice in running it. In this way they gain skills and experience and help to create a community that works for everyone.

The ideals which inspired Margaret are still very much alive.

APPENDIX

The Co-operative Movement of Margaret's Time: Some Useful Terms

Central co-operative bodies

Co-operative Union	The national body representing nearly all co-operative societies. It organised an annual Co-operative Congress and provided services for member societies.
Co-operative Central Board	Organised and ran the work of the Co-operative Union. It was made up of delegates from Sectional Boards (regional committees representing co-operative societies).
United Board	A smaller group drawn from the Central Board, which acted as the equivalent of an executive committee.
Central Education Committee (CEC)	Set up by the Co-operative Central Board, provided advice on education and ran classes.

Consumer co-operation

Consumer co-operative societies (also sometimes called 'industrial' or 'distributive')	Local societies which ran co-operative stores. Members owned shares, and each also received a dividend based on how much they spent. Each society had an elected management committee, and often also an elected education committee. Some also ran departments producing goods. Each branch of the Women's Co-operative Guild was linked to a local society.

Producer co-operation

Co-operative Wholesale Society (CWS)	A national, federal organisation whose members were mostly local consumer co-operative societies. It provided them with wholesale services, and also with goods produced in its own factories, workshops etc. Headed by a Board of Directors, who were responsible to quarterly meetings of delegates from member societies.
Producer co-operative societies	Individual co-operatively run organisations: workshops, factories etc.

ACKNOWLEDGEMENTS

This book would never have seen the light of day without a great deal of help.

I owe a huge debt to Chrys Salt, whose work on a planned biography of Margaret Llewelyn Davies was cut short some years ago. Having never met me before, Chrys happily sent me off with a whole file drawer packed with her research material, thus giving me a head start on the project. This was extraordinarily helpful, and I appreciate her generosity. I am also exceedingly grateful to Margaret Llewelyn Davies' great-niece Jane Wynne Willson and her daughters Emma Dogliani and Ruth Wilson. They have given me unlimited access to family papers, photographs and reminiscences, and I have greatly valued their interest and belief in the project.

The Ponsonby papers held at Shulbrede Priory have proved a vital source. I am extremely grateful to the late Laura Ponsonby and to Kate and Ian Russell for their hospitality, and for Laura's assistance in pulling out material about and by Margaret Llewelyn Davies from their voluminous collection. Staff in various archives have been most helpful; special thanks go to Stefan Dickers at Bishopsgate Institute, Kate Perry and Hannah Westall at Girton College Archive, Cambridge, Simon Wilson and staff at Hull History Centre, Sophie McCulloch at the National Co-operative Archive, Gillian Murphy at The Women's Library, LSE, and Maggie Cohen and staff at the Working Class Movement Library, Salford. Thanks, in addition, to Bodleian Library, University of Oxford; The Keep, Brighton; Kendal Archive Centre; Queen's College, and the TUC Library at London Metropolitan University. Thanks also go to Pat France at Kirkby Lonsdale, who located parish magazines for me to look through. Finally, I must record my appreciation of the wonderful British Library and its ever-helpful staff. Being lucky enough to live within easy reach, I have used it regularly and it has been an amazing resource.

Assistance of various kinds has been essential during the process of producing this biography. Rachel Summerson not only edited the final version, but provided support and expert advice whenever I needed it, at every point along the way. This made all the difference and enabled me to turn my research into what I hope is a readable biography. I owe a great deal, in addition, to Sheena Evans and Sybil Oldfield, for their insightful feedback on chapter drafts as I produced them. I cannot thank them all enough. I am also hugely grateful to June Hannam for her detailed and valuable comments on an earlier draft of the full text. A big thank you to Gillian Lonergan, who not only read and commented on a draft, but also produced the index. And to Daniel Lopez for vital computer support, and Anna Nesbit for help with photographs.

Among others who at various times have provided additional information, insights, comments on individual draft chapters and other support are Lucy Bland, Sheila Cohen, Anna Davin, Jean Gaffin, Melissa Llewelyn Davies, Phil Gagg, Rehana Malik, Frances Pine, Katharina Rowold, Andrée Rushton, Gillian Scott and Carl Taylor. Sincere thanks go to them all. Any errors or omissions are, of course, my own.

Quotations from Llewelyn Davies papers held at Girton College, Cambridge are reproduced by permission of The Mistress and Fellows of the College, and from Bertrand Russell's unpublished correspondence by permission of the Bertrand Russell Archives, McMaster University, Canada.

I am also most grateful to Tony Zurbrugg and Adrian Howe at The Merlin Press.

Finally, Richard Saffron has lived with Margaret Llewelyn Davies for more years than I care to remember. My thanks to him, for everything, go without saying.

BIBLIOGRAPHY

Primary Sources

Archives

Women's Co-operative Guild (WCG) archival material

Bishopsgate Institute Library Special Collections and Archives, Women's Co-operative Guild collection.
British Library of Economic and Political Science (BLPES): Coll. Misc. 0268, Women's Co-operative Guild: material relating to the work of the Guild and kindred interests; Archives Special Collections; The Women's Library.
Hull History Centre, Co-operative Women's Guild collection.
National Co-operative Archive, The Co-operative College.

Personal Papers:

Bertrand Russell Archives, McMaster University, copies accessed at Bodleian Library, University of Oxford.
Girton College Archives, University of Cambridge: Sarah Emily Davies personal papers and Llewelyn Davies personal papers.
Llewelyn Davies family papers in the possession of Jane Wynne Willson.
Monks House papers, University of Sussex, The Keep.
Shulbrede Papers: Diaries and correspondence of Dorothea and Arthur Ponsonby, in the possession of Kate and Ian Russell.
The Morgue: unpublished Llewelyn Davies family memoir, Peter Llewelyn Davies, in the possession of Jane Wynne Willson and Chrys Salt.

Other archives:

Kendal Archive Centre.
Queen's College Archive.
TUC Library, London Metropolitan University.
Archive, Society for Co-operation in Russian and Soviet Studies: Annual Reports and Executive Committee Minutes of the Society for Cultural Relations with the USSR.

Publications: WCG and related material

WCG Annual Reports 1889-1921

Books by Margaret Llewelyn Davies:

The Women's Co-operative Guild, 1883-1904, Kirkby Lonsdale: WCG, 1904.
'The claims of mothers and children', in Phillips, Marion, ed., *Women and the Labour Party*, London: Headley,1918.
Ed., *Maternity: Letters from Working Women*, London: Virago, 1978.
Ed., *Life as We Have Known It*, by Co-operative Working Women, London: Virago, 1977.

Selected Pamphlets by Margaret Llewelyn Davies:

The Relations between Co-operation and Socialistic Aspirations, 1890.
Co-operation in Poor Neighbourhoods, 1899.
A Co-operative Relief Column, 1900.
The Open Door, 1903.
The Co-operative Store Abroad, 1906.
A Co-operative Standard for Women Workers, 1908.
The Vote at Last! More Power to Co-operation, 1918.
Women as Organised Consumers, 1921.
The Inaugural Address Delivered at the 54th Annual Congress of the Co-operative Union, 1922.
With Lilian Harris: *The Platform and the Floor*, 1916.
With Honora Enfield:
Co-operation versus Capitalism, Memorandum on the Co-operative Movement and the Menace of Capitalism, 1919.
Co-operation and Labour Unrest, 1921.

Other selected WCG pamphlets:

Why working women need the vote, 1897.
Women as Co-operators and Citizens, 1900.
Wives' Savings, 1907.
The Position of Married Women, 1907.
Pull Together! Why our Women Employés should Organise, 1909.
A Minimum Wage Scale for Co-operative Women and Girl Employés, 1910.
Memorandum on the National Care of Maternity, 1917.
The Freedom of the Guild, 1922.

Other WCG books:

Webb, Catherine, *The Woman with the Basket*, Manchester: Women's Co-operative Guild, 1927.

Women's Co-operative Guild, *Working Women and Divorce, An Account of the Evidence Given on Behalf of the Women's Co-operative Guild Before the Royal Commission on Divorce*, London: David Nutt, 1911.

Other publications, primary sources

Arnold-Forster, H.O., *The Laws of Every-day Life*, London: Cassell, 1889.

Bondfield, Margaret, *A Life's Work*, London: Hutchinson, 1949.

Davies, Emily, *Collected Letters, 1861-75*, eds. A. Murphy and D. Raftery, Charlottesville: University of Virginia Press, 2004.

Davies, John Llewelyn, 'The Social Doctrine of F. D. Maurice', in Hunt, W.H., ed., *Sermons on Social Subjects*, London: Skeffington and Son, 1904.

Haldane, Elizabeth, *From One Century to Another, the Reminiscences of Elizabeth S. Haldane*, London: Alexander Maclehose & Co, 1937.

Llewelyn Davies, Margaret, 'The Marylebone Social Club for Young Men and Women' in *Eastward Ho!*, vol. iv, April 1886.

Mitchell, Hannah, *The Hard Way Up, The Autobiography of Hannah Mitchell, Suffragette and Rebel*, London: Virago, 1977.

Pankhurst, Sylvia, *The Home Front: a Mirror to Life in England during the World War*, London: Hutchinson, 1932.

Russell, Bertrand, *The autobiography of Bertrand Russell, vol.1*, London: George Allen and Unwin, 1971.

Russell, Bertrand, ed. Griffin, Nicholas A., *Selected Letters of Bertrand Russell, vol.1*, London: Allen Lane, The Penguin Press, 1992.

Stephen, Barbara, *Emily Davies and Girton College*, London: Constable, 1927.

Strachey, Ray, *The Cause, A Short History of the Women's Movement in Great Britain*, London: Virago, 1978.

Swanwick, Helena, *I Have Been Young*, London: Gollancz, 1935.

Thornton, William, *On Labour*, London: Macmillan, 1870.

Tweedie, Mrs Alec, *The First College Open to Women*, London: Queen's College, 1898.

Webb, Beatrice, *My Apprenticeship*, Cambridge: Cambridge University Press, 1979.

Webb, Beatrice, eds Mackenzie, Norma and Jeanne, *The Diary of Beatrice Webb, vol.1, 1873-1892*, London: Virago, 1982.

Woolf, Leonard, *Beginning Again*, London: Hogarth Press, 1965.

Woolf, Leonard, *Letters of Leonard Woolf*, ed. Spotts, Frederic, Weidenfeld and Nicholson, 1990.

Woolf, Virginia, ed. Nicolson, Nigel, *The Letters of Virginia Woolf*, vols.1, 2, 4 and 6, London: Hogarth Press, 1975-1980.
Woolf, Virginia, ed. Bell, Anne Olivier, *The Diary of Virginia Woolf*, vols.1 and 3, London: Hogarth Press, 1977, 1980.
Woolf, Virginia, ed. Bradshaw, David, *Carlyle's House and Other Sketches*, London: Hesperus Press, 2003.

Newspapers and periodicals

Clarion
The Common Cause
Co-operative News
Daily News
Hampstead and Highgate Express
Jus Suffragii
Labour Leader
The Labour Woman
Manchester Guardian
The Times
Trade Unionist

Official Publications

Royal Commission on Divorce and Matrimonial Causes 1909, *Report and Minutes of Evidence*, London: H.M.S.O., 1912.

Interviews

Interview with Theodora Calvert by Chrys Salt
Interviews with Jane Wynne Willson by the author

Secondary sources

Bibby, Andrew, *All Our Own Work, The Co-operative Pioneers of Hebden Bridge and their Mill*, London: Merlin Press, 2015.
Birkin, Andrew, *J.M. Barrie and the Lost Boys*, London: Constable, 1980.
Black, Naomi, *Social Feminism*, Ithaca and London: Cornell University Press, 1989.
Bland, Lucy, 'White Women and Men of Colour: Miscegenation Fears in Britain after the Great War' in *Gender and History*, vol.17, April 2005.
Blaszak, Barbara, *The Matriarchs of England's Co-operative Movement*, Westport: Greenwood, 2000.

Blaszak, Barbara, 'Martha Jane Bury (1851-1913): a case-study of class identity' in *Labour History Review*, 67(2) 2002

Eds, Bock, Gisela and Thane, Pat, *Maternity and gender policies, women and the rise of the European welfare states, 1880s-1950s*, London: Routledge, 1991.

Burnett, Jacky, 'Exposing "the Inner Life": the Women's Co-operative Guild's Attitude to "Cruelty"' in *Everyday Violence in Britain: Gender and Class*, ed. D'Cruze, Shani, Harlow: Pearson Education, 2000.

Caine, Barbara, *Victorian Feminists*, Oxford: Oxford University Press, 1993.

Ceadel, Martin, *Semi-detached Idealists: the British Peace movement and International Relations, 1854-1945*, Oxford: Oxford University Press, 2000.

Cole, G.D.H., *A Century of Co-operation*, Manchester: Co-operative Union, 1944.

Davin, Anna, 'Imperialism and Motherhood' in *History Workshop Journal*, Spring 1978, p. 9.

Dwork, Deborah, *War is Good For Babies and Other Young Children, a History of the Infant and Child Welfare Movement in Britain, 1880-1914*, London: Tavistock, 1987.

Davis, Mary, *Sylvia Pankhurst, A Life in Radical Politics*, London: Pluto Press, 1999.

Gaffin, Jean and Thoms, David, *Caring and Sharing, the Centenary History of the Women's Co-operative Guild*, Manchester: Co-operative Union, 1983.

Gleadle, Kathryn, *British Women in the Nineteenth Century*, Basingstoke: Palgrave, 2001.

Glendinning, Victoria, *Leonard Woolf*, London: Simon and Schuster, 2006.

Gurney, Peter, *Co-operative Culture and the Politics of Consumption in England, 1870-1950*, Manchester: Manchester University Press, 1996.

Hannam, June, *Isabella Ford*, Oxford: Basil Blackwell, 1989.

Hannam, June and Hunt, Karen, *Socialist Women, Britain, 1880s to 1920s*, London: Routledge, 2002.

Harrison, Brian, 'Bertrand Russell: the False Consciousness of a Feminist' in *Russell: The Journal of Bertrand Russell Studies*, vol. 4, 1984.

Harrison, J.F.C., *A History of the Working Men's College, 1854-1954*, London: Routledge & Kegan Paul, 1954.

Harrison, Royden, 'Professor Beesly and the Working-class Movement' in Briggs, Asa and Saville, John, eds., *Essays in Labour History*, London: Macmillan, 1967.

Hall, Lesley A., *Sex, Gender and Social Change in Britain since 1880*, Basingstoke: Palgrave Macmillan, 2013.

Hollis, Patricia, *Ladies Elect: Women in English Local Government*, 1865-1914, Oxford: Clarendon, 1987.

Holton, Sandra Stanley, *Feminism and Democracy, Women's Suffrage and Reform Politics, 1900-1918*, Cambridge: Cambridge University Press, 1986.

Lee, Hermione, *Virginia Woolf: A Biography*, London: Chatto & Windus, 1996.

Jones, Clara, *Virginia Woolf: Ambivalent Activist*, Edinburgh: Edinburgh University Press, 2015.

Koven, Seth, *Slumming: Sexual and Social Politics in Victorian London*, Princeton and Oxford: Princeton University Press, 2004.

Lewis, Jane, *The Politics of Motherhood: Child and Maternal Welfare in England, 1900 – 1939*, London: Croom Helm, 1980.

Liddington, Jill, *The Life and Times of a Respectable Rebel, Selina Cooper (1864-1946)*, London: Virago, 1984.

Liddington, Jill and Norris, Jill, *One Hand Tied Behind Us, the Rise of the Women's Suffrage Movement*, London: Virago, 1978.

Liddington, Jill, *The Long Road to Greenham, Feminism and Anti-Militarism in Britain Since 1820*, London: Virago, 1989.

Lygo, Emily, 'Promoting Soviet Culture in Britain' in *Modern Language Review*, 108, 2013.

MacGregor, O.R., *Divorce in England: a Centenary Study*, London: Heinemann, 1957.

Monk, Ray, *Bertrand Russell: The Spirit of Solitude*, London: Jonathan Cape, 1996

Moorehead, Caroline, *Bertrand Russell, A Biography*, London: Sinclair-Stevenson, 1992.

Norman, E.R., *The Victorian Christian Socialists*, Cambridge: Cambridge University Press, 1987.

Oldfield, Sybil, 'Margaret Llewelyn Davies and Leonard Woolf', in Chapman, Wayne K. and Manson, Janet M., eds., *Women in the Milieu of Leonard and Virginia Woolf*, New York; Oxford: Pace University Press, 1998.

Oldfield Sybil, ed., *Afterwords: Letters on the Death of Virginia Woolf*, Edinburgh: Edinburgh University Press, 2005.

Pedersen, Susan, *Eleanor Rathbone and the Politics of Conscience*, New Haven and London: Yale University Press, 2004.

Purvis, June, *A History of Women's Education in England*, Milton Keynes: Open University Press, 1991.

Rowbotham, Sheila, *Edward Carpenter, a Life of Liberty and Love*, London: Verso, 2008.

Rowbotham, Sheila, *Dreamers of a New Day*, London: Verso, 2010.

Salt, Chrys, Schweitzer, Pam and Wilson, Mervyn eds., *Of Whole Heart Cometh Hope: Centenary Memories of the Co-operative Women's Guild*, London: Age Exchange Theatre Company, 1983.

Scott, Gillian, 'Working Out Their Own Salvation: Women's Autonomy and Divorce Law Reform in the Co-operative Movement, 1910-1920' in Yeo, Stephen, ed., *New Views of Co-operation*, London: Routledge, 1988.

Scott, Gillian, *Feminism and the Politics of Working Class Women*, London: UCL Press, 1998.

Scott, Gillian, 'A "Trade Union for Married Women": The Women's Co-operative Guild, 1914-1920' in Oldfield, Sybil, ed., *This Working-day World: Women's Lives and Culture(s) in Britain, 1914-1945*, London: Taylor and Francis, 1994.

Scott, Gillian, 'The Women's Co-operative Guild and Suffrage' in ed. Boussabha-Bravard, Myriam, *Suffrage Outside Suffragism: Women's Vote in Britain 1880-1914*, Basingstoke: Palgrave Macmillan, 2007

Swartz, Martin, *The Union of Democratic Control in British Politics During the First World War*, Oxford: Clarendon Press, 1971.

Thane, Pat, *Foundations of the Welfare State*, Harlow: Longmans, 1996.

Thomson, Alistair, 'Domestic Drudgery will be a Thing of the Past' in ed., Yeo, Stephen, *New Views of Co-operation*, London: Routledge, 1988.

Tilghman, Carolyn, 'Autobiography as Dissidence: Subjectivity, Sexuality and the Women's Co-operative Guild' in *Biography*, 26:4, 2003.

Vorberg-Rugh, Rachael, 'A Woman's Place Begins at Home: Who Can Say Where it Ends?' Gender Tensions in the English Co-operative Movement, 1880-1920, unpublished MA thesis, Portland University, 2002.

Vorberg-Rugh, Rachael, 'Employers *and* Workers: Conflicting Identities in the British Co-operative Movement', in Black, Lawrence and Robertson, Nicole, eds., *Consumerism and the Co-operative Movement in Modern British History*, Manchester: Manchester University Press, 2009.

Vicinus, Martha, *Independent Women, Work and Community for Single Women, 1850-1920*, London: Virago, 1985.

Wilson, Duncan, *Leonard Woolf A Political Biography*, London: Hogarth Press, 1978.

Wiltsher, Anne, *Most Dangerous Women, Feminist Peace Campaigners of the Great War*, London: Pandora, 1985.

Wynne Willson, Jane, *The Chain of Love, a Victorian Family History*, Birmingham: Garland Publications, 2018.

Wynne Willson, William, *The Story of A Victorian Visit*, Birmingham: Garland Publications, 2007.

www.uk.co-op/economy, *The Co-operative Economy*, 2017 and 2019. radicalmanchester.wordpress.com, 2010, Irving, Sarah, *Alfred Barton: Nineteenth Century Anarchism and the Early Twentieth Century Labour Party*.

Oxford Dictionary of National Biography online

ABBREVIATIONS USED IN THE NOTES

AR: Annual Reports, Women's Co-operative Guild.

BLPES WCG: British Library of Political and Economic Science, Coll. Misc. 0268: Women's Co-operative Guild: Material Relating to the Work of the Guild and Kindred Interests.

BR Arch.: Bertrand Russell Archives, McMaster University Library, photocopies accessed at Bodleian Library, MSs. Facs. C. 111-113.

CC minutes: Central Committee minutes, Women's Co-operative Guild, held at Hull History Centre.

CN: Cooperative News.

FP: Llewelyn Davies family papers in the possession of Jane Wynne Willson.

GCPP Davies, Girton College Archive, Cambridge, personal papers of Sarah Emily Davies.

GCPP LLD: Girton College Archives, Cambridge, Llewelyn Davies personal papers.

LW Arch.: Leonard Woolf Archive, University of Sussex Special Collections.

M.Ll.D.: Margaret Llewelyn Davies.

Morgue: Peter Llewelyn Davies, *The Morgue, Some Davies Letters and Papers*, unpublished, n.d., in the possession of Jane Wynne Willson and Chrys Salt.

OWP: Our Women's Pages (women's pages of CN).

SP: Ponsonby family papers, Shulbrede Priory.

WC: Woman's/Women's Corner (women's pages of CN).

NOTES

1. Virginia Woolf, ed. Nigel Nicolson, *The Letters of Virginia Woolf*, vol. 2, London: Hogarth Press, 1976, Virginia Woolf to Janet Case, 7 June 1922.
2. G.D.H. Cole, *A Century of Co-operation*, Manchester: Co-operative Union, 1944, p. 371.
3. *OWP*, 10 June 1922.
4. *CN*, 10 June 1922.
5. M.Ll.D., *The Inaugural Address Delivered at the 54th Annual Congress of the Co-operative Union*, Manchester: Co-operative Union, 1922.
6. Virginia Woolf, loc.cit.
7. G.D.H. Cole, (1944), p. 218.
8. Leonard Woolf, *Beginning Again*, London: Hogarth Press,1965, p. 101.
9. M.Ll.D., *The Women's Co-operative Guild*, Kirkby Lonsdale: WCG, 1904, p. 21.
10. M.Ll.D., ed., *Life as we have known it*, London: Virago, 1977, p. 49.
11. *Manchester Guardian*, 24 June 1914.
12. *CN*, 22 November 1913, cited in Gillian Scott, *Feminism and the Politics of Working Class Women*, London: UCL Press, 1998, p. 1.
13. Virginia Woolf, ed. Nigel Nicolson, *The Letters of Virginia Woolf*, vol. 2, London: Hogarth Press, 1976, Virginia Woolf to Lady Robert Cecil, May 1913.
14. BLPES WCG, vol.1.
15. See William Wynne Willson, *The Story of A Victorian Visit*, Birmingham: Garland Publications, 2007.
16. Beatrice Webb, *My Apprenticeship*, Cambridge: Cambridge University Press, 1979, p. 149.
17. Royden Harrison, 'Professor Beesly and the working-class movement' in Asa Briggs and John Saville, eds. *Essays in Labour History*, London: Macmillan, 1967, p. 241.
18. *Oxford Dictionary of National Biography*.
19. ibid.
20. GCPP LlD, Lady Crompton to M.Ll.D, 30 April 1881.
21. Emily Davies, 'Family Chronicle', reproduced in *Morgue*, p. 153. This is the main source for this section.
22. Barbara Stephen, *Emily Davies and Girton College*, London: Constable, 1927, p. 271.
23. Muriel Bradbrook, 'That Infidel Place', quoted in Introduction to Emily Davies, *Collected Letters 1861-75*, eds. Murphy A. and Raftery D., 2004, Charlottesville: University of Virginia Press, 2004, p. xxiv.
24. ibid., Emily Davies to Henry Tomkinson, 7 November 1870.
25. J. F. C. Harrison, *A History of the Working Men's College, 1854-1954*, London: Routledge & Kegan Paul, 1954, p. 41.
26. E.R Norman, *The Victorian Christian Socialists*, Cambridge: Cambridge University Press, 1987, p. 24.
27. see Sheila Rowbotham, *Edward Carpenter, a Life of Liberty and Love*, London: Verso, 2008, p. 27. Carpenter was F.D. Maurice's curate.
28. *Morgue*, p. 112.
29. John Llewelyn Davies, 'The Social Doctrine of F. D. Maurice', in W.D. Hunt, ed., *Sermons on Social Subjects*, London: Skeffington and Son, 1904, p. 188. Thanks to

    Chrys Salt for this reference.
30 *Morgue*, p. 102.
31 Sir Charles Lucas, *The Cornhill Magazine*, October 1916.
32 GCPP LLD, Mary Davies to M.Ll.D., 3 June 1894.
33 Jane Wynne Willson, *The Chain of Love, a Victorian Family History*, Birmingham: Garland Publications, 2018, p. 15.
34 *Morgue*, Dorothea (henceforward Dolly) Parry to Peter Llewelyn Davies, 21 December 1945.
35 GCPP LLD, Mary Davies to M.Ll.D., 8 June 1990.
36 *Morgue*, p. 155.
37 GCPP LLD, Mary Davies to M.Ll.D., 20 April 1887.
38 Jane Wynne Willson, (2018), on which this chapter draws heavily, p. 28.
39 ibid., p. 22-23.
40 Jane Wynne Willson, (2018), p. 110.
41 GCPP LLD, Mary Davies to M.Ll.D., 29 September 1876.
42 ibid., 12 July 1877.
43 FP, Katherine Llewelyn Davies memoir of M.Ll.D., n.d.
44 GCPP LLD, Mary Davies to M.Ll.D., 30 June 1877.
45 1881 and 1891 censuses.
46 GCPP LLD, Mary Davies to M.Ll.D., 16 November 1882.
47 Jane Wynne Willson, (2018), p. 26.
48 GCPP LLD, Mary Davies to M.Ll.D., 4 July 1877
49 Personal communication, Jane Wynne Willson.
50 GCPP LlD, Mary Davies to M.Ll.D., 4 October 1882.
51 ibid,16 March 1877.
52 ibid, 29 September 1876.
53 Jane Wynne Willson, (2018), p. 44.
54 See June Purvis, *A History of Women's Education in England*, Milton Keynes: Open University Press, 1991.
55 F.D. Maurice, cited in Mrs Alec Tweedie, *The First College Open to Women*, London: Queen's College, 1898, p. 3.
56 ibid.
57 GCPP LLD, Mary Davies to M.Ll.D., 5 March probably 1874.
58 ibid., 5 August 1877.
59 FP., Rosalind Nash, *A memoir of Margaret Llewelyn Davies*, n.d.
60 Barbara Stephen, (1927), p. 276.
61 See GCPP LLD, Mary Davies to M.Ll.D., 20 February 1881.
62 ibid., 8 June 1882.
63 *Morgue*, Arthur Llewelyn Davies to Mary Davies, 12 June 1882.
64 Helena Swanwick, *I Have Been Young*, London: Gollancz, 1935, p. 122-123.
65 GCPP LLD, Mary Davies to M.Ll.D.,14 October 1882.
66 Rosalind Nash, (n.d.).
67 Girton College Archives, *Girton College Register*.
68 Martha Vicinus, *Independent Women, Work and Community for Single Women, 1850-1920*, London: Virago, 1985, p. 124.
69 GCPP LLD, Mary Davies to M.Ll.D, 17 April 1883.

70 ibid., 11 June 1883.
71 ibid., Jane Wynne Willson to Alison Duke, 18 March 1988.
72 *Oxford Dictionary of National Biography, Girton College Register.*
73 Jane Wynne Willson, (2018), p. 111. The letter refers to the Prince and Princess of Wales, and to pupils of state schools, run by local School Boards.
74 ibid., 30 October 1884.
75 GCPP LLD, Mary Davies to M.Ll.D., November 1883.
76 Beatrice Webb, (1979), pp. 179-80.
77 H.M. Hyndman and William Morris, '*A Summary of the Principles of Socialism*', quoted in Beatrice Webb, (1979), pp. 181-2.
78 Sheila Rowbotham, (2008), p. 79.
79 SP, M.Ll.D to Dolly Ponsonby, 18 August 1930.
80 GCPP LLD, Mary Davies to M.Ll.D., 3 October 1883.
81 M.Ll.D., 'The Marylebone Social Club for Young Men and Women', in *Eastward Ho!*, vol. iv, April 1886. Thanks to Anna Davin for this reference.
82 Elizabeth Haldane, *From One Century to Another, the Reminiscences of Elizabeth S. Haldane*, London: Alexander Maclehose & Co, 1937, p. 141.
83 M.Ll.D, (1886).
84 BLPES WCG, vol.1.
85 William Thornton, *On Labour*, London: Macmillan, 1870.
86 Andrew Bibby, *All Our Own Work, The Co-operative Pioneers of Hebden Bridge and Their Mill*, London: Merlin Press, 2015, pp. 7 and 59.
87 See Peter Gurney, *Co-operative Culture and the Politics of Consumption in England, 1870-1950*, Manchester: Manchester University Press, 1996.
88 In 1884 renamed the Women's Guild for the Spread of Co-operation, and by 1890 the Women's Co-operative Guild.
89 Catherine Webb, *The Woman with the Basket*, Manchester: Women's Co-operative Guild, 1927, pp. 20-21.
90 The Guild covered England and Wales only; a separate Guild came into being in Scotland.
91 M.Ll.D., ed., (1977), p. 37.
92 Cited in Jill Liddington, *The Life and Times of a Respectable Rebel, Selina Cooper (1864-1946)*, London: Virago, 1984, p. 56.
93 Catherine Webb, (1927), p.20-21; *WC*, 10 July 1886, cited in Barbara Blaszak, *The Matriarchs of England's Co-operative Movement*, Westport: Greenwood, 2000, p. 100.
94 *WC*, 29 June 1889.
95 ibid., 26 June 1886.
96 ibid., February-October 1885.
97 ibid., 1 March 1890.
98 Catherine Webb, (1927), p. 22.
99 *WC*, 6 August 1887.
100 GCPP LLD, Mary Davies to M.Ll.D, date unclear, 21? September 1887.
101 *WC*, 9 June 1888.
102 ibid.
103 *WC*,16 June 1888.
104 See *Contemporary Review*, June 1916. The memorial article written by his son Charles

states that Llewelyn was a Liberal Unionist: that is, he opposed Gladstone's Home Rule policy.
105 *The Times*, 5 January 1889.
106 Girton College Archives, GCPP Muir, papers of Margaret Alice (Meta) Muir, Meta Muir to Eva Muir, 9 September 1889.
107 Barbara Blaszak, (2000), p. 39, *WC* 12 January, 23 February and 23 March 1889.
108 National Cooperative Archive, Lawrenson Collection, Mrs Lawrenson to M.Ll.D., 13 May 1888. See also letters to Mrs Lawrenson from Miss Wilson and Miss Sharp, January and March 1889.
109 *WC*, 11 May 1889.
110 ibid., 22 November 1890.
111 GCPP LLD, Mary Davies to M.Ll.D, 28 November 1889.
112 *Morgue*, Mary Davies to Sylvia du Maurier, 3 November 1890.
113 *SP*, diary of Lady Maude Parry, 29 October 1890.
114 ibid., 17 October 1890.
115 *SP*, Diary of Dolly Parry (later Ponsonby), 20 March 1892.
116 *WC*, 17 August 1889.
117 See Gillian Scott, (1998), p. 17.
118 National Co-operative Archive, Lawrenson Collection, Mary Lawrenson to M.Ll.D., May 1888; also *WC*, 17 August 1889.
119 *WC*, 6 July 1889.
120 H.O. Arnold-Forster, *The Laws of Every-day Life*, London: Cassell, 1889.
121 *WC*, 1 November 1890.
122 *AR*,1889-1890.
123 GCPP LLD, Mary Davies to M.Ll.D., 16 November 1889.
124 M.Ll.D., *The Relations between Co-operation and Socialistic Aspirations*, Manchester: Co-operative Union,1890.
125 *CN*, 31 May 1890.
126 Beatrice Webb, eds, Norman and Jeanne Mackenzie, *The Diary of Beatrice Webb, Volume 1, 1873-1892*, London: Virago, 1982, entry 24 May 1890.
127 *Lunesdale and District Parish Magazines*, Kendal Archive Centre, April 1889.
128 *CN*, 1 July 1922, cited Gillian Scott, (1998), p. 40.
129 GCPP LLD, Mary Davies to M.Ll.D., 21 April 1891.
130 See Catherine Webb, (1927), p. 9.
131 See *CN*, 6 August 1891, 29 October 1892.
132 TUC Library, *Trade Unionist*, 3 October 1891.
133 ibid., 31 October 1891.
134 *AR*, 1891-1892.
135 M.Ll.D., (1904), pp.122-4.
136 *Trade Unionist*, 3 October and 10 October 1891.
137 ibid., 19 Dec 1891. This refers to an anti-slavery slogan which was also used in the labour movement.
138 M.Ll.D., (1904), pp. 121-3.
139 *AR*, 1891-1892.
140 e.g., M.Ll.D, (1904), p. 65.
141 GCPP LLD, Mary Davies to M.Ll.D., 2 August 1891.

142 ibid., 8 June 1889.
143 With thanks to Jane Wynne Willson.
144 See Susan Pedersen, *Eleanor Rathbone and the Politics of Conscience*, New Haven and London: Yale University Press, 2004, p. 163.
145 M.Ll.D., (1904), pp. 112-13.
146 GCPP LLD, Mary Davies to M.Ll.D., 3 June 1889.
147 *AR*, 1892-1893, *Manchester Guardian*, 26 July 1892, see also *WC*, 20 August 1892.
148 *CN* supplement, 6 August 1892.
149 *WC*, 20 August 1892.
150 CC minutes, June and July 1892.
151 *WC*, 20 August 1892.
152 *WC*, 13 August 1892.
153 ibid.
154 This section draws on Gillian Scott, (1998), pp. 17-19.
155 M.Ll.D., ed., (1977), p. 96.
156 *AR*, 1892-1893.
157 *AR*, 1893-1894.
158 *Daily Chronicle*, 29 December 1894, cited in *WC*, 12 January 1895.
159 *WC*, 14 July 1894.
160 *AR* 1893-1894.
161 *CN*, 20 and 27 February, 5 March 1892.
162 *WC*, 26 May 1894.
163 *CN*, 13 June 1892.
164 ibid., 22 September 1894, 16 January 1897.
165 *OWP*, 3 March 1928.
166 *Oxford Dictionary of National Biography*.
167 *WC*, 28 October 1893.
168 Bertrand Russell, ed. Nicholas A. Griffin, *Selected letters of Bertrand Russell, vol.1*, London: Allen Lane, The Penguin Press, 1992 (Bertrand Russell to Alys Russell, 12 October 1893, referring to M.Ll.D. having broken down because of her dedication to work).
169 *WC*, 6 January 1894.
170 ibid., 1 December 1894.
171 GCPP LLD, Mary Davies to M.Ll.D., 8 December 1893, 17 December 1894.
172 ibid., Harry Llewelyn Davies to M.Ll.D., 14 October 1894.
173 ibid., Mary Davies to M.Ll.D., 20 November 1894.
174 ibid., 28 December 1894.
175 ibid., 6 February 1895.
176 ibid., 30 June 1889.
177 *Morgue*, Dolly Ponsonby to Peter Llewelyn Davies, 21 December 1945.
178 GCPP LLD, Mary Davies to M.Ll.D., 29 September 1891.
179 *Lunesdale and District Parish Magazines*, January 1895, Kendal Archive Centre.
180 *WC*, 2 March 1895.
181 CC minutes, April 1897.
182 *WC*, 12 January 1901.
183 Rosalind Nash, n.d.

184 *CN*, 6 August 1892.
185 *WC*, 23 September 1899.
186 *WC*, 10 July 1897.
187 CC minutes, January to June 1901.
188 CC minutes, April/May 1901.
189 *WC*, 5 January 1901.
190 M.Ll.D., (1904), p. 21.
191 ibid, pp. 39-40.
192 *WC*, 5 January 1901; M.Ll.D., (1904), p. 40.
193 Jill Liddington, (1984), see especially p. 75.
194 D.H. Lawrence, *Sons and Lovers*, New York: Gramercy Books, pp. 46-7, cited in Rachael Vorberg-Rugh, 'A Woman's Place Begins at Home: Who Can Say Where it Ends?' Gender Tensions in the English Co-operative Movement, 1880-1920, unpublished MA thesis, Portland University, 2002.
195 M.Ll.D., (1904), p. 40, *WC*, 6 November 1897.
196 *WC*, 23 October 1897. M.Ll.D., (1904), pp. 102-3.
197 See e.g. Alistair Thomson, 'Domestic Drudgery will be a Thing of the Past', in Stephen Yeo, ed., *New Views of Co-operation*, London: Routledge, 1988.
198 M.Ll.D., (1904), p. 132.
199 see Arnold Bonner, *British Co-operation*, Manchester: Co-operative Union, 1970, pp. 120-21.
200 *WC*, 8 June 1895.
201 ibid., 20 July 1895.
202 See Jill Liddington and Jill Norris, *One Hand Tied Behind Us, the Rise of the Women's Suffrage Movement*, London: Virago, 1978.
203 M.Ll.D., (1904), pp. 144-5.
204 *Manchester Guardian*, 15 and 16 July 1897.
205 *AR* 1902-1903.
206 *WC*, 1 August and 10 October 1903. See also CC minutes.
207 ibid., 10 October 1903.
208 M.Ll.D., (1904), p. 143.
209 *Manchester Guardian*, 12 November 1903.
210 *CN*, 14 November 1903.
211 M.Ll.D., (1904), p. 150.
212 ibid., p. 36.
213 *WC*, 29 August 1896.
214 *WC*, 4 February 1905.
215 Rosalind Nash, n.d.
216 *WC*, 20 February 1904.
217 *WC*, 16 December 1905.
218 *CN*, 22 October 1891, cited Rachael Vorberg-Rugh, (2002), p. 58.
219 *AR* 1898.
220 M.Ll.D., *Co-operation in Poor Neighbourhoods*, 1899.
221 M.Ll.D., (1904) p. 77.
222 *AR* 1899-1900.
223 See e.g. *WC*, 10 February and 17 March 1900.

224 M.Ll.D., (1904), p. 78.
225 *WC*, 28 October 1899.
226 BLPES Archives Special, thanks to Chrys Salt for this reference.
227 *CN*, 5 June 1901.
228 1901 census shows Mrs Abbott was a former teacher.
229 BLPES WCG, vol. 6, J.C Gray to M.Ll.D., 11 February, 1902.
230 *WC*, 5, 12, 26 April and 3 May 1902.
231 National Co-operative Archive , M.Ll.D., *The Open Door*, 1903.
232 ibid., p. 30.
233 M.Ll.D., (1904), p. 91.
234 *AR* 1902-1903.
235 BLPES WCG, vol. 2.
236 *WC*, 20 December 1902 and 14 February 1903.
237 *AR*, 1902-1903, BLPES WCG, vol 2.
238 M.Ll.D., (1900).
239 BLPES WCG, vol. 2.
240 ibid., M.Ll.D., (1903).
241 ibid., cutting from *Daily News*, 10 February 1903.
242 ibid., C.M. Mayo to M.Ll.D., undated.
243 Gillian Scott, (1998), p. 99.
244 See *WC*, 19 November 1904.
245 ibid., 8 July 1905.
246 ibid., 19 November 1904.
247 ibid., 23 July and 12 November 1904, 8 and 15 July, 5 and 26 August 1905.
248 BLPES WCG, vol. 2., Mary Spooner to M.Ll.D., 2 December 1905.
249 ibid., Mary Spooner to M.Ll.D., 7 December 1905.
250 ibid., Ada Greener to M.Ll.D, December 1905.
251 ibid., Mary Spooner to M.Ll.D., n.d.
252 BLPES WCG, vols. 2-6.
253 BLPES WCG, vol. 2, "Nellie".
254 *WC*, 10 December 1904.
255 Cited Barbara Blaszak, (2000), p. 148
256 See Gillian Scott, (1998), p. 100.
257 *SP*, Dolly Ponsonby diary, 6 October 1922.
258 G.D.H. Cole, (1944), p. 223.
259 *WC*, 29 November and 6 December 1902.
260 M.Ll.D., (1904), p. 96.
261 Frederick Rogers, quoted in Duncan Wilson, *Leonard Woolf A Political Biography*, London: Hogarth Press, 1978, p. 51.
262 Jane Wynne Willson, (2018), p. 110.
263 *The Times*, 31 July 1905.
264 Jane Wynne Willson (2018), p. 115, Bertrand Russell, *The autobiography of Bertrand Russell, vol.1,* London: George Allen and Unwin, 1971, pp. 195-196.
265 *Lunesdale and District Parish Magazine*, August 1905.
266 Bertrand Russell, (1971), pp. 195-6 (Crompton Llewelyn Davies to Bertrand Russell, October 1905).

267 BR Arch., M.Ll.D. to Bertrand Russell, August 1905.
268 BLPES WCG vol. 6, Mary Spooner to M.Ll.D., 5 September 1905.
269 BR Arch., M.Ll.D.to Russell, 23 February 1906, Russell to M.Ll.D., 27 February 1906.
270 See e.g. Ray Monk, *Bertrand Russell: The Spirit of Solitude*, London: Jonathan Cape, 1996.
271 The rest of this chapter draws on *The Morgue*, Peter Llewelyn Davies, unpublished, n.d., with thanks to Jane Wynne Willson and Chrys Salt. For a comprehensive account, see Andrew Birkin, *J.M. Barrie and the Lost Boys*, London: Constable, 1980.
272 *Morgue*, Arthur Llewelyn Davies to M.Ll.D., 12 June 1906.
273 ibid., Arthur Llewelyn Davies to M.Ll.D., 27 March 1890.
274 ibid., Sylvia Llewelyn Davies to M.Ll.D., 16 July 1895.
275 *SP*, Dolly Ponsonby diary, August 1906.
276 *Morgue*, M.Ll.D. to John Llewelyn Davies, 14 June 1906.
277 ibid., p. 241.
278 *SP*, Dolly Ponsonby diary, August 1906, also *Morgue*, her letter to Peter Llewelyn Davies, 21 December 1945.
279 *Morgue*, p. 266.
280 ibid., Sylvia Llewelyn Davies to M.Ll.D., 5 July 1906.
281 ibid., Arthur Llewelyn Davies to John Llewelyn Davies, 21 September 1906.
282 BR Arch., M.Ll.D. to Bertrand Russell, undated ('October').
283 *Morgue*, M.Ll.D. note, 2 December 1906.
284 BR Arch., M.Ll.D. to Bertrand Russell, 3 January 1907.
285 *SP*, Sylvia Llewelyn Davies to Dolly Ponsonby, n.d., probably winter 1906/1907.
286 *Morgue*, Arthur Llewelyn Davies note, n.d.
287 BR Arch., M.Ll.D. to Bertrand Russell, 'Easter Sunday' (31 March 1907).
288 *Morgue*, Harry Llewelyn Davies to M.Ll.D., 11 May 1907.
289 ibid., M.Ll.D. to Peter Llewelyn Davies, n.d., p. 219.
290 BR Arch., M.Ll.D. to Bertrand Russell, 3 June and ? July 1907
291 *Morgue*, p. 441.
292 BR Arch., M.Ll.D. to Bertrand Russell, 1 December 1907.
293 *Morgue*, p. 439.
294 ibid., p. 295.
295 ibid., Emma du Maurier to May Coles, July 1910.
296 ibid., p. 546.
297 ibid., Emma du Maurier to May Coles, 1 August 1910
298 Theodora Calvert, interview with Chrys Salt, n.d.
299 ibid.
300 See e.g. Andrew Birkin, (1980), Piers Dudgeon, *Captivated: J.M. Barrie, the Du Mauriers and the Dark Side of Neverland,* London: Chatto and Windus, 2008, *The Lost Boys*, (BBC Television, 1978), *Finding Neverland*, (film, 2004).
301 *SP*, Dolly Ponsonby diary, 7 August 1911.
302 *Morgue*, George Llewelyn Davies to Peter Llewelyn Davies, 30 December 1914, Michael Llewellyn Davies to George Llewelyn Davies, 3 March 1915.
303 Virginia Woolf, ed. David Bradshaw, *Carlyle's House and Other Sketches*, London: Hesperus Press, 2003, p. 11. Thanks to Sybil Oldfield for this reference.
304 Bertrand Russell, ed. Nicholas A. Griffin, (1992), 2 April 1907.

305 ibid., M.Ll.D. to Bertrand Russell, (undated) August 1907, Bertrand Russell to M.Ll.D., 29 August 1907.
306 ibid., M.Ll.D. to Bertrand Russell, 11 June 1911.
307 BR Arch., folder 111.
308 See Caroline Moorehead, *Bertrand Russell, a Biography*, London: Sinclair-Stevenson, 1992, p. 95.
309 Theodora Calvert interview, n.d.
310 *SP*, M.Ll.D. to Dolly Ponsonby, 'Jan 2', content fixes as 1912.
311 CC minutes, 22 and 23 August 1912.
312 ibid., 15 November 1912.
313 Tom Paine, radical philosopher and activist, author of *The Rights of Man*; Bakunin, Russian anarchist thinker, Santayana the Spanish-American philosopher and humanist.
314 BR Arch., M.Ll.D. to Bertrand Russell, 4 May 1906.
315 ibid., M.Ll.D. to Bertrand Russell, undated, content indicates May 1908.
316 *SP*, Dolly Ponsonby diary, 1 April 1909.
317 LW Arch., M.Ll.D. to Leonard Woolf, n.d., contents indicate 1913.
318 Virginia Woolf, ed. Nigel Nicolson, (1976), Virginia Woolf to Katherine Cox, 18 March 1913.
319 LW Arch.., M.Ll.D. to Leonard Woolf, undated. This section draws on Sybil Oldfield, 'Margaret Llewelyn Davies and Leonard Woolf' in Wayne K. Chapman and Janet Manson, eds., *Women in the Milieu of Leonard and Virginia Woolf*, New York; Oxford: Pace University Press, 1998.
320 Victoria Glendinning, *Leonard Woolf*, London: Simon and Schuster, 2006, p. 193.
321 LW Arch., M.Ll.D., undated, probably 1913.
322 ibid, M.Ll.D. to Leonard Woolf, undated, probably 1913.
323 Leonard Woolf, (1964), pp. 102-3.
324 See Hermione Lee, *Virginia Woolf: A Biography*, London: Chatto & Windus, p. 328.
325 Virginia Woolf, *Letters*, (1975), Virginia Woolf to Janet Case, December 1910.
326 See Clara Jones, *Virginia Woolf: Ambivalent Activist*, Edinburgh: Edinburgh University Press, 2015.
327 *Manchester Guardian*, 25 June 1908.
328 BR Arch., M.Ll.D to Bertrand Russell, June 1908.
329 Leonard Woolf, (1964), p. 102.
330 G.D.H. Cole, (1944), p. 371, *ARs* 1904-1915 and 1913-1914.
331 Margaret Bondfield, *A Life's Work*, London: Hutchinson, 1949, p. 127.
332 Leonard Woolf, (1964), pp. 106 and 108, thanks to Chrys Salt.
333 Helena Swanwick, (1935), pp. 161-2.
334 *WC*, 30 June 1906.
335 ibid., 26 June 1909.
336 ibid., 29 June 1913.
337 ibid., 27 April 1912.
338 *CN* 16 July1910.
339 See *ARs* 1908-1909 and 1909-1910.
340 *The Times*, 13 May 1905.
341 *Morgue*, M.Ll.D. to Barbara Stephen, n.d., p. 144.
342 See Jill Liddington and Jill Norris, (1977).

343 *WC*, 23 July 1904.
344 See Sandra Stanley Holton, *Feminism and Democracy, Women's Suffrage and Reform Politics, 1900-1918*, Cambridge: Cambridge University Press, 1986, June Hannam and Karen Hunt, *Socialist Women, Britain, 1880s to 1920s*, London: Routledge, 2002.
345 *WC*, 28 January 1905, see Liddington and Norris (1978), p. 180-81.
346 *Clarion*, 30 December 1904.
347 ibid., 12 May 1905, cited June Hannam and Karen Hunt, 2002, p. 110.
348 Hannah Mitchell, *The Hard Way Up, The Autobiography of Hannah Mitchell, Suffragette and Rebel*, London: Virago, 1977, p. 139, Ada Nield Chew, *Clarion*, 30 November 1906.
349 *The Times*, 13 May 1905.
350 *WC*, 3 March 1906.
351 ibid., 26 May 1906.
352 ibid., 16 June 1906.
353 Ray Strachey, *The Cause, A Short History of the Women's Movement in Great Britain*, London: Virago, 1978, p. 305.
354 ibid., pp. 311-12.
355 *Manchester Guardian*, 2 November 1906.
356 BR Arch., M.Ll.D. to Bertrand Russell, 'Easter Sunday' 1907.
357 See *CN*, 30 June 1906.
358 Helena Swanwick, (1935), p. 193.
359 Ray Strachey, (1978), p. 306.
360 27 October 1906, thanks to Chrys Salt.
361 *Manchester Guardian*, 5 December 1906.
362 BR Arch., M.Ll.D. to Bertrand Russell, 12 January 1908.
363 *WC*, 8 May 1909.
364 BR Arch., M.Ll.D. to Bertrand Russell, 31 March 1907. See Brian Harrison, 'Bertrand Russell: the False Consciousness of a Feminist' in *Russell: The Journal of Bertrand Russell Studies*, vol. 4, 1984, thanks to Gillian Scott for this reference.
365 BR Arch., Bertrand Russell to M.Ll.D, 2 April 1907, M.Ll.D. to Bertrand Russell, 12 May 1907.
366 BR Arch., M.Ll.D. to Bertrand Russell, October 1908.
367 *The Times*, 15 February 1909.
368 *SP*, Dolly Ponsonby diary, 1 April 1909.
369 See June Hannam and Karen Hunt, (2002), p. 123.
370 *The Common Cause*, 21 October 1909.
371 ibid., 9 December 1909.
372 BR.Arch., folder 111.
373 See Sandra Stanley Holton, (1986), Chapter 3.
374 *WC* 26 June 1909.
375 This summary of Mrs Bury's background and earlier life draws on Barbara Blaszak, 'Martha Jane Bury (1851-1913): a case-study of class identity' in *Labour History Review* 67(2), 2002, and on 1891 and 1901 censuses.
376 Quoted M.Ll.D., (1904), p. 61.
377 *WC*, 9 February 1895, 30 June 1906.
378 ibid., 23 October, 13 November, 27 November 1909.
379 ibid., 8 January 1910.

380 ibid., 27 November 1909 and 1 January 1910.
381 BR Arch., Helena Swanwick to Bertrand Russell, 27 November 1909.
382 BR Arch., M.Ll.D. to Bertrand Russell, undated, probably 1911.
383 *Manchester Guardian*, 27 January 1912.
384 *WC*, 14 December 1912.
385 ibid.,18 January 1913.
386 *Labour Leader*, 6 February 1913.
387 LW Arch., M.Ll.D. to Leonard Woolf, "Sunday". Content indicates June/July 1913.
388 Thomas Hood, *The Song of the Shirt*, 1843.
389 See Rachael Vorberg-Rugh, 'Employers *and* Workers: Conflicting Identities in the British Co-operative Movement', in Lawrence Black and Nicole Robertson, eds., *Consumerism and the Co-operative Movement in Modern British History*, Manchester: Manchester University Press, 2009 (original emphasis in title).
390 *WC*, 30 June 1906.
391 ibid., 27 June 1896.
392 *WC*, 29 June 1907.
393 *CN*, 13 June 1908.
394 *A Co-operative Standard for Women Workers*, paper read by M.Ll.D. at the 1908 Women's Co-operative Guild Congress, thanks to Chrys Salt for this reference.
395 *AR* 1908-1909.
396 *Pull together! Why our Women* Employés *Should Organise*, paper for WCG spring conferences, 1909, thanks to Chrys Salt.
397 *WC*, 30 July 1910.
398 *WC*, 9 December 1911.
399 BLPES WCG, vol.1, M.Ll.D. and Lilian Harris, *Peaceful Campaigns, by Two Old Campaigners*, n.d.
400 Cited in Catherine Webb, (1927), p. 120.
401 *AR* 1913-1914.
402 *WC*, 14 October 1911.
403 Catherine Webb (1927), pp. 99-100.
404 *Wives' Savings*, paper for sectional conferences, 1907.
405 BR Arch., M.Ll.D. to Bertrand Russell,1 December 1907.
406 *AR*, 1911-1912.
407 June Hannam and Karen Hunt, (2002), p. 69.
408 BR Arch., M.Ll.D. to Bertrand Russell, 17 November 1907.
409 *SP*, Dolly Ponsonby diary, 16 November 1910.
410 O.R. MacGregor, *Divorce in England: a centenary study*, London: Heinemann, 1957, p. 25.
411 Women's Co-operative Guild, *Working Women and Divorce, An Account of the Evidence Given on Behalf of the Women's Co-operative Guild Before the Royal Commission on Divorce*, London: David Nutt, 1911, p. 42.
412 See ibid., pp. 44-8.
413 Royal Commission on Divorce and Matrimonial Causes 1909, *Report and Minutes of Evidence*, London: H.M.S.O., 1912, Cd. 6481, vol. 111, 'Miss Llewelyn Davies', p. 151.
414 ibid.
415 ibid., p.156 and pp. 166-7.

416 ibid., pp. 169-70.
417 See Sarah Irving, *Alfred Barton: 19th Century Anarchism and the Early 20th Century Labour Party*, radicalmanchester.wordpress.com, 2010.
418 Royal Commission on Divorce and Matrimonial Causes (1912), Cd. 6481, 'Mrs. E. Barton', pp. 171-2.
419 *The Times*, 10 November 1910.
420 *WC*, 20 April 1912.
421 Royal Commission on Divorce and Matrimonial Causes (1912), Cd. 6478, 'Minority Report', p. 177.
422 *The Times*, 14 November 1912.
423 LW Arch., M.Ll.D. to Leonard Woolf, undated, 1913.
424 Women's Co-operative Guild, *Working Women and Divorce, An Account of the Evidence Given on Behalf of the Women's Co-operative Guild Before the Royal Commission on Divorce*, (1911).
425 *WC*, 19 April 1913.
426 *WC*, 7 June 1913.
427 BR Arch., M.Ll.D. to Bertrand Russell, 6 June 1913.
428 *WC*, 21 June 1913.
429 BR Arch., M.Ll.D. to Bertrand Russell, undated, 1913.
430 Cited in Lesley A. Hall, *Sex, Gender and Social Change in Britain since 1880*, Basingstoke: Palgrave Macmillan, 2013, p. 71.
431 *The Spectator*, 16 November 1912.
432 *The Times*, 28 November 1912.
433 Cited in Gillian Scott, 'Working Out Their Own Salvation: Women's Autonomy and Divorce Law Reform in the Co-operative Movement, 1910-1920', in ed. Stephen Yeo, (1988), p. 129.
434 *AR* 1913-1914.
435 ibid.
436 This account of the Central Board discussion is taken from Gillian Scott, (1988), pp. 137-9. See also *CN*, 6 June 1914, which reports that three Guild branches had written dissociating themselves from the Guild position.
437 *WC*, 20 June 1914.
438 LW Arch., M.Ll.D. to Leonard Woolf, undated, content indicates 1914.
439 ibid., undated.
440 ibid.
441 Jacky Burnett, 'Exposing "the Inner Life": the Women's Co-operative Guild's Attitude to "Cruelty"', in ed. Shani D'Cruze, *Everyday Violence in Britain: Gender and Class*, ed. Shani D'Cruze, Harlow: Pearson Education, p. 137.
442 Gillian Scott, (1998), pp. 129-30.
443 Lesley Hall (2013), p. 62, see also Carolyn Tilghman, 'Autobiography as Dissidence: Subjectivity, Sexuality and the Women's Co-operative Guild', in *Biography*, 26:4, 2003
444 Dorothy Sheepshanks, *WC*, 6 November 1915.
445 *AR* 1910-1911, cited Gillian Scott, (1998), p. 111.
446 Mrs Layton, 'Memories of Seventy Years' in ed. M.Ll.D, (1977), p. 49.
447 See e.g. *WC*, 15 April and 27 May 1911.
448 *The Times*, 24 June 1911.

449 LW Arch., M.Ll.D. to Leonard Woolf, undated. See also *AR* 1912-1913.
450 Margaret Bondfield, (1949), pp. 36-7, 126.
451 *WC*, 16 May 1914.
452 *The Times*, 26 and 29 July 1913; see also detailed discussion in Gillian Scott (1998), p. 115-17.
453 LW Arch., M.Ll.D. to Leonard Woolf, 'Wednesday evening'.
454 Catherine Webb (1927), p. 127.
455 *Manchester Guardian*, 7 August 1913.
456 Cited in Gillian Scott, (1998), p. 116.
457 *AR* 1914.
458 See Gillian Scott, (1998), p. 117.
459 See Pat Thane, 'Visions of Gender in the Making of the British Welfare State: the Case of Women in the British Labour Party and Social Policy, 1906-1945' in eds., Gisela Bock and Pat Thane, *Maternity and Gender Policies, Women and the Rise of the European Welfare States, 1880s-1950s*, London: Routledge, 1991, p. 101.
460 Cited in Jane Lewis, *The Politics of Motherhood: Child and Maternal Welfare in England, 1900–1939*, London: Croom Helm, 1980, p. 100.
461 ed. M.Ll.D., (1978), pp. 61-2.
462 ibid., pp. 23-4.
463 ibid., p. 45.
464 ibid., p. 49.
465 ibid., pp. 28-9.
466 M.Ll.D., 'The Claims of Mothers and Children' in ed. Marion Phillips, *Women and the Labour Party*, London: Headley, 1918, p. 29.
467 Census 1871.
468 The scheme is outlined in ed. M.Ll.D., (1978), p. 209.
469 *WC*, 11 April 1914.
470 See *The Times*, 28 March and 9 April 1914, BR Arch., M.Ll.D to Bertrand Russell, 17 May 1914.
471 *Manchester Guardian*, 8 July 1914.
472 Reprinted in *Public Health*, June 1914.
473 *SP*, Dolly Ponsonby diary, 4 July 1909.
474 LW Arch., M.Ll.D. to Leonard Woolf, 13 March, content indicates 1914.
475 BR Arch., M.Ll.D. to Bertrand Russell, 17 May 1914, LW Arch., M.Ll.D. to Leonard Woolf, undated.
476 *AR* 1914-1915.
477 *WC* 24 October 1914, BLPES WCG vol.1, *Peaceful Campaigns, by Two Old Campaigners*.
478 *AR* 1914-1915.
479 Ed. M.Ll.D., (1978).
480 ibid., pp. 1-17.
481 *AR* 1915-1916.
482 *WC*, 6 November 1915.
483 *Memorandum on the National Care of Maternity*, London: Women's Co-operative Guild, 1917.
484 *The Times*, 3 July 1917.
485 *WC*, 6 April 1918.

486 *AR* 1914-1915.
487 *WC*, 8 January 1915.
488 M.Ll.D. in ed. Marion Phillips, (1918), pp. 29-37.
489 Helena Swanwick (1935), p. 241; BR Arch., Bertrand Russell to M.Ll.D., 'Monday', August 1914.
490 LW Arch., M.Ll.D. to Leonard Woolf, 2 May, content indicates 1916.
491 LW Arch., M.Ll.D. to Leonard Woolf, undated.
492 BR Arch., M.Ll.D. to Bertrand Russell, 12 July 1916; *SP*, M.Ll.D. to Dolly Ponsonby, undated, content indicates 1916.
493 *The Times*, 23 May 1916, 17 September 2015, *Hampstead and Highgate Express*, 27 May 1916.
494 BR Arch., Bertrand Russell to M.Ll.D, 19 May 1916.
495 According to his grandson Peter, at the end of his life Llewelyn believed that the war was 'the work of the Jews', *Morgue*, p. 587.
496 *SP*, Dolly Ponsonby diary, 15 March undated, likely 1909 or 1911.
497 Sylvia Pankhurst, *The Home Front: a Mirror to Life in England during the World War*, London: Hutchinson, 1932, p. 161.
498 *CN*, 27 June 1914.
499 ibid., Co-operative Congress report, 29 May 1915.
500 *WC*, 19 June 1915.
501 *CN*, 10 June 1916.
502 *WC*, 22 July 1916.
503 ibid., 16 February 1918.
504 M.Ll.D., *The Vote at Last! More Power to Co-operation*, 1918.
505 *WC*, 14 December 1918.
506 *AR* 1918-1919.
507 LW Arch., M.Ll.D. to Leonard Woolf, undated, probably 1915.
508 Quoted in Martin Swartz, *The Union of Democratic Control in British Politics During the First World War*, Oxford: Clarendon Press, 1971, p. 106.
509 *Jus Suffragii*, 1 January 1915.
510 Jill Liddington, *The Long Road to Greenham, Feminism and Anti-Militarism in Britain Since 1820*, London: Virago, 1989, Chapter 5; Anne Wiltsher, *Most Dangerous Women, Feminist Peace Campaigners of the Great War*, London: Pandora, 1985.
511 Quoted in Mary Davis, *Sylvia Pankhurst, A Life in Radical Politics*, London: Pluto Press, 1999, p. 51.
512 *WC*, 25 September 1915.
513 *AR* 1917-1918.
514 BR Arch., Bertrand Russell to M.Ll.D., 15 April 1918.
515 *WC*, 22 June 1918.
516 ibid.
517 *WC*, 23 June 1918.
518 *CN*, 6 July 1918.
519 *WC*, 16 November 1918.
520 LW Arch., M.Ll.D. to Leonard and Virginia Woolf, 'Sunday evening'.
521 10 October 1891, thanks to Chrys Salt for this reference.
522 GCPP LLD, Mary Davies to M.Ll.D., probably March 1892.

523 *The Labour Woman*, July 1944, The Women's Library, BLPES.
524 *OWP*, 17 June 1944.
525 Virginia Woolf, ed. Nigel Nicolson (1976), Virginia Woolf to Saxon Sydney Turner, 30 September 1916.
526 Virginia Woolf, ed. Anne Olivier Bell, *The Diary of Virginia Woolf, vol. 1*, London: Hogarth Press, 1977, 8 March 1918 and 15 November 1919.
527 *SP*, Arthur Ponsonby Diary, 6 March 1936.
528 Virginia Woolf, ed. Nigel Nicolson, (1976), Virginia Woolf to Vanessa Bell, 24 September and to Sidney Saxon Turner, 30 September 1916.
529 Theodora Calvert interview, n.d.
530 *SP*, M.Ll.D. to Dolly Ponsonby, 27 August, undated, probably 1917.
531 *CN*, 1 February 1919.
532 G.D.H. Cole, (1944), p. 299.
533 M.Ll.D. and Honora Enfield, *Co-operation versus Capitalism, Memorandum on the Co-operative Movement and the Menace of Capitalism*, 1919, BLPES Archives Special, HD/E17.
534 *AR* 1919-1920.
535 CC minutes, circular 15 April 1920.
536 *The Observer*, 25 April 1920, Lucy Bland, 'White Women and Men of Colour: Miscegenation Fears in Britain after the Great War, *Gender and History*, vol.17 no.1, April 2005, esp. pp. 39-43.
537 *OWP*, 17 April 1920.
538 *OWP*, 6 November 1920 and 26 March 1921.
539 Catherine Webb, (1927), p. 173.
540 *OWP*, 27 August 1921.
541 *OWP*, 29 October 1921.
542 CC minutes, 11 and 12 October 1919.
543 LW Arch., Leonard Woolf to M.Ll.D, 5 April 1920.
544 Barbara Stephen, (1927), p. 355.
545 LW Arch., M.Ll.D. to Leonard and Virginia Woolf, 31 May 1921.
546 ibid, M.Ll.D. to Leonard Woolf, n.d., probably August or September 1921.
547 CC minutes, 22 September 1921.
548 ibid.
549 *OWP*, 22 October 1921.
550 As was relatively common practice in her generation, Margaret either destroyed most personal letters she received, or eventually returned them to the writer. After Margaret's death, Lilian deposited the letters discussed here as part of a collection of Guild-related papers, BLPES Coll. Misc. 0268.
551 CC minutes, 14 and 15 December 1921.
552 *OWP*, 19 November 1921.
553 *OWP*, 18 February 1922.
554 *CN*, 10 June 1922.
555 Leonard Woolf, *Letters of Leonard Woolf*, ed. Frederic Spotts, Weidenfeld and Nicholson, 1990, Leonard Woolf to M.Ll.D, 21 April 1922.
556 BLPES WCG, vol. 9.
557 *CN*, 10 June 1922.

558 *The Freedom of the Guild*, 1922, thanks to Chrys Salt for this reference,
559 Virginia Woolf, ed. Anne Olivier Bell, *The Diary of Virginia Woolf, vol.3*, 1980, 17 May 1925. See also 15 November 1921 and 28 February 1923.
560 ibid., 11 March 1930.
561 SP, M.Ll.D. to Dolly Ponsonby, 11 August 1933.
562 SP, Dolly Ponsonby diary, 10 November 1927.
563 LW Arch., M.Ll.D. to Leonard Woolf, undated, content confirms 1922.
564 OWP, 6 September 1923.
565 MLl.D., *Commonplace Book 4*, loose pages.
566 SP, M.Ll.D. to Dolly Ponsonby, 'March 2 Saltdean', probably 1929.
567 The original edition, by the Hogarth Press, was republished by Virago in 1977; page references in these notes are to the 1977 edition.
568 M.Ll.D. ed., (1977), p. 140.
569 Virginia Woolf, ed. Nigel Nicolson, *The Letters of Virginia Woolf, vol. 4*, London: Hogarth Press, 1978, Virginia Woolf to M.Ll.D., 6 June 1929.
570 SP, M.Ll.D. to Dolly Ponsonby, probably 1933.
571 See e.g. Clara Jones, *Virginia Woolf: Ambivalent Activist*, Edinburgh: Edinburgh University Press, 2016.
572 Virginia Woolf, ed. Nigel Nicolson, *The Letters of Virginia Woolf, vol. 6*, London: Hogarth Press, 1980, Virginia Woolf to M.Ll.D, 8 June1938.
573 Thanks to Sybil Oldfield for this point.
574 SP, M.Ll.D. to Dolly Ponsonby, undated, probably January 1924.
575 SP, DP diary 17 June 1924.
576 See Executive Committee minutes and Annual Reports, 1924-1928 of the Society for Cultural Relations with the USSR, held by the Society for Co-operation in Russian and Soviet Studies (SCRSS). See also *Manchester Guardian*, 11 July 1924.
577 SP, M.Ll.D to Dolly Ponsonby, undated, 1925.
578 SP, Dolly Ponsonby diary,10 June 1924.
579 Michael David-Fox, *Showcasing the Great Experiment: Cultural Diplomacy and Western Visitors to the Soviet Union*, 1921-1941, Oxford: Oxford University Press, 2012, pp. 82-3, cited in Emily Lygo, 'Promoting Soviet Culture in Britain', *Modern Language Review*, 108 (2013).
580 SP, M.Ll.D. to Dolly Ponsonby, 27 June 1927.
581 SP, M.Ll.D. to Dolly Ponsonby, 18 August 1930.
582 SP, Dolly Ponsonby diary, 10 October 1927.
583 SP, Dolly Ponsonby diary, 30 July 1928.
584 SP, M.Ll. D. to Dolly and Arthur Ponsonby, 19 December, content confirms 1929.
585 SP, Dolly Ponsonby diary, 8 January 1930.
586 LW Arch., M.Ll.D. to Leonard Woolf, 1 September, probably 1919 and 1 October, probably 1922.
587 M.Ll.D. (1890), discussed in Chapter 4.
588 See chapter 3.
589 M.Ll.D., *Commonplace Book 1*, attrib. there to H. Wolfe.
590 LW Arch., M.Ll.D. to Leonard Woolf, 8 March 1920.
591 M.Ll.D., *Commonplace Book 1*.
592 BLPES WCG, vol. 1, *Peaceful Campaigns, By Two Old Campaigners*.

593 OWP, 20 January 1934, Jean Gaffin and David Thoms, *Caring and Sharing, the Centenary History of the Women's Co-operative Guild,* Manchester: Co-operative Union, 1983, p. 100.
594 Hull History Centre, photograph U DCW/6/10/19.
595 *SP,* M.Ll.D. to Dolly Ponsonby, 11 August 1933.
596 See *Commonplace Book 3.*
597 *Commonplace Book 2.*
598 See Jill Liddington (1989), Chapter 8.
599 *SP,* M.Ll.D. to Dolly Ponsonby, 27 December 1936.
600 *Manchester Guardian,* 28 September 1938. Margaret was still remembered well enough for her name to be included in the printed list; Lilian no doubt was among the '100 others' who also signed.
601 GCPP LLD, Janet Potts, *The Llewelyn Davies and Fletcher Families,* unpublished.
602 Wynne Willson (2018), p. 55.
603 *SP,* M.Ll.D. to Dolly Ponsonby, 16 December, content indicates 1935.
604 *SP,* Rosalind Nash to Dolly Ponsonby, 23 March, undated.
605 *SP,* M.Ll.D. to Dolly Ponsonby, 3 January 1933.
606 *SP,* Arthur Ponsonby diary, 12 May 1940.
607 Theodora Calvert interview, n.d.
608 ibid.
609 *SP,* M.Ll.D. to Dolly Ponsonby, 'Patterdale', undated.
610 Cited in Sybil Oldfield, (1998), p. 23. See also Oldfield, ed., *Afterwords: Letters on the Death of Virginia Woolf,* Edinburgh: Edinburgh University Press, 2005
611 M.Ll.D. *Commonplace Book* 4. See Sybil Oldfield (1998) for a fuller discussion of the Commonplace Books.
612 *SP,* Rosalind Nash to Dolly Ponsonby, 14 April 1944.
613 Thanks to Jane Wynne Willson for details about legatees.
614 Theodora Calvert interview, n.d.
615 ibid.
616 *CN,* 24 June 1944. See also *SP,* Mary Davies (Margaret's niece) to Dolly Ponsonby, 16 June 1944.
617 *Manchester Guardian,* 2 June 1944, *The Labour Woman,* July 1944, TWL @LSE
618 Ed. M.Ll.D., (1977 and 1978). In 2012 Virago repackaged the two books in new editions, with slightly different titles: "*Life as We Have Known It, The Voices of Working Class Women,* and *No-one but a Woman Knows, Stories of Motherhood before the War.*
619 Jean Gaffin and David Thoms, (1983).
620 Gillian Scott, (1998).
621 Barbara Blaszak, (2000).See Jutta Schwarzkopf review, *Labor History,* 42 (1), February 2001.
622 J.F.C Harrison, (1984), Sybil Oldfield, (1998), Clara Jones, (2016).
623 Jean Gaffin and David Thoms, (1983).
624 *The Co-operative Economy* 2019, www.uk.co-op/economy/2019.
625 http://reports.uk.coop/economy/2017.

INDEX

M.Ll.D.: Margaret Llewelyn Davies
W.C.G.: Women's Co-operative Guild

Abbot, Mrs, 85, 118
Acland, Alice, 34, 36, 37, 58
Adult Suffrage Society, 132
Allen, Mrs, 199
Amalgamated Union of Co-operative
   Employees, 141, 144, 146, 147, 148-49,
   224
Anderson, Adelaide, 48, 61
Anderson, Elizabeth Garrett, 7, 13, 63, 77
Anson, Sir William, 159
Anti-Sweating League, 140
Asquith, Herbert Henry
   divorce reform, 173, 160
   manhood suffrage, 134, 137, 138
   women's suffrage, 122, 128, 130-31
Austria, 213-14

Balfour, Lady Frances, 158-59
banners, 33, 56, 218, 232
Barnes, Sir John Gorell (Lord Gorell), 153,
   156
Barrie, J.M.
   adoption of M.Ll.D.'s nephews, 4, 102,
   103-04
   Arthur and Sylvia Llewelyn Davies, 97-98,
   99, 100, 101,
   women's suffrage, 133
Barton, Alfred, 158
Barton, Eleanor
   divorce reform, 157-58, 159, 160, 166
   international co-operation, 214
   parliamentary candidate, 219
   peace, 195, 198, 200
   W.C.G. President, 191
   work for W.C.G., 218, 232
Bective, Earl and Lady, 43
Beesly, Emily (earlier Emily Crompton),
   9, 49
Beesly, Professor Spencer, 9
Bell, Isabel, 68
Besant, Annie, 8
Black, Clementina, 57
Blair, Anna, 161-62
Blaszak, Barbara, 240
Bodichon, Barbara, 11, 16, 25
Bolton, 61-62, 71, 176
Bondfield, Margaret
   divorce reform, 160
   maternity campaign, 175, 176, 180
   minimum wages, 147
   national insurance, 172-74, 175
   peace, 187
   relationship with M.Ll.D., 180
   tribute to M.Ll.D., 239
   women's suffrage, 132
   work for W.C.G., 112, 171-72, 190, 232
Booth, Charles, 10, 85
Booth, Meg, 95
Booth, Mrs, 162
Breedon Housing Co-operative, 241
Brierfield, 73
Bright, John, 78
Bristol, 89-91
British Medical Journal, 183
Brown, Mrs, 133
Browning, Robert, 7, 28
Bury, Mrs

conflict with M.Ll.D., 119, 136
divorce reform, 159, 161, 166
minimum wage, 140, 141
women's suffrage, 78, 134-35
Bye, Mrs, 162

Campbell-Bannerman, Sir Henry, 122, 126
capitalism, 2, 211-12
Carpenter, Edward, 30
Case, Janet
  correspondence with Virginia Woolf, 115
  friendship with M.Ll.D., 109, 113, 235
  Girton College, 25, 27, 28, 29
  women's suffrage, 131-32, 133
Cecil, Lord Robert, 174
charitable work, 14, 17, 181, 184
Charity Organisation Society, 14
Chew, Ada Nield, 125, 151
children
  care by women, 151-52
  divorce, 162
  employment, 75-76, 86
  health, 118-19, 175-86
  maternity grant, 168-75
Christian Socialism
  co-operative movement, 32
  F.D. Maurice, 13
  John Llewelyn Davies, 13-14, 19, 31, 45, 69, 87, 188
  M.Ll.D., 45, 69, 87, 188, 220, 230
  Queen's College, 21
Churchill, Winston, 78
citizenship campaign, 76
Clantman, Mrs, 145-46
Clarion, 124
class
  classes working together, 3, 69
  co-operation and the poor, 81-93
  effects of taxation, 78
  middle class leadership of W.C.G., 45, 85, 92
  separation of classes, 17, 225
  suffrage, 123-24
  working class organiser in Bristol, 90
  working class women and national insurance, 168, 170
Close, Mrs, 200

Cole, G.D.H., 2, 92
Common Cause, The, 132
Communist Party, 227
Comte, Auguste, 8-9
Cooper, Selina, 72-73
Co-operation in Poor Neighbourhoods, 82-83
Co-operative Commonwealth, 32, 33, 212
Co-operative Congress
  1890 prize paper competition, 49-50
  divorce campaign, 164
  implementation of decisions, 144
  links with labour movement, 108
  M.Ll.D. as Congress President, 1-2, 218-20, 223
  M.Ll.D. attendance, 71
  minimum wages, 131-43, 148
  resolution on W.C.G., 60
  responses to poverty, 82, 84
  role of women, 61
  suffrage, 129
  withdrawal of W.C.G. grant, 191, 194
co-operative movement
  attitudes to W.C.G., 71, 84, 163-67, 191, 194
  boycott of sweated goods, 141
  changes post first world war, 211
  Co-operation Versus Capitalism, 212
  co-operative education, 33, 68, 74-75, 92
  Co-operative Education Committee, 75
  co-operative housing, 32, 33, 241
  co-operative principles, 34
  development, 32-34, 240-41
  dividends, 81, 82, 83, 149-52
  employee conditions, 57, 74, 78, 141-49
  international, 112, 212-15
  international women's organisations, 214-15, 216, 223, 233, 238
  M.Ll.D.'s early interest in, 28, 32
  members, 33, 192
  membership costs, 82, 85, 86, 91
  prices, 52, 81, 85, 86, 87, 88-89
  response to poverty, 81-93
  role of W.C.G., 60, 164-67, 191, 194
  social activities, 92
  terms, 242
  trade unions, 51-53, 57, 211-12
  women members, 32, 33-36, 74, 149-52

INDEX

women employees, 84
women on committees, 59, 74, 117, 146, 219
Co-operative News (see also *Woman's Corner* and *Our Women's Pages*)
  capitalist menace, 212
  joint meeting on taxation, 78
  Manchester Festival, 58
  M.Ll.D. as Congress President, 2, 219, 220
  minimum pay scales, 146
  obituary of John Llewelyn Davies, 188
  obituary of M.Ll.D., 239
  peace, 233
  role of W.C.G., 191
  Russia, 227
  W.C.G. activities, 84, 120, 190, 232-33
  writing by Leonard Woolf, 113
Co-operative Parliamentary Committee, 129, 150, 171
Co-operative Party, 192, 194, 219
Co-operative Relief Column, A, 84
Co-operative Standard for Women Workers, 143, 152
Co-operative Union
  description, 242
  grant to W.C.G., 60, 189-91, 194
  response to poverty, 82, 83
  taxation, 78
  The Vote at Last! More Power to Co-operation, 194
Co-operative Wholesale Society, 145-49, 212, 219, 219, 242
Co-operative Women's Guild (see Women's Co-operative Guild)
Cottrell, Mrs, 219
Crompton/Llewelyn Davies family tree, 6
Crompton, Albert (M.Ll.D.'s uncle), 9
Crompton, Carrie (M.Ll.D.'s aunt), 8, 18, 19, 22, 53
Crompton, Lady Caroline (M.Ll.D.'s grandmother), 7-10, 16, 17, 26
Crompton, Sir Charles (M.Ll.D.'s grandfather), 9-10
Crompton, Charley (M.Ll.D.'s uncle), 8, 17
Crompton, Emily (M.Ll.D.'s aunt later Emily Beesly), 9, 49
Crompton, Florence (M.Ll.D.'s aunt), 8

Crompton, Harry (M.Ll.D.'s uncle), 8, 9
Crompton, Mary (M.Ll.D.'s mother later Mary Davies), 12, 14-15
Crompton, Ned (M.Ll.D.'s uncle), 9

Daily Chronicle, 58, 59
Daily News, 88, 174
Davenport, Lucy, 68, 69, 70
Davidson, Emily, 138
Davies, Arthur Llewelyn (M.Ll.D.'s brother)
  childhood, 8, 17
  death, 96-101, 109, 110, 128, 129, 140, 141, 143
  death of wife, Sylvia Llewelyn Davies, 101-04
  J.M. Barrie caring for children, 103-04
Davies, Charles Llewelyn (M.Ll.D.'s brother), 7, 8, 17, 19, 24, 234
Davies, Crompton Llewelyn (M.Ll.D.'s brother)
  Cambridge University, 25, 49, 94
  childhood, 17, 18, 22
  death, 234
  death of brothers, 95, 99, 100
  family difficulties, 216
  support for M.Ll.D., 49, 62, 209
Davies, (Sarah) Emily (M.Ll.D.'s aunt)
  background, 10-12, 69
  death, 216
  Girton College, 7, 11-12, 22, 23-26
  relationship with M.Ll.D., 19
  women's education, 7, 15, 20
  women's suffrage, 43, 121, 122
Davies family, 2, 15, 17-20, 94-104
Davies, George Llewelyn (M.Ll.D.'s nephew), 103, 104
Davies, Henry Llewelyn (M.Ll.D.'s brother), 17, 20, 26, 63, 100, 234
Davies, Canon John (M.Ll.D.'s grandfather), 10
Davies, Rev. John Llewellyn (M.Ll.D.'s father)
  background, 7, 10, 12-14
  Christian Socialism, 13-14, 19, 31, 45, 69, 87, 188
  death, 187-89, 191, 192, 196, 205
  death of sons, 95, 96

death of wife, 64, 66, 67-68
dependence of M.Ll.D., 30
education, 13
family life, 10, 18-19
health, 91, 99, 109, 111, 123, 187
Kirkby Lonsdale reading room and institute, 69
marriage, 12-15
move to Kirkby Lonsdale, 39, 43
Queen's College, 21
relationship with M.Ll.D., 68, 69, 91, 108-09, 111-12, 171, 187-89, 191, 192
retirement, 108-09
support for women, 13, 19, 69, 122
views on divorce, 189
W.C.G. Congress, 69
work in London, 12-14

Davies, Margaret Llewellyn
activities after retirement, 215, 222-41
attitude to royalty, 46, 70, 77, 229, 233
caring for father, 123, 171, 175, 196
caring for nephews and nieces, 98, 99, 100, 101-02, 111, 128
childhood, 16-23
Christian Socialism, 45, 69, 87, 188, 220, 230
class antagonism towards, 161
commonplace books, 223-24, 230-31, 233, 234, 236
conflict with W.C.G. Central Committee, 134-36, 210
congratulations from W.C.G. Central Committee, 148
Co-operative Congress paper, 49-50
Co-operative Congress President, 1-2, 218-20, 223
death and will, 237-38
death of Arthur Llewelyn Davies, 96-101, 109, 110, 128, 129, 140, 141, 143
death of brothers Charles, Crompton, Henry and Maurice, 234
death of father, 187-89, 191, 192, 196, 205
death of mother, 64, 67-69
death of Theodore Llewelyn Davies, 95-96, 110, 125-26
dependence on parents, 30, 39, 43-44, 49
description, 1-4, 19-20, 23, 29, 80, 111, 115
domestic role, 22, 26-27, 65, 68-69, 108-09
education, 20-27
effect of war, 210, 223
elected W.C.G. General Secretary, 44-53
family, 6, 7-15, 216
F.D. Maurice's ideas, 13
financial contribution to W.C.G. activities, 87, 190
Freedom of the Guild, 221
friends and their marriages, 53-55, 204-05
gardens, 228, 234, 237
health, 46, 62-64, 68, 111
health and retirement, 209-10, 211-12, 214, 216, 222, 223, 228, 234-36
impartiality, 79-80
international work, 212, 223
joining co-operative society, 32
joining Women's Co-operative Guild, 34-39
Labour Party, 185-86
legacy, 239-41
Life as We Have Known It, 223-25
London venture, 49
Manchester Festival, 56-58
Margaret Llewelyn Davies Close, Redditch, 241
move to Dorking and Patterdale, 234-37
move to Kirkby Lonsdale, 39, 43-36, 108-09
move to London, 109-10
music, holidays and reading, 228-31
peace work, 194-201, 212-13, 233-34
photograph of Guild office, 70
positivism, 15, 230
relationship with Beatrice Webb, 181-82
relationship with Emily Davies, 19
relationship with father, 68, 69, 91, 108-09, 111-12, 171, 187-89, 191, 192
relationship with grandmother, 10, 20
relationship with Lilian Harris, 202-05
relationship with Margaret Bondfield, 180
relationship with Millicent Fawcett, 77, 112, 130

relationship with mother in youth, 18, 19, 22, 23, 25-27
relationship with mother when adult, 28, 29, 30, 46, 53-54, 56, 63-69, 179
relationship with Sylvia Davies, 96-104
relationship with Virginia Woolf, 109, 113-16, 222, 225, 229, 230
religion, 156, 229, 236
reminiscence on the W.C.G., 232
responsibility to W.C.G. Central Committee, 80
retirement, 3, 4, 209-21
romance, 54-55, 64-65, 111, 204-05
settlement work, 86-89, 90-93
social clubs, 30-32, 88
social life, 110, 112
socialist ideas, 30, 32, 49-50, 112-13
Society for Cultural Relations with the USSR, 226-28
sources of information, 4, 243-52
support for Leonard Woolf, 114
support for W.C.G. workers, 90
temperance, 50-51
trade unions and co-operatives, 51-53
W.C.G. coming of age history, 71-72, 77, 79, 205, 222-23
W.C.G. education, 48
William Morris, 87, 101, 231
work for suffrage, 121-39
workload, 61-63, 68, 111-12, 143, 210
Davies, Mary (M.Ll.D.'s grandmother), 10-11, 19
Davies, Mary (M.Ll.D.'s mother)
background, 14-15
death, 64, 67-69
family, 14-15, 17-18, 22-23
financial support for W.C.G. organizer, 61, 67
health, 18, 19, 26-27, 28
Lilian Harris, 51, 203
marriage, 12, 14-15
relationship with M.Ll.D. in youth, 18, 19, 22, 23, 25-27
relationship with M.Ll.D. when adult, 28, 29, 30, 46, 53-54, 56, 63-69, 179
religion, 19

servants, 17-18, 22, 179
visit to grandparents, 7-10
W.C.G. administration work, 67
women's movement, 15, 122
Davies, Maurice Llewelyn (M.Ll.D.'s brother)
childhood, 10, 17
children, 201, 216
death, 234
death of wife, 99, 111
support for M.Ll.D., 234, 235
Davies, Michael Llewelyn (M.Ll.D.'s nephew), 103, 104, 216
Davies, Peter Llewelyn (M.Ll.D.'s nephew), 97-98, 99, 101, 103, 104
Davies, Roland Llewelyn (M.Ll.D.'s nephew), 201
Davies, Sarah Emily (M.Ll.D.'s aunt), see Emily Davies
Davies, Sylvia Llewelyn (M.Ll.D.'s sister-in-law), 96-104
Davies, Theodore Llewelyn (M.Ll.D.'s brother),
childhood, 17, 26, 28
commenting on M.Ll.D.'s writing, 49
death, 94-96, 110, 125-26
Davies, Theodora Llewelyn (M.Ll.D.'s niece), 205, 237, 238
Dibdin, Sir Lewis, 156-57, 159, 166
Dickenson, Mrs, 60
Dickinson, W.H., 122, 129
dividend in co-operatives, 81, 82, 83, 149-52
divorce law reform, 3, 153-67, 178, 189
domestic abuse (see divorce law reform)
Duckworth, Gerald, 183

East London Federation of Suffragettes, 121, 139
Eccles, Mrs, 162
education
co-operative education, 33, 68, 74-75, 92
Davies family, 17, 18, 20
religious education, 13
Sunderland settlement, 88
women, 7, 8, 9, 11, 20-27, 35-36

W.C.G., 37, 48, 72-3, 74-75, 171, 191, 210
Eliot, George, 7, 8, 16
employment conditions, 57, 74, 78, 141-49, 190
Enfield, Honora, 211, 212, 214, 215, 218

Fabian Society, 113, 115, 180, 181
factory inspectors, 60-61
fair trade, 3, 74
family allowance, 151
family wage, 149-52, 175
Fawcett, Millicent
  Queen Victoria's Jubilee, 77
  relationship with M.Ll.D., 77, 112, 130
  women's suffrage, 78, 121, 122, 127, 131, 192, 195
feminism, 2-3, 11-12, 113
Fidkin, Mrs, 140-41
Fletcher, Caroline
  (see Crompton, Caroline)
Freundlich, Frau Emmy, 213-14, 232, 239
friendly societies, 170

Gaffin, Jean, 240
Galsworthy, John, 133
Gaskell, Elizabeth, 8
Gasson, Mrs, 77-78, 128, 133, 150-51, 214
Gibson, Mrs, 162
Girton College, Cambridge, 7, 8, 11-12, 22, 23-27
Glendinning, Victoria, 114
Globe, The, 9
Gorell, Lord (Sir John Gorell Barnes), 153, 156
Gration, Miss, 119, 154, 162, 200
Greener, Ada, 90

Haldane, Elizabeth, 31
Hardie, Keir, 89, 124
Hardy, Thomas, 8
Harris, Lilian
  activities after retirement, 222-41
  bequest from M.Ll.D., 237
  description, 204, 225
  Freedom of the Guild, 221
  gardens, 228, 234
  health, 53, 202, 221, 222, 234-35
  international work, 223
  minimum wage campaign, 142, 151
  move to Dorking and Patterdale, 234-37
  move to London, 110, 189, 203
  national insurance, 168, 173
  peace work, 195, 198, 200
  photograph of Guild office, 70
  relationship with M.Ll.D., 202-05
  relationship with parents, 202-03
  retirement, 4, 51, 203, 209-21
  Sunderland settlement, 87
  support for M.Ll.D., 99, 110, 111
  temperance, 51, 202
  W.C.G. democracy, 191
  W.C.G. work, 51, 62, 64, 78, 202-04, 215, 232
  women's suffrage, 129, 133, 138
  writing with M.Ll.D., 211
Haworth, Mrs, 118
health
  campaigns, 74, 86
  district health visitors, 180
  housing conditions, 184
  maternity campaign, 175-86
  maternity grant, 168-75, 179
  poverty, 118-19
Henderson, Arthur, 132, 137
Hobhouse, Emily, 132
Hobhouse, Leonard, 226
Hodgett, Mrs, 126, 146
Hodgson, Mary, 98, 101-02
Holland, 71
Holyoake, Emilie, 45
Hood, Mrs, 218
Hopkinson, Mary (later Mary Davies), 10-11
housing co-operatives, 32, 33, 241
Howard, Mary, 28, 46
Hughes, Thomas, 13, 32
Huxley, T.H., 7
Hyndman, H.M., 29

Independent Labour Party (see also Labour Party), 72, 73, 194
Insurance Act 1911, 107-08

INDEX

International Co-operative Alliance, 214, 237
International Co-operative Women's Committee, 214-15
International Co-operative Women's Guild, 214, 216, 223, 233, 238
International Socialist Congress, 62
International Women's Peace Congress, 195-96, 197
Ireland, 213, 216, 231
Isaacs, Sir Rufus, 169
Italy, 54

Jamaica, 8, 9
Jex-Blake, Katherine, 27
Jones, Annie (Mrs Ben Jones)
  trade unions and co-operatives, 52
  votes for women, 57
  W.C.G. and public work, 58, 61
  W.C.G. Central Committee, 45, 47
  women's work, 36
Jones, Ben, 50, 52
Jones, Kate, 68-69, 90

Keynes, J.M., 133, 226, 227
Kidd, Harriet, 119, 148-49, 210, 224
King's College, 21
Kingsley, Charles, 7
Kirkby Lonsdale
  Davies family move, 39, 43-46, 108-09
  description, 43
  entertainments and lectures, 43
  information board on M.Ll.D., 241
  reading room and institute, 69
  temperance, 50-51
  transport, 61, 110
  W.C.G. office, 51, 70
Knott, Mrs, 45-46
Kollontai, Alexandra, 3, 116
Labour Department, 75
Labour Leader, 138, 183
Labour Party, 124, 132, 137, 138, 139, 185-96
Lancashire and Cheshire Women Textile and Other Workers Representation Committee, 121, 123

Law, Bonar, 108
Lawrence, D.H., 73, 224, 228
Lawrenson, Mary, 34, 44-45, 48
Lawton, Mrs, 184
Layton, Mrs, 35, 169
League of Nations, 212-13
Lewes, G.H., 8, 16
Life as We Have Known It, 223-25, 240
Lisson Grove social club, 30-31
Llewelyn Davies (see Davies)
Lloyd George, David
  national insurance, 168-75, 179, 182
  social security benefits, 107-08
  women's suffrage, 122, 131, 137
London
  John Llewelyn Davies's work, 12-14
  mass suffrage meeting, 138
  M.Ll.D. in London, 16-23, 49, 109-10
  poverty, 29, 85
  separation of classes, 17
  social clubs, 30-32
  trade unions and co-operatives, 52-53

Macarthur, Mary, 79, 114, 132, 137
Macdonald, Margaret, 79, 142
Macdonald, Ramsay, 173, 174, 195
McArthur, Ellen, 27
Manchester
  Free Trade Hall, 78
  Manchester Festival, 56-58
  Manchester Guardian
    death of M.Ll.D., 239
    Life as We Have Known It, 224-25
  Manchester Festival, 58, 69
  M.Ll.D. as Congress President, 218-20
  maternity, 173, 174, 180
  W.C.G., 3, 116, 148
  women's suffrage, 127
Mann, Tom, 51-52
marguerites, 218
Marlborough, Duchess of, 184
Married Women's Property Act, 150
Martineau, Harriet, 8
Marx, Karl, 7, 9
Marylebone W.C.G. branch, 34-39
Masefield, John, 133

Masterman, Charles, 173
Maternity: Letters from Working Women, 3, 183-84, 240
Maternity and Child Welfare Act, 185
maternity campaign, 3, 35, 175-86
maternity grant, 168-75
Maurice, F.D., 7, 13, 21
Maurier, George du, 96
Maurier, Mrs, 99, 102
Maxwell, William, 141, 199
May, Henry, 226, 227
Mayo, Catherine, 68
Mill, J.S., 7, 8, 122
minimum wage campaign, 142-51
Mitchell, Hannah, 125
Morris, William, 28, 29, 30, 54, 101, 231
Mothers' Union, 160
Moxon, Mrs, 197
Muir, Meta, 44

Nash, Rosalind (see also Smith, Rosalind Shore)
  bequest from M.Ll.D., 237
  friendship with M.Ll.D., 109, 204-05, 239
  M.Ll.D.'s health, 234-35, 237
  M.Ll.D.'s life, 69, 80
  national insurance, 168
  support for M.Ll.D. on death of her brothers, 95
  Woman's Corner, 68
  women's suffrage, 129, 131-32, 133
Nash, Vaughan, 53, 131-32
National Council Against Conscription, 197
National Council for Adult Suffrage, 193
National Federation of Women Workers, 79, 132, 169
national insurance, 168-75
National Society for Women's Suffrage, 76-77
National Union of Women's Suffrage Societies
  alliance with Labour Party, 137-38, 139
  differences in approach to W.C.G., 129, 131, 133
  formation, 121, 127

International Women's Peace Conference, 195, 196
  maternity care, 185
  wartime suspension, 192-93
  work with W.C.G., 130, 185
Netherland Co-operative Women's Union, 71
New Statesman, 174, 182
Newnham College, 223
Nightingale, Florence, 25
No Conscription Fellowship, 197

Observer, The, 219
Open *Christmas Letter*, 195
Our Women's Pages (earlier *Woman's Corner* and *Women's Corner*)
  retirement of M.Ll.D. and Lilian Harris, 209, 217, 218
  International Co-operative Women's Guild, 214
  death of M.Ll.D., 239
Owen, Robert, 32, 33, 81

Pankhurst, Christabel, 121, 127
Pankhurst, Emmeline, 121, 127
Pankhurst, Sylvia, 121, 139, 176, 190, 193, 196
Parry, Lady Maude, 46-47, 70
peace campaigns, 187, 188, 194-201, 212-13, 223, 233-34
Peace Pledge Union, 233, 234, 237
penny banks, 86, 87
pensions, 107
People's Suffrage Federation, 122, 132-33, 135, 138-39, 171, 193
Peterloo, 125
Polovtseva, Varvara, 227, 230
Ponsonby, Arthur, 131-32, 197, 204, 223, 226, 229
Ponsonby, Dolly
  correspondence with M.Ll.D., 111, 224, 225, 227, 229
  description of John Llewelyn Davies, 189
  description of M.Ll.D., 97, 153, 226, 229, 230
  description of visit to Kirkby Lonsdale, 65

friendship with Sylvia Llewelyn Davies, 97, 98, 102
M.Ll.D. and Beatrice Webb, 181-82
M.Ll.D.'s health, 209, 222, 236
women's suffrage, 131-32
Poor Law, 59, 73, 76, 107, 118, 135
Positivism, 8-9, 15, 230
Potter, Beatrice (see Beatrice Webb)
Potts, Janet, 234
poverty
  campaign by W.C.G., 3, 81-93
  causes, 29, 82, 83, 85
  health, 118-19
  maternity, 177-78, 183, 184
  wartime distress, 190
public speaking, 72-73, 116, 117

Queen Victoria, 77
Queen's College, 20-22

radical suffragists, 121, 124, 129, 130
Railway Women's Guild, 185
Rathbone, Eleanor, 151
Reddish, Sarah
  barriers to co-operative office, 117
  Bolton Guild branch, 71, 176
  maternal and infant health, 176
  textile industry information, 75, 76
  W.C.G. Central Committee, 47
  W.C.G. organiser, 61-62, 63, 64, 67
  women's suffrage, 77, 121, 123, 134
Redhouse, Mrs, 235, 237, 238
Reeves, Maud Pember, 148
Reigate, 63-64
religion
  Christian Socialism, 13-14
  Davies family, 10-11, 19
  John Llewellyn Davies, 12-14
  M.Ll.D., 156, 229, 236
  opposition to divorce, 155, 156, 159, 160, 161, 163-64
  religious education, 13
  Unitarianism, 9, 19
Rendel, Rose, 28
Reynolds News, 173
Rhondda, Lord, 183-84

Rigby, Mrs, 75
Roberts, George, 173, 174
Robertson, Professor George Croom, 31
Robinson, Mrs, 119
Rochdale Pioneers, 33, 74
Romilly, Lucy, 8
Rowntree, Seebohm, 85
Royal Commission on Divorce Law Reform, 153
royalty, 46, 70, 77, 229, 233
Ruskin, John, 7
Russell, Alys, 110-11, 133
Russell, Bertrand
  correspondence with M.Ll.D. at time of family illness, 99, 100, 101
  correspondence with M.Ll.D. on divorce, 161
  correspondence with M.Ll.D. on socialism, 112-13
  correspondence with M.Ll.D. on suffrage, 127, 130, 131, 132, 136, 151
  correspondence with M.Ll.D. on W.C.G., 116
  correspondence with M.Ll.D. on women's wages, 151, 152
  friendship with M.Ll.D., 110
  marriage, 110-11
  Society for Cultural Relations with the USSR, 226, 227
  Theodore Llewelyn Davies, 95, 110
  war, 187, 197, 199
  women's suffrage, 133
Russell, Edith, 111
Russia
  civil war, 213
  international trade, 212
  Russian revolution, 198-99, 211, 226, 230
  Society for Cultural Relations with the USSR, 226-28

Salford Diocese Catholic Federation, 163-64
Samuel, Herbert, 182, 183
Sargant, Ethel, 25, 27, 43, 63, 64
savings
  dividend, 81, 82, 83, 88-89
  penny banks, 86, 87

wives' savings, 150-52, 158
Schreiner, Olive, 30, 38
Scott, Gillian, 166, 240
self-help, 33
servants
  Davies family, 17-18, 22, 68-69, 98, 111
  Girton College, 25
  national insurance, 170
settlements, 85, 86-89, 204
Sharp, Evelyn, 116
Sheffield, 45-46
Sheppard, Reverend Dick, 233
shop workers' conditions, 57, 74, 78, 172
Sickert, Helena (see also Swanwick, Helena), 27
Smith, Rosalind Shore (see also Nash, Rosalind)
  friendship with M.Ll.D., 28, 53-54, 64
  Girton College, 25, 26, 27
  marriage, 53
  London venture, 49
  W.C.G., 54, 62
  Woman's Corner, 54, 68
Snowden, Philip, 147, 174
social clubs, 30-32
Social Democratic Federation, 30
socialism, 30, 49-50
Society for Cultural Relations with the USSR, 226-28
Spectator, The, 163
Spooner, Mary, 64, 74, 90-91, 202
Standing Joint Committee of Industrial Women's Organisations, 190
Stephen, Leslie, 8
Strachey, Ray, 126
strikes, 108, 119
suffrage, 3, 9, 12, 57, 73, 76-77, 78
  equal, 122
  male, 122, 124, 130, 131, 134, 137, 138
  married women, 128, 138
  property qualification, 9, 123, 128, 132
  suffragettes, 108, 127, 192
  universal, 123, 124, 128, 130, 131, 193
  W.C.G. and other campaigns, 121-39
  women's, 3, 12, 57, 73, 76-77, 78, 122-39, 192-94
Sunderland, 86-89, 91-93, 204
Swanwick, Helena (see also Sickert, Helena), 117-18, 136, 139, 187, 197
sweated goods, 74, 84, 140-41
Switzerland, 62, 110

Tandy, Annie, 68-69
taxation, 71, 78, 107, 192
Taylor, Mrs, 184
temperance, 50-51, 202
Thoms, David, 240
Times, The
  divorce reform, 159, 160, 163
  maternal health, 180, 182, 183
  national insurance, 170
  obituary of John Llewelyn Davies, 188
  obituary of Theodore Llewelyn Davies, 94-96
  support for co-operatives, 83
  women's suffrage, 127, 131, 158-59
Tomlinson, Annie Bamford, 217
Thornton, William, 32
Tillett, Ben, 52
Toynbee, Gertrude, 87
Trade Union Congress, 59
trade unions
  co-operators and trade unionists, 51-53, 211-12
  Crompton family support, 8, 9
  national insurance, 170
  strikes, 59, 60
  women, 38, 59, 62, 71, 75, 148-49
Trevelyan, Charles, 110, 197
Trinity College Cambridge, 12, 24
Tweddell, Thomas, 129
unemployment, 29, 86, 107-08, 168
Unitarianism, 9, 19
United Board, 74, 84-85, 144, 163-67, 218-20, 242

Vote at Last! More Power to Co-operation, The, 194
votes for women (see suffrage)

Wakeham, Mrs, 217-18
war

approach of second world war, 233-34
death of George Llewelyn Davies, 187
death of Roland Llewelyn Davies, 201
effect of war on M.Ll.D., 210, 223
mothers and babies, 182-86
outbreak of first world war, 187
post first world war conditions, 211-13
peace, 187, 188, 194-201, 212-13, 223, 233-34
second world war conditions, 235
travel, 192
wartime relief, 190, 298
women's work, 190
Webb, Beatrice (earlier Beatrice Potter)
concern about poverty, 29
Co-operative Congress, 50
Positivism, 8
relationship with M.Ll.D., 181-82
welfare provisions, 181-82
women's 'inertia', 60
women's suffrage, 133
Webb, Catherine, 60, 142, 223
Webb, Sidney, 82, 133
West, Rebecca, 163
Whitby, Miss, 118
white poppy, 233
Whitehead, Alfred North, 110, 218-19, 236
Whitman, Walt, 38
Wilkinson, Ellen, 149
Willson, Jane Wynne (see Wynne Willson, Jane)
Wimhurst, Mrs, 112, 119, 191
Winter Circular, 48
Woman with the Basket, 232
Woman's Corner (later *Women's Corner* then *Our Women's Pages*)
aims of W.C.G., 36
commencement, 34
Co-operation in Poor Neighbourhoods, 83
death of Mary Davies, 67
descriptions of M.Ll.D. and her work, 46, 62, 67, 69, 71, 130
divorce reform, 159, 161, 162
edited by Rosalind Nash, 54, 68
election of M.Ll.D., 45

Manchester Festival, 57-58
maternity campaign, 185
minimum wages, 146-47
peace, 197, 199, 200-01
W.C.G. campaigns, 74, 76, 85, 89, 91
W.C.G. leadership, 80
W.C.G. meetings, 72
W.C.G. office, 70
W.C.G. progress reports, 37, 38
women's income, 151
women's pages as source, 4
women's rights, 36
women's suffrage, 124, 126, 128, 135, 136, 138
writings by Mary Lawrenson, 44-45
women (see also Women's Co-operative Guild)
activity outside the home, 34-35, 60
as property of husband, 156, 158, 172-75
care for children, 151-52
citizenship campaign, 76
co-operative committees, 59, 74, 117, 146, 219
Crompton family support for education, 7, 8, 9
developing role, 11-12, 58-60
divorce, 153-67
domestic role, 130, 149-52
economic independence, 174-75, 186
education, 11, 20-27, 35-36
equal pay, 142, 144, 146, 152
friendship and romance, 53-55, 204-05
International Women's Peace Congress, 195-96, 197
lives of women, 2-4
married and unmarried mothers, 184, 186, 224
married women's rights, 149-52
maternity campaign, 175-86
maternity grant, 168-75
minimum wages, 140, 141-49
national insurance, 168-75
parliamentary vote, 3, 9, 12, 38
politicisation, 3
public bodies, 76

responsibilities, 38
rights, 36
trade unions, 38, 59, 62, 71, 75, 148-49
unpaid domestic labour, 3, 11, 36, 170, 173, 181
wages for housework, 149-52
wives' savings, 150-52, 158
women's movement, 11-12, 27
work experience used in debates, 75-76
work outside the home, 12, 34-35, 45, 86, 181, 190
working conditions, 79-80, 84, 124, 141-49
Women's Co-operative Guild (see also individual names and campaigns)
50th anniversary, 232-33
acting on resolutions, 57
administration, 51, 67-68, 70-71, 210
aims, 36, 58-59
annual reports, 70
bequest from M.Ll.D., 237
branch organisation, 72, 210
campaigns, 3, 51-53, 71, 72, 73-80
central committee clashes, 44-45
classes for children, 38-39, 57
closure, 240
co-operative member recruitment, 57, 74
criticism of divorce reform, 159
D.H. Lawrence description, 73
democracy, 38, 47, 70, 119, 190
development, 37, 58-60, 71-72, 116-17, 210
divorce reform, 153-67, 191
education, 37, 48, 72-73, 74-75, 117, 191, 210
effect on members, 3, 74, 76, 116-18, 165, 223-25
employment of organizer, 61-62, 67
experiences of members of W.C.G., 3, 223-25, 240
experiences of members on divorce, 154-59, 160, 166-67, 178
experiences of members on maternity, 176-86
finances, 60, 163-67, 189-91, 194
formation, 34

Freedom of the Guild for M.Ll.D. and Lilian Harris, 221
history, 71-72, 77, 79, 205, 222-23, 240
independence, 164, 190
international co-operation, 198-99, 200, 212-15
leadership, 34, 35, 37-39, 44-45, 47, 62, 79-80, 134-36, 161
Manchester Festival, 56-58
M.Ll.D.'s vision, 2-4
maternity campaign, 175-86
maternity grant, 168-175
members, 2-4, 34-35, 191, 210
memorial for M.Ll.D., 239
national insurance, 168-75
northern towns, 45, 72
office, 51, 70, 109, 189, 210
opposition to activism, 83-84, 120
paid secretary, 112
peace, 194-201, 212-13, 233-34
profile, 77-78
protest against French African troops, 213
public speaking, 72-73, 116, 117
publications for debate, 72
role of General Secretary, 44-53
role of W.C.G., 60, 164-67, 191, 194
social activities, 37, 38, 58, 50, 73
structure, 34, 38, 47, 48, 51, 58, 79, 134-36, 215
support for Austria, 213-14
survey on divorce 154-55
survey on maternity grant, 169
training for activism, 72-73, 117
vote of thanks to M.Ll.D. and Lilian Harris, 78
Women's Co-operative Guild Congress
administration, 71, 79-80, 98
divorce reform, 161-63, 164
minimum wages, 143
peace, 198, 199-200
poverty, 84, 89, 119
retirement of M.Ll.D. and Lilian Harris, 216, 221
structure, 215
suffrage, 123, 124, 129, 134-35, 136, 139
visitors, 69, 113-14

withdrawal of grant, 190-92
women joint head of household, 151
Women's Corner (see *Woman's Corner*)
Women's Enfranchisement Bill, 125
Women's Industrial Council, 75, 142, 169
Women's International League, 196, 213
Women's Labour League, 79, 132, 142, 169, 173, 176, 180, 185, 215
Women's League for the Spread of Co-operation (later W.C.G.), 34
Women's Liberal Association, 9
Women's Liberal Federation, 163
Women's Peace Crusade, 198, 200
Women's Social and Political Union, 121, 127, 131, 133, 137, 138, 139
Women's Suffrage Society, 135
Women's Trade Union Association, 57
Women's Trade Union League, 71, 169
Wood, Mrs, 70
Woolf, Leonard
  admiration for M.Ll.D., 2
  capitalist menace, 211
  correspondence with M.Ll.D., 112, 113-17, 128, 160, 165, 174, 195
  friendship with M.Ll.D., 230, 231
  Life as We Have Known It, 224-25
  M.Ll.D. as Congress President, 220
  Society for Cultural Relations with the USSR, 226-28
  support of M.Ll.D., 188, 191, 192, 215, 216, 223
  Theodore Llewelyn Davies, 95
Woolf, Virginia
  description of M.Ll.D., 3, 220
  Life as We Have Known It, 224-25
  Lilian Harris, 204
  Maternity: Letters from Working Women, 183
  M.Ll.D. as Congress President, 1, 220
  relationship with M.Ll.D., 109, 113-16, 222, 225, 229, 230
Wootton, Barbara, 230
worker co-operatives, 32
Workers and Soldiers Convention, 198
working class
  family life, 34-35, 53, 86

membership of W.C.G , 2-3, 34-35
national insurance, 168, 170
organiser in Bristol, 90
working women, 34-35
Wynne Willson, Jane, 4, 6, 241, 243

York, Archbishop of, 159, 163
young people's social clubs, 30-32

Zimmern, Alice, 27